The role of the military in politics

The role of the military in politics
A case study of Iraq to 1941

Mohammad A. Tarbush

Foreword by A. H. Hourani

This is a modest testimony to the role of
Wilfrid Knapp in my education.
With lots of affection,

Mohammad

Paris 1983

Kegan Paul International
London, Boston, Melbourne and Henley

First published in 1982
by Kegan Paul International Ltd
39 Store Street, London WC1E 7DD,
9 Park Street, Boston, Mass. 02108, USA,
296 Beaconsfield Parade, Middle Park, Melbourne,
3206, Australia, and
Broadway House, Newtown Road,
Henley-on-Thames, Oxon RG9 1EN
Set in Press Roman by
Hope Services, Abingdon, Oxon.
and printed in Great Britain by
The Thetford Press Ltd
Thetford, Norfolk
© Mohammad Tarbush 1982

Library of Congress Cataloging in Publication Data

Tarbush, Mohammad, 1945-
The role of the military in politics.
Revision of thesis (Ph. D.) – Oxford, 1978.
Bibliography: p.
Includes index.
1. Iraq – Armed Forces – Political activity.
2. Iraq – Politics and government.   I. Title.
DS79.T37 1982   332'.5'09567   82-4698

ISBN 0-7103-0036-0

Contents

Contents

Illustrations

Tables

Map

Foreword

In 1936 the government of Iraq, installed in accordance with constitutional forms, was overthrown by a military *coup d'état*, starting a process which has continued in Iraq, as in other countries of the 'Third World', until today. It is a process much discussed by writers on the sociology of politics, who have put forward many theories to explain it, but until now there have been few detailed studies of particular revolutions in particular countries. Mohammad Tarbush's book on the sequence of military coups in Iraq from 1936 to 1941 is therefore to be warmly welcomed.

As he shows, what happened in Iraq needs to be explained in terms of the nature of Iraqi society, of the Iraqi state, and of the army. Iraq in its present form was created by the British after the First World War. Its population was not united by ethnic identity, religious adherence or common historical experience; its countryside was not controlled by urban officials or elites, but, precariously, by tribal shaikhs. When the British government decided in 1920 that it would try to preserve ultimate control over the country by means of indigenous institutions, it had to begin by creating a political elite strong enough to govern, but not strong enough to challenge the British presence. The monarch was an essential element in the elite but could not be the whole of it; neither could the tribal shaikhs, whose support was essential but who lacked the knowledge and skills needed for national politics and government. It was therefore necessary to co-opt urban notables and former Ottoman officers and officials. This group included too many members for the available offices; not being controlled by firmly held convictions, public opinion, or organized political parties, their struggle for power was carried on through the medium of fragile systems of alliance and patronage, looking for support to the British and the Palace.

In the 1930s, after Iraq obtained a greater measure of independence within the British system of control, a third source of power was added to these two. This was the army, new, without firmly established military traditions, with a sense of national mission increased by its actions in suppressing internal disturbances, open to penetration by politicians seeking support in their conflicts with each other, and also by the powerful ideologies of the age.

The movement which made the coup of 1936, that of Bakir Sidqi, was composed of three elements: ambitious army officers, politicians seeking to oust their rivals, and a group of educated men wedded to the ideas of parliamentary democracy and moderate social reform, the *Jama'at al-Ahali*. The revolution of 1941, that of Rashid 'Ali, was made by similar groups, but the relationship between them had changed. The army officers had moved to the centre of the political process, and governments could not be formed without them; and they were exposed to an idea more powerful than those of the *Ahali* group, that of Arab nationalism. The circumstances of the War seemed to hold out the possibility of obtaining complete independence from the British, but those same circumstances made it possible for the British to use force to defeat what they saw as a direct challenge to their position in the Middle East.

Dr Tarbush's treatment of this subject is based on a careful study of British and Iraqi archives, on information given him by survivors from the period he is describing, and on wide reading in Arab political memoirs. It is informed by a lively understanding of the way in which political decisions are made and one thing leads to another. It is a valuable contribution to our knowledge of what happened in Iraq at that time; but, in spite of his modest limitation of what he is saying to one country and one era, it will also help us to understand similar events in other places and at other times.

Albert Hourani

Note on transliteration

I have adopted for Arabic names and words a transliteration which is
simple and consistent, and which takes account both of the way in
which they are spelt in literary Arabic and of the way in which they are
pronounced in Iraq.

Because of the circumstances in which the book was set, it was not
possible to use a special sign for the Arabic letter *'ain*. I have therefore
used an ordinary apostrophe; I also use the same sign for *hamza* when it
comes in the middle of a word, but have omitted it when it comes at
the beginning or end of a word.

I have used the familiar English form for some names and words
(e.g. 'Mosul' instead of 'Mousil').

Abbreviations

Air	Air Ministry Files
BHCF (New Delhi)	Baghdad High Commission Files
CO	Colonial Office Files
FO	Foreign Office Files
LP & S	India Office, Letters, Political and Secret
WO	War Office

Acknowledgments

This book is a revised version of a thesis that was submitted for the degree of Doctor of Philosophy in the University of Oxford in 1978. In compliance with the rigorous academic standards of the university, extensive quotes were used to document all views and interpretations advocated in this work. In my research I relied a lot on the reports of the British Embassy although my use of these was not uncritical. How objective, for example, was the British Ambassador's analysis of political events in the country? Some documents contain blatantly racist and condescending references to leading Iraqi politicians of the period under study, and it is, therefore, not unlikely that their emphasis had been distorted by personal bias and prejudices. However, bearing these reservations in mind, I found the most comprehensive and useful British official records on Iraq to be the FO/371 series, with the exception that, for the year 1941, Embassy dispatches from Iraq were, perhaps owing to the atmosphere of urgency that characterised this era of crisis, rather sketchy and, in contrast with those documents relating to the 1936 coup, for example, certainly less analytical.

Apart from these Foreign Office files, I also found the Air Ministry archives to be of some value, particularly in relation to biographical information. The Colonial Office files too were very useful, and include important data on the formation of the Iraqi army as well as the circumstances surrounding the formation of Iraqi cabinets. In the main, however, important dispatches in the Air Ministry or Colonial Office files were almost invariably repeated to the Foreign Office, and thus can be found in the FO/371 series. Thus, future researchers might find the FO/371 series quite adequate for any investigation of the development of the Iraqi polity.

In any case, alternatives to British archives were found to be limited. Although I benefited greatly from the insight given to me by veteran Iraqi politicians, particularly Muhammad Hadid and Husain Jamil, my benefit from the Iraqi State Archives was very limited.

On the whole, secondary sources on Iraq proved much more useful for my present inquiry. Particular mention should be made here of *Tarikh al-Wizarat al-'Iraqiya* (History of the Iraqi Cabinets) by 'Abd al-Razzaq al-Hasani,[1] which offers in ten volumes a comprehensive chronology of the political history of Iraq from 1920 to 1958. Although this voluminous work suffers from an evident lack of theme (in spite of its rather precise title) or any scholarly structure, it is still possible to reconstruct from it a fairly systematic account of significant political events during the period covered by my inquiry. A more scholarly work, though comparatively less useful for the period under study, is Hanna Batatu's comprehensive analysis of Iraq's social classes.[2] Other secondary sources that, like the present study, are based largely on British documents, and which were found useful for the understanding of the circumstances determining the nature of the Iraqi state, were Klieman's book on the Cairo Conference[3] (particularly on British attitudes towards the crowning of Faisal as King of Iraq), Mejcher's work on the *Imperial Quest for Oil*[4] (especially its emphasis on the strategic importance of Mosul and the settlement of the northern boundary in Iraq's favour, and its stress of the fragility of the Iraqi political structure), and finally Sluglett's study of Britain in Iraq, 1914–32[5] (particularly its emphasis on the disunity of Iraq and on the immense changes brought about by British intervention, which helped to ensure the concentration of political power in the hands of a small class of officials and bureaucrats, supported by local tribes or rural leaders whose powers had been greatly enhanced by grants and protected, together with British interests, by rather excessive use of the British Royal Air Force).

While researching for and writing the present work, and generally during my studies in England, I was helped by a number of people. No verbal or written expression can convey the genuine depth of appreciation that I have for their support.

The most consistent and characteristically generous support towards my education at Oxford came from His Excellency Muhammad Mahdi al-Tajir, the current UAE Ambassador in London. I am also indebted to the following personalities and institutions who have helped me financially at different stages of my studies: the late King Faisal of Saudi Arabia, Shaikh Zayed Bin Sultan al-Nahyan, President of the United Arab Emirates, Shaikh Salem al-Sabah, former Kuwaiti Ambassador to London and now Minister of Defence, the late 'Abd al-Hamid Shuman, founder and chairman of the Arab Bank, Mr Yusif al-'Abd al-Aziz al-Fulaij, Mahmud Yusif al-Hibbiya, Director of the Makkasid Society in Jerusalem, the British Council, and finally Banque Arabe et Internationale d'Investissement, who through the understanding and foresight of their former director, Roger F. 'Azar, have helped me at a particularly crucial stage of my research.

No less profound is my gratitude to those scholars who, in a variety of degree, have been the architects of my intellectual development. For the present work, I am deeply grateful for the supervision by A. H. Hourani of St Antony's College, Oxford, whose gentle guidance and incisive comments enabled me to negotiate intellectual zig-zags which had appeared impassable. Very special thanks must also go to W. F. Knapp and to the staff and students of St Catherine's College (particularly Dr M. Leask and Miss D. Dorman), who have all provided me with an endless source of intellectual stimulus as well as being helpful in every way.

In Baghdad and Beirut I have benefited greatly from discussions I had with Messers Sadiq Shanshal, Yusif Yazbak, Khayri al-'Umari, Fadhil Husain and Najdat Safwat.

The following persons have also helped me in a number of significant ways: Mr Nazih Karram, Dr P. Sluglett, Mr L. Whitehead, Mr C. Reynolds, Professor P. J. Vatikiotis, Dr R. Owen, Mr A. G. al-Dalli, Dr D. Sandole, Mr M. Cavey, and Mr P. J. Sharp.

Finally, special thanks go to Marie-France Belthé who dedicated some of her talents to organising and typing the manuscript of the present work.

Introduction
The army in politics: questions and problems

This book attempts to explain how and why the Iraqi military intervened in the affairs of state between 1936 and 1941. The intention is
not to describe the various coups of this period, but to explain the
gradual assumption of a political role by the Iraqi army. It is primarily
an 'historical' explanation that is being attempted, rather than an application of any theoretical model of the role of the army in politics. It
may therefore be appropriate first to explain why I regard this approach
as more suitable to this subject, and to discuss the limits within which
theoretical explanations can be useful.

There are a number of meanings of the term 'model'.[1] They range
from the type of mathematical model characteristic of science, in which
postulates, variables and relationships are specified in order to induce
through a rigorously deductive argument possible hypotheses capable of
empirical test, to idealised or abstract conceptual frameworks, which
are intended to be suggestive or to enable further empirical inquiry. In
both these senses the use of models strictly constitutes a technique. For
example, a mathematical model consists of, or incorporates, a set of
propositions referring to an idealised situation expressed in mathematical
terms, and it is the relationships within the model itself that are important. Such relationships within the confines of the quantified
variables may yield knowledge that was not apparent through extant
explanations or observation. The model itself is neither a theory nor an
explanation. But from it theoretical deductions or inferences can be
made which assist in formulating a hypothesis capable of an empirical
test. The essential feature of such models is that they make it possible
to formulate and test hypotheses with greater precision than would
otherwise be possible. If a model simply correlates variables or factors
without producing empirically testable hypotheses, then it is useless as a

method of advancing empirical knowledge. This implies that variables must be both identifiable and quantifiable. Whether the chosen model is a good or bad one depends upon its relationship to an adequate explanation.

To be useful, however, a model should not be a conceptual scheme or a comprehensive general theory of human behaviour in society. If it is this, then we may well ask whether it can produce empirically testable hypotheses. There are many examples of model-building in the social sciences that shade off into general conceptual frameworks; and, indeed, in the absence of explanatory hypotheses capable of an empirical test, it is hard to make any criticism of this kind of theorising, other than to say that it is non-explanatory. In my view, models are at best adjoints to such an inquiry, and their value seems to be in direct proportion to the number of fruitful conjectures that can be elicited from them. The conjectures that they elicit are initially neutral. That is to say, they are guidelines, and not positive directions for an inquiry. If they dominate an investigation, or are taken to be assumptions rather than questions, then inevitably the inquiry becomes either circular or loaded.

Most of the models in the field of the military in politics consist of an idealised set of categories related to various conjectures. For example, Janowitz discusses four model 'states':[2] the aristocratic, the democratic, the totalitarian and the garrison state. These correspond to a typology of idealised 'states' characterised by the relation of the political and military elites to the state.[3] As they stand they amount to idealised descriptions, which correspond only very loosely to reality and are thus non-explanatory. Janowitz's categories consist of class, elite and structure, together with dynamic factors such as technological influences and external political pressures. The conjectural element consists of postulating possible developments or metamorphoses of these models. The central idea is to extrapolate from 'reality' and then to proceed on the assumption that, if the real world is like the model, then the model can explain 'reality'. The circularity in such attempts is evident. We know what a garrison state model is, either as a form of historical description limited in space and time or as an abstract set of definitions and relations. But the systematic fabrication of these into a set of categories and variables does not add to knowledge if we cannot proceed to formulate testable hypotheses. The model merely repeats what we already know or assume about given states of affairs involving the military in politics. In brief, the central objection to these models is that they do not advance an explanation. But, of course, the relevant explanation would be of a general theoretical nature from which empirically verified general propositions about the role of the military in politics could be made. No such theory is yet forthcoming, and it is beyond the scope of this inquiry to go into the problems associated with the formulation of general theories.

It may be, however, that models derived from a comparative study of a number of cases will be useful in an inquiry on the military in politics. The studies that have been made suggest a number of propositions which appear to correspond to empirical experience. For example, the notion that the army is a modernising influence in developing states has had a fair currency.[4] This notion has been heavily criticised by Hurewitz[5] and also by Janowitz,[6] on the grounds that, while it appears to be verified by the Turkish and Egyptian experience, it does not fit Syria or, more importantly for this study, Iraq. Its value as a generalisation is thus mitigated by the considerable exceptions to it. And indeed, the role of the army in Iraqi politics in this admittedly early period does not support the idea that the military is the vanguard of social change. Clearly, other factors existed that were more important in establishing the army's role in Iraq, and the notion of social cleavage, for example, put forward by Hurewitz[7] as a more significant determinant, appears to be more fruitful in providing an explanation.

In short, the fragmented nature of Iraqi society and the divisive factor of the British presence, both features peculiar to Iraqi politics, seem to be more relevant. But even so these factors are contingent, and it is difficult to see how the notion of social cleavage can be extended into a general hypothetical basis for an explanation of the role of the army in politics. Similarly, Janowitz, while equally critical of the direct application of concepts and hypotheses more appropriate to the European and Anglo-Saxon experience than to the Middle East, puts in their place the notion of historical tradition and the evolution of an ideology peculiar to the army. It is certainly true that ethnic and religious elements are extremely important in any explanation of the activities of the Iraqi army in the state; but, again, it is the specifics of the case rather than the general category that is important in advancing an explanation. In other words, while such criticisms are undoubtedly valid, they contain alternative hypotheses - in the case of Hurewitz, the notion of social cleavage and relative social homogeneity; and in the case of Janowitz, a notion of historical development - which are far from being free of ambiguity. They require further empirical support if they are to prove explanatory in the case of Iraq. Is, for example, the Iraqi army a product of, or a contributing factor to, social divisions in

Iraq? What is the concept of homogeneity in empirical terms? Is it merely descriptive? Similarly, the vagueness of the concept of historical tradition (like that of 'political culture', for example[8]), in its relation to sectarian loyalties, militates against a clear explanation of the role that religion played in the development of the Iraqi army and its political activities.

A further comment about the use of models and comparative theories in explaining the role of the military in the politics of developing countries is that they sometimes depend upon a normative basis. There are two difficulties here. One, which has been pointed out by Hurewitz, is that the use of comparative concepts, such indeed as the very term 'development', presupposes the primacy of the European and American experiences. That is, the notion of a state used in such models is derived from the kind of polity typical of the 'developed' areas with strong central government, an absence of sectarian or ethnic regional groupings of any major political consequence, constitutionally prescribed relations between the army and the government, etc. Both as an ideal type for comparison and as a prescribed goal for development, this normative basis is deficient in its application to the Middle East, because it assumes that the Western 'model' is not necessarily applicable to the Middle East. Moreover, the notion that this type of polity is an end product implies a general theory of development in which the necessary and sufficient conditions are known and can be stipulated, so as to induce or interpret various stages in the developmental process. In other words, there is an implicit theory of development underlying the use of comparative models which needs to be explicitly stated and tested. So both value judgments and misleading methodological implications are implicit in references to idealisations based on Western experiences.

All of this is not to say that there is no value in such theorising. Useful insights may be derived from it. Indeed, the very conjectural element in it provides a number of questions that act as a focus for inquiry. Given that they are questions and not answers, they do not necessarily prejudice an investigation into the role of the army in politics. But throughout this study, those significant factors and elements that will be stressed are, in my view, for the most part unique to Iraqi society and politics in the period under study. That is why my approach will be largely historical, in that references to the temporal context of Iraqi politics and society will have pre-eminence over reference to theoretical categories. Hence terms such as 'weakness', 'instability', etc., when used in reference to the political regime of the Iraqi state, are intended to be descriptive and not theoretical in nature.

Bearing all of these reservations in mind, I have conceived the Iraqi state as a set of cross-cutting relations in which the army gradually assumed a predominant role. Circumstances unique to Iraq played a part in shaping this role. The extent to which these relationships were manipulated by the army or the central government provides us with an index as to relative power and, indeed, to the nature of the developing polity. In particular, the way in which change was 'organised' gives us an indication as to the 'effectiveness' of the state as a polity.

In addition to the possession of agreed boundaries and a population with a sense of its own political autonomy, a means of enforcement is also a necessary component of the modern state. Indeed, the monopoly of violence is considered by some to be one of the chief attributes of the state. External defence and internal security are considered two major functions of a stable government. The extent to which the means of enforcement are controlled by the central government is an index of its 'power' and 'stability', that is, its ability to 'organise change'. *Coups d'état*, the intervention of the armed forces in areas that, ostensibly, at least, are beyond its formal jurisdiction, the necessity of military support to sustain government or to administer the state, the role of the military in political decision-making – are all phenomena that testify to the political significance of the armed forces, and to the corresponding weakness of the civil state.

A broad understanding of the role of military intervention in politics must of necessity, therefore, involve an analysis of the nature of the state in question. The more unstable, ineffective, and divided the civil polity becomes, the greater is the likelihood of military intervention. But it may be that the existence of a 'state within a state', that is, an autonomous source of authority (in this case the army), contributes to the general conditions of instability, especially if it adopts an interventionary role. The degree to which this autonomous condition exists provides an indication as to the political significance of the army, whether this is latent or actual. As our evidence should show, the state of Iraq lacked the prerequisites for the effective mobilisation of change in terms of decision-making and control over resources. This inherent weakness stemmed from the state's artificial geographical and structural foundations. Its unsettled boundaries, the ethnic heterogeneity of its population, the corruption of a high percentage of its officials, the archaic land tenure system, the striking economic inequalities, the traditional opposition of the tribal system, and the state's almost total dependence on the political and military support of a foreign power – all in varying degrees contributed to the inherent instability of the Iraqi government, and therefore provided a suitable environment for the intervention of the army in the affairs of the state. This is why this study begins with an inquiry into these structural conditions and their effect on the developing polity. Within this structure, the ever-growing importance of the army was due to the way in which the Iraqi state evolved right from its inception. I will attempt to show that the frequent occasions on which the state deployed the army in a political role indicate both the failure of the state itself to create a civil polity, and the growing political importance of the armed forces. In a sense, the army had a political role from the very origins of the new state.

The weakness of the central government, particularly after the death of King Faisal (especially *vis-à-vis* British pressure), and its concern for extending its control over the diverse elements of the polity, could be expected to give the army a pivotal significance on politics. Again, the absence of a basic bureaucratic development and of a communications system could be expected to strengthen this role. Hence an examination of the actual functioning of the army and its involvement in the civil administration of Iraq might provide evidence of a developing autonomy.

The involvement of the British government in Iraq also had a determining effect on the 'politicisation' of the Iraqi army. Given this involvement, and the consequent restrictions placed on both the authority of the government and the development of the Iraqi army, it would be reasonable to suggest that there was tension between Britain's larger concern for security and the Iraqi government's concern for its power and prestige. From this we could expect the Iraqi army to act as a focus for nationalist sentiments arising out of the relative impotence of the central government and the British presence. Yet the government was also dependent on the army for its authority in the provinces, and the army was dependent on the British for its supplies, equipment and training. Tensions between these different demands can be regarded as being unique to Iraq, and some examination of them is clearly necessary to explain the army's political role.

In short, all of these considerations have made it inevitable that an understanding of the political role of the Iraqi army include a thorough investigation of the development of the Iraqi polity itself. Thus, after a brief chronological summary, chapter II deals with the structural and geographical distribution of the population, which was a major factor determining the instability of Iraq during the period under study. Chapter III indicates how the state was governed by a 'closed' elite, where the privileged position of this ruling class in the socio-political hierarchy was rooted in the past (at least in the sense that the majority of its members had been in the service of the Turkish and/or the Sharifian authorities). Chapters IV and V contain a description of the creation and expansion of the army and of the increasing reliance of the government on the armed forces and the subsequent augmentation of the army's involvement in the affairs of state. Chapter VI, VII and VIII contain an analysis of the circumstances leading to the first Iraqi coup in 1936 and the series of coups that followed, culminating in that of 1941. Finally, chapter IX summarises my conclusions.

Chapter 1

The beginning of the state

The region of Mesopotamia* within which the modern state of Iraq was established has been ruled by many successive empires from the earliest recorded periods of history. It was ruled in turn by the Babylonians, the Assyrians, the Persians and the Greeks. In 247 BC it fell once more into Persian hands and remained under their control until its conquest by the Arabs in AD 636. Within a little over a century Iraq had become the centre of Arab civilisation, and its newly created capital, Baghdad, became and remained the seat of the Abbasid Caliphs until the final disintegration of the Abbasid Empire in 1258.

This Arab influence left a lasting impression on the country, which neither the devastating invasion of Hulaku Khan nor almost four centuries of Ottoman rule could eradicate. During the last years of Ottoman rule, when the Ottoman Empire was starting to fragment, some Arabs of Mesopotamia, undoubtedly inspired by the upsurge of contemporary nationalist feeling in many areas, and perhaps both resenting and admiring the Ottomanism of the Young Turks, started to revive and assert their Arab identity. (It should be pointed out, however, that many Iraqi officers and officials continued to work in the Ottoman framework until its final collapse.) A large proportion of the Iraqi personalities who were later to occupy the highest public offices started their political careers working for secret Arab nationalist societies, and fighting with the Sharifian Arab army in alliance with the British against the Turks during the First World War. For example, two-thirds of the Iraqis who held the position of premier between 1920 and 1936 had actively participated in the armed revolt against the Turks.

One of the secret nationalist societies of this period, al-'Ahd, was

* Mesopotamia is a word of Greek derivation meaning 'between the rivers'.

formed exclusively by Mesopotamian Arabs[1] with the avowed aim of securing the 'independence of Mesopotamia from all foreign control'.[2] However, with the end of the war the aspirations of these nationalists were frustrated. Mesopotamia's potential oil resources,[3] coupled with its acknowledged strategic importance[4] as the vital overland route through which commercial and postal traffic to India and the Far East must pass, resulted in Britain's failing to keep her wartime pledges of complete independence for her Arab allies, although it had been agreed that southern Mesopotamia would remain under British rule. But, far from being abandoned, the cause of the Arab nationalists received fresh impetus with the publication in 1918 of President Wilson's '14 points', and by the Anglo-French declaration preceding it, reiterating the intention of the two governments to establish among those 'people so long ... oppressed by the Turks ... national Governments and Administrations drawing their authority from the free choice of indigenous populations'.[5]

The markedly varied responses to these declarations shown by different sectors of the Mesopotamian population foreshadowed the development of what would come to be dominant trends in the evolution of the Iraqi polity. While the nationalists busied themselves discussing various schemes for the setting up of an Arab government in the form of either a monarchy or a republic, the majority of the tribal shaikhs called for the continuation of British administration.[6] (This was particularly true of the 'Amara tribes, who had been under British occupation for a relatively longer period and who had materially benefited from it. (There were other tribes who also favoured British occupation, either because their shaikhs were recipients of British favours or because of their fears that the Arab government would most likely be dominated by Sunnis.) The *mujtahids* (Shi'a clergy with the sole authority to interpret Islamic law) called for the establishment of an Islamic state, while the Kurds called for an autonomous Kurdistan and the Jewish community, which formed over one-third of the population of Baghdad, 'sent a petition asking to be allowed to become British subjects'.[7] While the debate in Iraq continued, the San Remo Conference assigned the Mandate for Iraq and Palestine to Great Britain, news of this agreement reaching Iraq in June 1920.

No sooner had the Mandate been announced in Baghdad than the divergence of views dwindled into insignificance. Most significantly, a rapprochement was reached between the Sunni and Shi'a communities (who jointly constituted 92 per cent of the population). Political meetings were held in various parts of the country, and recitations of patriotic poetry, to which the 'Arab is so peculiarly susceptible'[8] were organised. These gatherings represented the initiation of a process of politicisation that culminated in the popular uprising of 1920.[9] After fierce fighting, with considerable human and economic losses to both the British and the Iraqis, hostilities ceased and the process of setting up a national state was set in motion. This is how the new situation was summed up in a confidential conversation between the British Foreign Secretary and the French Ambassador in London:[10]

> The position in Mesopotamia was this, the British Government had encountered difficulties in Mesopotamia which had involved them in overwhelming responsibilities, in constant and fierce criticism in Parliament and in the Press, and in the expenditure of money, which it was altogether out of reason to expect that we could continue to bear. In these circumstances, we had publicly announced our intention . . . to let the Arabs of Mesopotamia set up their own Government.

In Iraq itself, with the cessation of hostilities and the intense political activities and manipulations by diverse political factions that followed,[11] the old contradictions re-emerged, expressing themselves in seemingly irreconcilable notions and aspirations. For example, the British High Commissioner described the attitude of some sectors of the population of Mesopotamia towards the proposed nation-state as follows:[12]

> In Basra willayets I found no enthusiasm for the idea of a national Government. The merchants and people of Basra itself have grown rich, their trade is prospering, they fully appreciate the advantages of British administration and have no actual desire for a material change. In Qurnah, Qal'at Salih, and 'Ammara division itself, the Shaikhs and landlords, though obliged to pay revenue regularly, do so willingly now that they are secure in their tenure and immune from the necessity of periodically bribing officials. . . . In Baghdad, and Mosul willayets, the type and temper of people are different. They are not to the same degree immersed in commerce, and they are in closer touch with the West. . . . Among them there is a very general and impatient desire for a greater share in the administration and early establishment of a national Government. The majority of the intelligentia [sic] are no doubt strong nationalists, but, realising that they cannot walk alone, are inclined to trust in our assurances and look forward to gradual formation of a national administration under our auspices.

In further dispatches the High Commissioner provided evidence that the attitude of the mercantile community of Baghdad, particularly the Jews, towards the setting up of a national government was similar to that of their counterparts in Basra. Thus it was reported that, in a conversation with the High Commissioner, Sha'ul Haskail, one of the leading merchants of Baghdad (and brother of Sassun Haskail, then the Minister of Finance in the provisional government), expressed grave doubts about the commercial future of Mesopotamia under an Arab government; doubts[13]

> which he says are widely shared by the Jewish mercantile community.
> . . . He himself contemplates disposing of all his interests in the
> country and settling permanently in Europe, and he believes that
> this course will be followed by others, not only Jews but
> Mohammedans, who are in a position to pursue it, unless the assur-
> ance speedily gains ground that the British Mandate will be exercised
> so as to ensure stable political conditions. He admits that the dis-
> appearance in this manner of capital and commercial enterprise
> would be a serious blow to the prospects of the country.

In the Muntafiq division, the situation was summed up as follows:[14]

> The events of the past months have resulted in driving every landlord
> into support of the British Government. . . . In the face of general
> hostility, the tribal shaikh, in order to maintain his position, has
> been forced into an unfriendly or at least neutral attitude towards
> us [Britain] . On the other hand the Chiefs of big confederations
> have in most cases felt themselves strong enough to defy public
> opinion and support Government, relying in turn on government
> support. The prospect of native public institutions causes them
> considerable uneasiness.

In spite of this opposition, however, the British government gave way to the generally more pressing arguments in favour of setting up a national government. Underlying her new attitude was the policy that the status of Iraq should not 'be defined . . . in the usual mandate form but in the form of a treaty'.[15] In order to secure this, Britain set about actively looking for a 'suitable' Arab leader to rule Iraq, a search that ended in the decision to invite Amir Faisal to become king.

However, the mere creation of the monarchy could in no way pro-duce the social cohesion that was necessary for its survival. The pre-dominantly tribal rural population that constituted over two-thirds of the population had a traditional hostility towards any form of govern-ment. Perhaps more important, some tribes were in open conflict with one another, either over land issues or because of conflicting allegiances. In some cases there were even conflicts within the same tribe, such as those that occasionally existed between the shaikhs and the *sarkals*. All of these factors added to the considerable difficulties of ruling the tribal areas, and, as a typical intelligence report remarked as late as 1930, many of the tribal shaikhs were 'regretting the 1920 revolt which brought it [the Government] to power';[16] in the aftermath of the 1920 rebellion a number of tribal areas lapsed back into anarchy, refusing to pay taxes and scarcely recognising the central authority in Baghdad.[17]

In the case of the Shi'a tribes, this general lawlessness was given added momentum by the *'ulama*, who persisted in their opposition to the central government and the king. This is how their attitude to the 1923 elections, for example, was summed up:[18]

> First they desire a weak Government which will allow their ignorant theocracy to rule the tribes and to exploit them. . . . (if all goes well) the king and the Iraq Government will be able to claim that their authority is based on the will of the people and will gain in strength and no longer have to defer to the 'Ulama. They believe that the Turks would be better for their interests, because they would inevitably be weak. Secondly, they feel that, if the Government continues as at present constituted, the Shi'ah will have no influence in it. The Electoral Law was so framed that elections must be hopelessly gerrymandered in favour of the Sunnis. . . . Thirdly they seem to have some personal dislike of the King.

In addition to this tribal dissension and the manipulation of the *'ulama*, as will be seen in later sections, some minority groups, particularly the Kurds and the Assyrians, continued their call for complete autonomy and secession from Iraq, a call that frequently developed into armed conflict between the nationalists and government troops. Furthermore, the country's boundaries were still unsettled, particularly in the oil-rich Mosul area, resulting in a succession of armed clashes between Turkish and Iraqi forces. This dispute was not settled until July 1926, when Mosul was allocated to Iraq on the undertaking that Turkey would receive a 10 per cent share of any royalties accruing to the Iraq government from its oil deposits over the next twenty-five years.

The new state set up in 1920 was thus subject to a variety of pressures and contradictions which threatened its stability and political success. On the one hand, Iraq was only partially independent and was still heavily influenced by the British civil and military presence. All Iraqi governments were therefore subject to the charge of being in the stranglehold of British imperialism. On the other hand, many Iraqis had little confidence in their own political leaders and doubted their ability to set up a viable independent state. Thus the regime was faced with the general problem of 'legitimacy', and although the accession of Faisal did something to mitigate this, the strains and stresses within Iraqi society remained acute and explosive. More specifically, the government was faced with the problem of imposing and maintaining control over a rebellious and heterogeneous population. Among Middle Eastern states, Iraqi society was notable (though not exclusively so) for its tribal, ethnic and religious heterogeneity.

Chapter 2

Structural instability

The structure and distribution of the population

On becoming a state in 1920, Iraq had a population of 2,849,000.[1] In terms of absolute numbers, the majority of the population (about 56 per cent) were Shi'a, while the Sunnis (both Arabs and Kurds) constituted around 36 per cent; the remainder were Assyrians, Christians, Jews, Yazidis and other numerically smaller religious and ethnic groups. Most of the Shi'a population lived in the southern parts of the country, while the Sunni Arabs, the Christians and the Jews lived mainly in the two major urban centres (Baghdad and Mosul). The Kurds were concentrated in the north-east region, and the Yazidis lived in the proximity of Jabal Sinjar, fifty miles west of Mosul. As should become clear in the course of this book it was mainly the Sunnis who provided the cadre for the administration of the country. This was due primarily to the relatively advantageous position they held in the country's social hierarchy, which in turn must have been due to the fact that they had been traditionally more urban and therefore more modern than their Shi'a counterpart; a fact that can be attributed, at least partly, to the Shi'as' more conservative religious doctrine.

As we shall see, the differences between Sunnis and Shi'as and Arabs and Kurds were to be of great importance in the political life of Iraq. Nevertheless, the basic division that the British faced when they occupied Iraq was between rural and urban sections of the population. That such a discrepancy existed is of course not unique to Iraqi society. However, in Iraq this division, which was manifested in cultural as well as in economic and political matters, was so profound as to constitute one of the main underlying causes of the internal conflict characteristic of the period under study. A reconciliation between the two sectors was

14

a task requiring carefully considered long-term programmes and policies. But, as will be seen below, the average life of the cabinet during the first sixteen years of the state's existence was just over eight months, making long-term policies difficult to plan or carry out.

In addition to the general rift between the rural and urban population, these sectors were also divided within themselves; politicians working against their colleagues, shaikhs perpetuating their traditional rivalries and enmities, *fallahin* (land cultivators) resenting the exploitation of urban landlords and tribal shaikhs alike, and, most significantly, the army suppressing the armed uprisings of tribes from which most of its troops originated, and with which they still identified. Not infrequently, members of the armed forces, when sent by the government on reprisals against the tribes, would abandon their units and join the rebels. This is how a confidential report described one such incident:[2]

> but the Government . . . hesitated . . . by no means sure that the army would fight. Many of the officers are believed to be in sympathy with the Government's opponents, and the majority of the rank and file, being Shi'ah . . . some few officers actually refused to proceed to the front, and the men of the punitive column . . . were reduced to tears by the appeals of the women not to shed the blood of their brother Arabs and coreligionists.

To the urban elite, the rural population, whose members cultivated most of the country's agricultural land and manned the newly established national army, remained as obscure as it had been during the chaotic period of Ottoman rule. Analysing the human material that was to provide the governing body of the emergent state in 1920, a British government report claimed that:[3]

> the intelligentsia from top to bottom neither have any knowledge of rural conditions nor have they begun to realise that these must be studied and known. . . . Except for the families of tribal descent . . . the Baghdadi . . . regards the whole tribal population, on which the economy of Mesopotamia ultimately rests, with a mixture of fear and disdain.

According to this same report, this feeling of resentment was mutual, and the inhabitants of the provinces were[4]

> jealous of the Baghdadi; and resent his being placed exclusively in authority. . . . The townsman . . . is reluctant to serve in provincial

15

posts and the Baghdadi landlord in nine cases out of ten has never set eyes on his estates outside the town.

Did this antagonism diminish with the evolution of the state during the period under review, and how did it influence the distribution of privileges and national resources? It is hoped that some of the answers will emerge from the discussion that follows.

There does seem to have been some change in the relative proportion of the urban and rural population. At the beginning of the period of British occupation, the Iraqi population was predominantly rural, with only 22 per cent living in urban areas. It is not known what proportion of this urban population was living in Iraq's three major cities in 1920, but estimates for 1930[5] show that those cities together accommodated 344,000 – 38 per cent of the total urban sector, and a mere 12 per cent of the total population of Iraq. Of the 344,000 inhabitants of the three major cities, 64 per cent lived in Baghdad, 23 per cent in Mosul, and the remaining 13 per cent in Basra.

According to the estimates available for the first decade of the state's existence, it appears that there was a *negative* annual growth rate of population, averaging −0.8 per cent; thus, by 1930 the population was estimated at 2,824,000. This negative growth rate might reflect the difficulties of census-taking in the absence of stable administration, but it could also be attributed to Iraq's low standard of public health,[6] to emigration, and to the state's frequent armed incursions against the tribes and some minority groups. Although there are no statistics to indicate the state of health in rural areas, it is clear that their share of the country's medical facilities was considerably smaller than that of urban areas. Over two-thirds of the hospital beds in Iraq in 1922 were distributed between the three main cities, and although by 1930 the number of hospital beds in rural areas had risen to half that of the cities, the disparity between the two sectors was still marked: while there was one hospital bed for every 418 city dwellers in 1930, there was only one bed to every 5,794 people living outside the cities.[7]

Some drift of population away from the rural parts to the towns may have also been caused by the government's suppression of the recurring tribal uprisings. There were numerous skirmishes between the government forces and the armed tribes, and the frequency of these clashes increased after King Faisal's death in 1933, escalating into open war during 1935 and 1936 and only temporarily subsiding with the overthrow of the government by members of the armed forces in 1936. An indication of the scale of these conflicts is the fact that, from the time of King Faisal's accession to the throne in August 1921 until the independence of the state in 1932, there were 130 occasions [8] when the RAF came to the government's aid, making raids that sometimes involved the dropping of as much as ten tons of bombs, not infrequently resulting in villages being 'practically destroyed . . . the debris being completely burnt up by incendiary bombs and Verey lights'.[9] It seems likely that the tribal rebellions and the social instability caused by them must have played some part in changing the traditional distribution of population.

The extent of emigration from Iraq is harder to ascertain. Although there are no reliable figures, the dispatches of the British Embassy in Baghdad make frequent reference to groups of people, particularly Assyrians, Kurds and Yazidis, who were regularly moving between Iraq and neighbouring countries. While there is no indication as to the numbers of those who stayed permanently outside Iraq, it is known that, by 1933, 9,000 of the Assyrian population had left the country and settled elsewhere.[10]

For these reasons, although there was an overall decline in the total population during the ten years in question, the estimated figures show that there was an increase in the urban sector, from 640,000 in 1920 to 895,000 by 1930, bringing the proportion of the population that was urban to 32 per cent. An indication that this increase was not due to natural growth alone is the fact that the total number of births in the three major cities in 1928–30 exceeded the total number of deaths by a mere 639, giving an average population increase of 71 persons per annum for each city. It is, therefore, justifiable to assume that the increase in the urban sector was due to a shift of population from the rural areas towards the towns.

This trend towards urbanisation may be explained not only by those factors driving the inhabitants away from the countryside, but also by the positive attraction of towns and the rising political and commercial influence of the cities, and not least by the state's establishment in 1920 of the army and police force, the combined strength of which had reached 25,000 by 1930. The majority of the rank and file in the army came from the rural areas, and thus inevitably came to be exposed to modern ideas and trends. To these people, a career in the army involved abandoning their traditional costume and adopting a modern appearance. Furthermore, it frequently entailed the learning of a new skill, which made it easier for them to find employment in the metropolis once their service in the forces ended.

In addition to the indirect role of the army and police force as recruiting agencies of urbanisation, the spread of modern means of communication and education played an important role in bridging the gap between the urban and rural sectors of the population. It is claimed that in 1878 the cost of transporting £1 worth of grain from Hilla to Baghdad – a distance of about 60 miles – was £1.50. [11] However, shortly before the outbreak of the First World War, the Ottoman government, with the help of Germany, had completed the construction of a small section of railway estimated to be 130 miles long.[12] This was later expanded by the British, and by 1920 extended from Baghdad to Basra in the south, and to Khanaqin and Kirkuk in the north-east, reaching a total length of 1,139 miles.[13] This gave the country a ratio of 1 mile of railway to 4,500 inhabitants, whereas in India, for example, whose railway had been established about seventy years before, there was 1 mile to 11,000 inhabitants. As an indication of the increasing use of the railways for both personal travel and the transportation of goods, the number of passengers increased by 44 per cent between 1923 and 1928, and, despite the economic depression of the late 1920s, increased a further 8 per cent between 1928 and 1930. Figures for the increase in the transport of freight by rail during these two periods are 43 and 11 per cent, respectively. The system of river steamers, another major means of transport, is also reported to have been improved. Although no figures are available for years earlier than 1927, later figures show that the number of steamers had increased by 9 per cent between 1927 and 1930.

There is more solid evidence regarding the expansion of education. Under the Ottomans, education in Iraq had been provided only by the mullah (religious) schools, the curriculum of which was based entirely on recitation of the Koran. Even when modern elementary schools were established during the early years of this century, 'every boy attending school was compelled to wear the local travesty of the European dress and a fez, to salute the Turkish flag, and to receive instruction in Turkish'.[14] These regulations resulted in a boycott of such schools by most sectors of the population, and particularly by members of the Shi'a community, who, in addition to these restrictions, objected to Sunni religious instruction being a compulsory part of the school curriculum. However, these widely resented impositions in the schools were brought to an end with the collapse of Ottoman rule, and by the time the state emerged in 1920, 88 primary schools had been established with an attendance of 8,001. By 1925 the figures had increased to 213 and 20,512, respectively, and by 1930 to 314 and 34,220.

The proportion of annual government expenditure devoted to education also showed a gradual rise during the years in question, from 2.3 per cent of the total expenditure in 1920, to 4.2 per cent in 1925 and 7.5 per cent 1930 (table 1). However, as with medical facilities, this expansion was not evenly distributed between the various sectors of the population. Although there was an increase of 33 per cent in the number of pupils attending schools in rural areas during the period under study, it is clear that the urban share of educational facilities was much larger. As shown in table 1, 40 per cent of the schools in Iraq in 1922 were located in rural areas, and while the rural share of school buildings had risen to just over half by 1930, 57 per cent of the total number of pupils came from urban areas. This disparity was even more marked in the field of secondary education, where 86 per cent of those attending secondary schools in 1927 still came from the urban sector; this figure was reduced slightly to 82 per cent by 1930.[15]

The tribes and the system of land tenure[16]

The slow process of urbanisation described above had little effect on the bulk of the population, which remained predominantly agrarian: over 80 per cent of the rural inhabitants depended on agriculture as the main source of livelihood. (This figure excludes the nomads, who are estimated to have formed 10 per cent of the population in 1920 and about 8 per cent in 1930.) It is significant that the greater part of the agricultural sector was composed of settled tribes or semi-settled nomads. Both before and after the emergence of the state in 1920, their shaikhs, the tribal chiefs, formed an important part of the power structure of Iraq. Most of this power was derived from the land tenure system and the control that it enabled the shaikhs to exercise over their *fallahin*, particularly when it is borne in mind that about four-fifths of the families of Iraq owned no land whatever.[17]

The fertility of the land of ancient Mesopotamia and the advanced nature of its irrigation works support the belief that, in the neo-Babylonian and Abbasid periods, Mesopotamia supported a population of about 30 million.[18] The advanced irrigation system on which the country's prosperity largely depended started to decay in the Middle Ages, especially after the Mongol invasion of 1258, which virtually destroyed settled urban life.

During the following five centuries, this progressive disintegration was never effectively halted, while at times it was given added momentum

Table 1 *Number of government elementary and primary schools in Iraq in 1922, 1925 and 1930*

Liwas	1923				1925				1930			
	Schools	Pupils	% of total Schools	Pupils	Schools	Pupils	% of total Schools	Pupils	Schools	Pupils	% of total Schools	Pupils
Baghdad	18	1,925	11.9	12.6	24	3,788	11.2	18.4	39	7,396	12.4	21.6
Basra	10	1,232	6.6	8	20	2,038	9.3	9.9	33	3,580	10.5	10.4
Mosul	63	6,576	41.7	43	68	6,637	31.9	32.3	73	8,525	23.2	24.9
Others	60	5,542	39.7	36.2	101	8,049	47.4	39.2	169	14,719	53.8	43
Total	151	15,275	<100>	100	213	20,512	100	100	314	34,220	100	100
Education budget (ID)		146,543				171,532				288,075		
% of total expenditure		3.6				4.2				7.5		

by severe epidemics and the existence of an almost continuous state of war. The country's geographical situation between rival states was a major cause of its witnessing 362 major battles between 1258 and the outbreak of the First World War.[19]

During this long process of increasing economic depression and the decline of the major cities of Mesopotamia, most of the former urban population returned to a semi-nomadic way of life, and the power of the tribes began to revive. Their resurgence went unchecked, and was virtually unchallenged by the weak authority of the government in Baghdad. In comparison with their other Arab provinces, the Ottomans always experienced particular difficulty in maintaining control over the Iraqi tribes, and the direct influence of the Ottomans was limited to the larger cities, their immediate hinterland and some vital garrison towns, as well as the imperial road from Istanbul along the Tigris Valley. Elsewhere, large areas had to be controlled mainly through political manipulation of the tribes.

The deep changes that occurred in the traditional Ottoman institutions, and which are generally characterised as 'decay', were manifested in Iraq, as elsewhere, by a general weakening of control. In addition, Iraq was considered 'Turkey's Siberia', and no Turkish official was keen to serve there. Those appointed as governors, including Midhat Pasha, were usually 'out of favour, and their tenure of office was deliberately kept short, so that they would not consolidate their power and seek independence'.[21] This contributed to the ineffectiveness of governmental authority, and to the virtual fragmentation of the country into a number of tribal confederations, with the result that Iraq became, in effect, a conglomeration of rival miniature states. The most prominent of these was the Muntafiq confederation in the Euphrates region, which consisted of Bani Malik and al-'Ujoud tribes, and the 'Amara confederations of Albu Muhammad, Bani Lam and Bani Rabi'a.[22]

Although these general weaknesses of Ottoman rule were an important factor in giving the power of the tribal shaikhs free rein, the main source of that power lay in their hold over the land. Under the Ottomans, almost all available land was classified as *miri* – that is to say, its ultimate ownership lay with the state. Tenants were obliged to pay a land tax, which they in turn collected from individual cultivators. However, as most of these cultivators were simultaneously members of tribes with acknowledged leaders whose authority within the tribe superseded that of the government, the state could succeed in collecting her revenue only through those chiefs. But big shaikhs and absentee landlords, in their turn, had to rely on local agents for the collection of their share, a fact that led to the emergence of a 'class' of intermediaries who were mostly 'minor' shaikhs, and who became known as *sarkals*. Owing to the financial and social rewards attached to such appointments, inter-mediary shaikhs were forced to bid against one another in order to obtain *sarkal* privileges.[23] In practice, therefore, whether the landlord was the state or an absentee owner, the 'unit' of cultivation was the *sarkal*. This is how a British report described the interrelationship existing between these three units:[24]

> In settled areas, where the power of the proprietor was strong and his rights enforceable in the law courts, the Government looked normally to the owner for the payment of revenue; but if the owner chose to contract with the farmer that he should pay revenue, Government dues were collected from the latter without reference to the proprietor. If a sarkal defaulted, the ordinary procedure was to send a posse of gendarmes to live with him as his 'guests' until he had paid his revenue in full. This course was only possible in areas in which the Turkish Government was strong enough to enforce its rights. Elsewhere a bargain was more or less deliberately struck with the tribes, who agreed to pay just so much revenue as would suffice to make the movement of troops to recover the balance unremunerative. The ability of a landlord to collect his rent depended on his relations with the local executive authorities and partly on his power of bargaining with the shaikh. If the executive desired to assist, they would lend gendarmes and treat debtors of the proprietor as if they were debtors of the State. More usually a bargain was entered into with the shaikh, who, it is asserted, often succeeded in wringing from the landlord half the amount collected from the fallah.

Thus, neither the authority of the state nor that of the absentee landlord could always be enforced, and therefore, the *sarkals* became almost independent of the authority of either, imposing their own scale of taxation and passing on a mere fraction of taxes collected. In this way, the *sarkals* grew to be *de facto* owners of the land. Unrestricted by the weak central authority in Baghdad, the power of the tribes over the land became almost absolute. However, the move towards reform in the Ottoman Empire during the early part of the nineteenth century, the disbanding of the janissaries in 1826 and the establishment of a new conscript army, combined with the introduction of steam navigation and telegraphic communication in 1861, confronted the tribes with a serious threat. This challenge was symbolised by the appointment of the vigorous Ottoman reformer, Midhat Pasha, as the new governor in

Baghdad. Soon after his arrival in 1869, he started to pay much attention to the problem of the tribal areas, a major step in this direction being the implementation of the new Ottoman land code, which had been promulgated in Istanbul ten years earlier. This law stipulated that all *miri* land was subject to registration in return for a fee (*mu'ajjala*) to be paid immediately to the state.[25] This registration of land could provide an incentive for the purchasers of these *tapu sanads* (as the registration documents were called) to farm their land more intensively and, equally important, might result in the breaking up of tribal con-federations and in bringing them within the sphere of central authority. However, Midhat Pasha's reforms could have produced results only over a considerable period of time, and in the short term, at least, he had necessarily to rely on those instruments of government inherited from his predecessors, which were inevitably riddled with corruption. Thus, not infrequently, those shaikhs who did accept the new land regulations found that they had been given land that was already occupied by other tribes, leading to inter-tribal friction and sometimes to wars.

The majority of shaikhs, however, resisted purchasing these *tapu sanads* altogether, fearing that to do so would bring their hitherto successful evasion of taxes to an end,[26] and would make it increasingly difficult for them to avoid conscription. Consequently, many of the *sanads* were sold to city merchants and government officials,[27] who found a general refusal on the part of the shaikhs (the effective owners of the land) to recognise their authority. Thus, when these[28]

> new urban owners tried to assert their rights, they were opposed by
> the tribesmen, who refused to recognise the alienation of their lands.
> The conflict was usually settled by the relative power of the Govern-
> ment and the tribes: near the towns the new owners were upheld
> and the tribesmen reduced to tenants, while in the more remote
> regions the new owners were not allowed to take possession. Nor
> were matters made easier by confused and conflicting tribal claims,
> the chaotic state of the Ottoman registers, and the ignorance and
> corruption of the officials.

This failure of the new governor's reforms led to a change in policy towards the tribes, but it was to prove equally unsuccessful. Having failed to control the tribes, he now hoped at least to weaken them by adopting a policy of calculated favouritism, thereby aggravating inherent inter-tribal rivalries. He thus sought an alliance with the most influential Sunni shaikhs, the Sa'duns, giving them *tapu* rights over large areas of *miri* land traditionally controlled by the tribes, particularly in the

Muntafiq region. The tribes who were adversely affected by this move never acquiesced in this change, and[29]

> Acute agrarian unrest kept the Muntafiq district in constant
> rebellion, attempts to suppress the insurgents ended very commonly
> in the discomfiture of Ottoman arms and . . . neither the State nor
> the Sa'dun succeeded in collecting more than a fraction of their rent.

This tribal unrest continued, and in the ensuing years, 'group was pitted against group, tribe against tribe, section against section, until in the welter which ensued neither the Turkish tax-gatherers, nor merchant, nor traveller, could secure safe passage'.[30]

In this atmosphere of general hostility and lawlessness, no more than one-fifth of cultivable land had been registered as *tapu* land by 1892, while the remaining four-fifths remained as *miri* land, in which the state retained both property (*raqaba*) and usufruct (*tasarruf*) rights, which meant that it could rent it out to cultivators while reserving the right to evict them at any time.[31]

However, the introduction of *tapu* registration was only partially responsible for the general atmosphere of hostility and lawlessness in late Ottoman time that the British found when they came to Iraq. The main underlying factor seems to have been the significant change that the tribal system itself was undergoing. Whereas, in the past, the *dira* (area claimed by the tribe) had been regarded as belonging jointly to all its members, its revenues being used mainly for communal purposes such as the upkeep of the tribal militia and the entertainment of guests,[32] the position of the shaikh and members of his tribe had now changed. With the introduction into Iraq of modern means of communication in the late nineteenth century, formerly localised agricultural products found new trading outlets, giving the shaikhs new profits and advantages. It is estimated that, as a result, the volume of Iraqi trade 'increased eighteen-fold between 1870 and 1914'.[33]

This spurt of economic development, coupled with the new role that some shaikhs acquired through becoming *tapu* holders,[34] resulted in the *fallah* acquiring an additional value to his shaikh, which superseded his traditional worth as a fighter.[35] In order to protect his role as an entrepreneur, the shaikh became more vigilant, relying on his *hawshiya* (armed police) to exact the obedience of his tribesmen.[36] This aroused the resentment of members of the tribe. 'To Baghdad I want to escape from this tribe that cares not for its afflicted nor has pride',[37] ran a song in Albu Muhammad, one of the most influential tribes. However, owing to the *fallah*'s total dependence on his agricultural skills and the scarcity of farming jobs in the proximity of the cities, his 'escape' was more often confined to his movement to another tribe,[38] thereby adding a new dimension to inter-tribal conflict. Some of these *fallahin* settled, however, on *miri* land held by absentee landlords, and formed their own miniature tribes. Thus, when the British occupied the Basra area in 1914, for example, they found around the junction of the Euphrates and Tigris 'congeries of tribal fragments occupying *tapu* . . . land owned by absentee landlords'.[39] In the Baghdad vilayet alone, they reported finding at least 110 independent tribes made up of 1,186 sections,[40] while in the Mosul area they found most settled *fallahin* unwilling to build decent houses for fear that they might be evicted at any moment.[41]

With no patriarchal shaikh to control them or be responsible for them, these 'deserters' posed a serious problem to British administration. As late as 1920, it was noted that 'Rural communities which have broken away from the tribal system present the greatest difficulty, and the adjustment of relations between absentee landlords and cultivators is a problem that must be faced.'[42] British officials were aware of the exploitation existing between the *sarkals* and the *fallahin* respectively, and to have re-settled those 'deserters' back in the tribal areas could have polarised the situation even more.[43]

> I believe it is true that the fallah is absolutely in the hands of his sarkals, that to refuse to obey his sarkal would mean certain death, whereas to obey or attack means a possible chance of loot, and a chance at any rate, of life. The sarkals seem to me to be like the Feudal Barons. Many of them were small men of no account made powerful and rich and they now have a great deal of power in their hands and think they can rule. . . . The unity of purpose and lack of dissensions between the big shaikhs and sarkals is curious.

However, Britain's concern for the welfare of the Iraqi *fallah* was at best secondary to her overall interests in the country, which she thought could best be served by preserving the power of the shaikhs together with their intermediaries, the *sarkals*. 'The policy we pursued', stated an official report candidly, 'was to reconstruct and support the power of the shaikh.'[44] In order to achieve this, the shaikhs were extended extra privileges[45] while being allowed to maintain their existing ones. [46]

> The danger is lest the already rapidly moving process of disintegration be accelerated, and the power of the shaikh weakened. It was felt that this danger could be averted by insisting, wherever possible, on

the responsibility of the shaikh for his sarkals and by giving him a financial interest in the collection of revenue in his area. In pursuance of this policy certain rebates of the Government share were made in such a way as to give the shaikh a share.

Furthermore, the British authorities assigned the shaikhs responsibility for the administration of their areas,[47] and introduced the Tribal Criminal and Civil Disputes Regulations,[48] which left the powers of the shaikhs virtually intact and gave them almost complete administrative autonomy from the central government. As mentioned earlier, however, the shaikhs' main source of power was the control they traditionally enjoyed over tribal land, which enabled them to exert influence on members of their tribe. British officials were naturally fully aware of the economic and political importance of land: 'Our financial stability depends on our ability to collect land taxes and if revenue-paying districts do not accept the Government that we set up, we shall at once be bankrupt.'[49] In fact, although tax remissions and favoured treatments were extended to co-operative shaikhs, such as the shaikhs of Bani Rabi'a, who were requested to pay only one-third of their dues for the years 1920 and 1921,[50] land revenue was collected with such efficiency by the British authorities that the thoroughness of the work has been adduced as one of the major causes of the rising of 1920.[51]

Because the British wished to minimise the risk of any 'undesirable' persons gaining control of *miri* land, the Political Officer was given full discretionary powers in interpreting the Land Regulations and individual claims to the land. Thus, Proclamation no. 34 of the Civil Administration stated that:[52]

the Political Officer or any officer deputed by him may after due inquiry decide who has the best claim to cultivate such lands and at what rent . . . and if in his opinion no one has a valid claim to cultivate such lands the Political Officer may lease such lands on a yearly tenancy to such persons as he thinks fit upon such terms as he thinks reasonable.

As regards *tapu* land, the attitude of the British administration was based on similar political considerations:[53]

The Tapu Code was vital to the maintenance of the principles on which Turkish land tenure was based, and it remained under the Iraq Code the law of the land. The decision has proved valuable. The wealth of Mesopotamia has been in the past, and still continues to be, derived almost exclusively from agriculture. Any sudden change in Turkish procedure in a matter of such fundamental importance as title in land was to be deprecated. Moreover, Midhat Pasha's settlement was conceived . . . on wrong lines. It was impossible to proceed to its immediate amelioration, but to have enforced it, as the courts would have been bound to enforce it, on purely legal reasoning must inevitably have resulted in political unrest. Reference to Tapu brought disputes into the cognizance of the Revenue Department, which was in a position to take a wider view of the issues involved, and had the advantage of exercising its authority locally through Political Officers, who were able to get first-hand evidence on the spot and to judge of and make allowance for the political significance of all claims that might arise.

These policies, together with Britain's avowed aim of preserving the power of the shaikhs, were the underlying explanation of the fact that the shaikhs (who had constituted a mere 6 per cent of the deputies representing Iraq in the last Turkish Majlis of 1914) made up 41 per cent of the members of the first Iraqi Constituent Assembly in 1924. In addition to their political power, the tribes were also relatively well armed:[54] even as late as 1933 King Faisal is reported to have complained that the tribes possessed seven times as many rifles as the government. [55] Government attempts to collect rents and land taxes were therefore futile, and in most areas no such attempts were made until 1926.[56]

This virtual absence of governmental authority in the tribal areas is amply documented by intelligence reports. Even as late as 1930, in describing the prevailing conditions of the powerful Muntafiq region, one such report claims that[57]

in 1926 few officials dared to move off the road . . . four years of non-too-good administration has not done very much to tame the inhabitants. . . . It is just as well . . . to admit that this considerable area of potential unrest does exist.

In spite of the demonstrable inability of the government to collect regular revenue from the tribal areas, it is significant that no efforts were made by the government to reform the inherently chaotic Land Regulations that formed the basis of the power of the tribes. Apart from the government's fear of antagonising the tribal shaikhs and their British patrons, their inactivity in that direction may also be attributed to the rise of a new class of landowners with a vested interest in preserving the customary land tenure system.[58] 'The greater part of newcomers into agriculture', wrote the British Inspector of Agriculture, 'have been active politicians. . . . They have been granted very extensive tracts of valuable Government land, not only without payment, but also with revenue privileges.'[59] Although no statistics indicating the actual area of land acquired by individual urban politicians are available, frequent reference was made by British officials, and later by interested experts, to the abuses of the land laws by these politicians, and to the manipulation of those laws for their personal advantage.[60] In 1925, for example, Naji al-Suwaidi (Minister of Justice), who, like other politicians, had now become a large landowner, was reported,[61]

> with other Ministers interested in land, [to] desire without any enquiry to get rid of the Iraqian [sic] head Surveyor of the Tapu and land record [sic] who has incurred the hostility of many influential personages owing to his refusal to countenance notorious abuses and to allow Government land to be included in private properties. Tapu Department is under the British Director Royds and under the general control of the Ministry of Justice. Director declares that the official attached is one of the few honest men in the department. . . . Ministers [sic] regarding whose properties large Tapu transactions are pending alleges that he has heared tales of official's corrupt conduct but refuse to substantiate them in official enquiry. . . . Cabinet hurriedly passed Resolution day before my British High Commissioner return to Baghdad directing the dismissal of the official.

Even when land legislation was passed, it amounted to little more than an official sanction of the system that had in practice obtained during the latter part of the Ottoman period. The first such law, the Land Settlement Law, was not promulgated until 1930. This law classified *miri* land into three categories: the first was the land previously acquired by *tapu sanads*, whose tenure now amounted to full ownership; the second, to be known as *lazma*, referred to 'land cultivated by the claimant for at least 15 years';[62] while the third class, termed *sirf*, was land with 'no previously established tenancy'.[63] By 1933, 47 per cent of the total area of land available was *sirf*, 31 per cent *lazma*, and 18 per cent *tapu*, while the remaining 4 per cent was *mulk* of various kinds, including *waqf* and *matruka* (land reserved for public use).[64]

This legalisation of agrarian anarchy was followed in 1933 by a Law Governing the Rights and Duties of Cultivators, the promulgation of which led the British Inspector of Agriculture to declare that 'such a state of affairs is almost invariably followed sooner or later by revolution'.[65] Given the virtual absence of government in the late nineteenth and early twentieth centuries and the chaotic conditions then prevailing, the *fallah* had at least been able to abandon his tribe and move to another. However, under the new legislation, the *fallah* was denied even the freedom to leave his land. 'Since he cannot leave the land', wrote the same agricultural inspector, the *fallah* 'is in reality reduced to the status of a slave'.[66] Proceeding to analyse the implications of this law, he expressed concern that the landowner now became the[67]

> agricultural authority (Article 3) and, unfitted though he may be, gives his orders for sowing, irrigating and harvesting, orders which the fallah is obliged under severe penalties to carry out (Article 18). All advances made to the fallah, all charges incurred by the farm-owner, are to be regarded as an 'Agricultural Debt' recoverable from the fallah (Article 10). These charges and these advances will be incurred whether the venture is a success or not, but if, even by bad farming and bad direction on the part of the farm owner, a loss is incurred, then that loss becomes the fallah's debt to the farm owner. So long as such a debt exists, he is legally incapacitated from seeking employment on either a more successful farm, or in Government Departmental Service or in Municipalities or Registered Companies (Article 15). . . . Under Article 13, an indebted fallah may even have his plough and plough animals confiscated unless he continues to work on the same estate. . . . Practically every disaster that can occur to a crop, damage by flood, damage by locusts, etc., etc., can be (and most frequently is) attributed to the negligence of the fallah. . . . The share of the fallah is such that unless he has got his 'customary perquisites', such as free grazing for a goat or two, free firewood, a certain amount of free vegetables and a certain amount of 'stolen' produce, it is doubtful if he could exist.

But while the *fallah* was clearly at a disadvantage in relation to his *sarkal* and absentee landlord, the *sarkal* himself was in turn being exploited by the shrewd town merchants on whom he had to depend for his supply of seed. This seed was invariably bought on credit terms, and in cases where crop failure made the *sarkal* unable to honour the terms of payment, the merchants would charge no less than 50 per cent and often up to 100 per cent interest for every year's delay.[68] With the accumulation of debts thus acquired,[69]

> a new system has therefore become almost universal . . . the sarkals have given sanads to the money lenders making over to the latter the whole sarkal's share of the crops for a given number of years. . . .

> Ridiculous sanads, by which the sarkal agrees to surrender all his crops to the merchant and yet pay taxes himself, render it impossible for him to fulfill his obligations as a tenant.

These makeshift arrangements between the *sarkals* and the merchants, together with the land legislation discussed above, increased the political and economic disparities between the different sectors of the population, while the land laws clearly reinforced the privileged position already enjoyed by the 'landowners', and increased the advantages that had been acquired by members of the new ruling elite.

Summary

Until Midhat Pasha's appointment, all land in Mesopotamia was *miri*, whose users, at least in theory, had to pay rents to the state. In the second half of the nineteenth century Midhat Pasha implemented a new Ottoman Land Code, which enabled buyers of *tapu sanads* to claim semi-private ownership of land. Contrary to Midhat Pasha's aim, however, these *tapu sanads* were bought mainly by merchants and government officials, and therefore his hope of bringing the tribes within the sphere of government control was frustrated. By the end of the nineteenth century, therefore, about four-fifths of the cultivable land was still *miri* and was therefore theoretically controlled by the government, while the remaining one-fifth was, again at least theoretically, controlled by holders of *tapu sanads*. However, as most of the cultivable land in fact lay in the tribal areas, whether the landlord was the state (renting out *miri* land) or an absentee landlord (renting out land held by *tapu sanads*, for which high registration fees or bribes had to be paid), direct control of this land lay with the *sarkals* and the paramount shaikhs. Thus, when Ottoman rule came to an end, the British, who took over the administration of Mesopotamia, considered it appropriate to preserve the position of the *sarkal* and shaikh together with the existing Land Regulations. These British policies were not challenged, but rather were reinforced by the Iraqi ruling elite that came to power in 1921, most members of which became landowners. Thus these Land Regulations were maintained virtually intact throughout the period under study.

Chapter 3

The creation of the state

A review of British interests in Iraq between the two world wars

The state of Iraq was created by Britain, to which the Mandate had been given, and it is therefore natural to expect that the nature of that state and of its system of government should, in the last resort, be determined by the British government, or at least should not be incompatible with British interests.

Britain's interests in Iraq may be divided into strategic and economic. The three main strategic elements were communications, the British bases, and oil. Since Britain acquired a dominant interest in India, one of the main reasons for her concern with the Middle East was that it lay across what was by far the shortest route between Britain and her South Asian and Far Eastern possessions. Egypt, of course, lay across the sea route, particularly after the construction of the Suez Canal in 1869, but Iraq held a similar position in relation to the partly land-based route and also, by the second quarter of the twentieth century, the most convenient air route.[1] Technical changes in aircraft design would reduce the importance of the latter factor in the future, but at this period it was considerable. This makes the insistence on safeguarding 'lines of communications' in the Anglo–Iraqi Treaty most explicable. A large part in the denouement of Anglo–Iraqi relations in the period covered by this book is due to the fact that both land and air communications could only be secured either by a genuine political will in the country concerned or by the military occupation of it. These considerations would largely determine Britain's attitude towards Iraqi governments throughout the period under study. It followed from the growing importance of aviation, both for military and civil purposes,

31

that Britain attached great importance throughout this period to having air bases in Iraq. A number of bases were in fact constructed and used during the Mandatory period, and the Anglo-Iraqi Treaty of 1930 stipulated that Britain should have two of them (Habbaniya and Shuaiba).

Initially, the British RAF units in Iraq had a three-fold purpose: to deter external aggression and, when and if this failed, to provide a skeleton organisation whereby His Majesty's government could aid Iraq; to support the authority of the Iraqi government by their very presence and, if unsuccessful in this aim as well, directly to assist the Iraqi government in restoring internal order; and, lastly, in an internal emergency, to protect British lives and property.[2] But to some extent these aims were counter-balanced, as the Foreign Office was aware, by the fact that these bases and the privileges and immunities that the RAF personnel 'necessarily' enjoyed formed the 'main bugbear of the pure Iraqi nationalists'.[3] By the 1930s, however, British officials were inclined to believe that certain factors mitigated these objections: first, the fear inspired by Italy's conquest of Abyssinia (though how Italy would have carried out an equivalent campaign in Iraq is not clear); and, second, the success of British diplomatic efforts in smoothing over the petty grievances over RAF privileges, especially after the Iraqis realised that no attempt would be made to prevent them dealing with religious minorities in their own way.[4] It was claimed (by the Foreign Office) that in fact the only remaining point of dispute was over the guards at the bases, which were supposed to be supplied by Iraq yet were still Levies employed directly by Britain. Nevertheless, throughout this period the British were seriously worried by the threat to the security of these bases and the safety of those therein, posed by even relatively disorganised popular action, let alone by an antagonistic Iraqi government using the military forces under its command. That is why, as we shall see,[5] the coup of 1936 was initially viewed with some foreboding by the Foreign Office, which feared that[6]

the new regime may stultify the alliance by refusing to follow the lead and accept the advice of His Majesty's Government in foreign affairs, the possibility of a further disturbance of Anglo-Iraqi relations as a result of internal troubles in Iraq must be held prima facie to be greater. This in its turn increases the risks . . . that in the event of any dispute with His Majesty's Government the shock-absorber which formerly existed in the form of the wiser and more experienced politicians will no longer be present. Thus in the event of serious Anglo-Iraq friction developing . . . the military security of the Royal Air Force units might be found to be in greater danger than before.

However, it is perhaps curious that, almost at the same time of concluding the above analysis, the Foreign Office was making determined efforts to acquire landing rights to Imperial Airways to Lake Habbaniya, which the Sulaiman government was very reluctant to accept.[7] This was the only suitable refuelling point for the large flying boats with which it was intended to operate the air mail service to India, the Far East and Australia. The shoals of the Rivers Tigris and Euphrates rendered them unsuitable for this purpose, and the lake was conveniently situated only four miles from the new RAF base at Dhibban.

Ironically, although the exact reasons for Iraqi obduracy in this case are not known, one objection raised over Imperial Airways' request to use Lake Habbaniya was its proximity to the RAF base at Dhibban.[8] The Dhibban base had been built to replace the ones at Mosul and Baghdad, because, for reasons of security, it was thought preferable to have the bases away from large centres of population. This is an indication of the fact that the possibility of an anti-British movement led by the armed forces was always in British minds. This is also why the Foreign Office was reluctant in 1936 to sanction a proposal by General Muhammad Jawad, the Chief of the Iraqi Royal Air Force (IRAF) to double the size of the IRAF, thus rendering it superior both in numbers and quality to the local RAF units.[9]

An example of the difficulties created by the RAF bases can be seen from a somewhat plaintive letter from the British Consul in Mosul on the matter of a Mills bomb, which was apparently stolen from the armoury of the RAF squadron and thrown at the British Military Service Club in Mosul. The Mutasarrif of Mosul resisted strong hints made by the British Consul that bodies such as the local branch of the League of Muslim Youth should be investigated, and stated that, more likely, the bomb was thrown by a member of a minority group wishing to discredit the local Muslims. He based this belief on two grounds: first, that the Assyrian Levies would, and the army would not, have access to such weapons; and, second, the rather comical boast, that 'bomb-throwing, in particular, was not a local speciality'.[10] But the Consul regarded the Mutasarrif's theory disparagingly as a 'typical oriental reaction',[11] and thought the prospects of the culprit being found were slight.

In the light of various discussions of this matter, it would appear that by the 1930s the general Foreign Office opinion was that there were two reasons against, but one for, the retention of the RAF bases in Iraq. The reasons against were (1) that the above sort of disruption was equally likely to happen, treaty or no treaty, and (2) that the steady technical advance in aviation might soon lead to the aircraft cutting out the detour to Baghdad and flying direct from Egypt to Basra, or even Karachi. Thus they would miss or only just touch Iraqi soil. Flying boats might be able to go down the Red Sea and across the Arabian Sea/Indian Ocean (though this in itself would seem somewhat of a detour).

To understand the strategic interest in retaining the RAF bases, one must remember that northern Iraq had long been recognised as one of the world's major oil fields. Although only partly in British ownership, it was under British control and therefore represented an important British strategic as well as economic interest,[12] given the overwhelming importance of oil in powering modern warfare by air, land and sea. This was already known when the British occupied Iraq, but it became even more important when the Kirkuk oil fields began to be exploited by the Iraq Petroleum Company (IPC) and when the pipeline to the Mediterranean was completed in 1934. It should also be remembered that whoever controlled the Shatt al-'Arab in southern Iraq controlled the egress of oil from the vast Abadan refinery in Iran, and that is why it was important for His Majesty's Government to have military bases as near as possible to the wells and refinery of the Anglo-Iranian Oil Company. This was perhaps the main argument for the RAF presence in Iraq.

Turning to the more general British economic interests in Iraq, we find that, prior to the first World War, Britain occupied a paramount position in the trade of what later became Iraq. Of the total import trade, the United Kingdom's share was between 45 and 50 per cent, and India's 25 per cent, while the United Kingdom was also the principal customer, taking some 35 per cent of the exports.[13] Most shipping into Basra, and the service up-river from that part to Baghdad, was also in British hands. Ironically, during the period we shall be studying, while Britain's political influence in Iraq increased so dramatically, her share of Iraqi trade declined. By 1932-3 Britain's share of Iraqi exports was admittedly marginally higher than twenty years previously (37 and 36 per cent respectively), but her share of imports now averaged 35 per cent.[14] Nevertheless, postwar growth had added many other interests. His Majesty's Government were directly concerned with Basra port and Iraqi railways (where 124 British subjects were employed); two and a half of the only three banks in the country were British;[15] and, of course, so much British capital was invested in the oil industry. Summing up Iraq's economic value to Britain, a Foreign Office document[16] states that

> with the single exception of Egypt, there is no foreign country in
> the Near and Middle East where British commercial interests are . . .
> so well established and of such extensive scope as Iraq. It is difficult
> to estimate accurately the amount of British capital invested in the
> oil industry alone. The capital of the Iraq Petroleum Company
> (£6,500,000) and its subsidiary, Mediteranean Pipe-Lines (Limited)
> (£9,178,000), is owned as to 23.75 per cent, by the Anglo-Persian
> Oil Company, and as to a further 23.75 per cent by the Anglo-Saxon
> Petroleum Company (Royal Dutch-Shell group), French and United
> States interests owning 47 per cent of the balance. It is specified
> in the Company's Convention that it shall remain a registered
> British Company, and that its chairman shall at all times be a British
> subject. The majority of the company's technical employees are
> British and all other responsible positions in Iraq are filled by British
> subjects. The machinery and material necessary to its operations are
> predominantly of British manufacture.

During the 1930s, the main threat to Britain's favourable economic relations with Iraq came from the German and Japanese competitors, with the former obviously also having political connotations. The Germans were in the habit of hiring cinemas – ironically, mainly from Jews (who at that time owned all but one of the six cinemas of Baghdad) – in order to show films about the work and products of German companies such as Bayers, the chemical and pharmaceutical concern. These efforts, together with a flood of pamphlets, catalogues and circulars, seemed to have 'a marked effect on the attitude of Iraqi officials, especially in the Public Works Department; Iraqi merchants too are coming to look upon the German products as at least being equal in quality to United Kingdom products'.[17] In addition to these commercial activities, the German authorities were making determined and quite successful efforts to bring Iraqis in touch with German culture and to encourage them to visit Germany. In 1936, the Olympic Games offered a main attraction, and several Iraqi notables, 'including the brothers Naji and Taufiq Suwaidi, have availed themselves of official invitation and . . . the total number of Iraqis going to Germany this summer is over 150'.[18] The same report continues to refer to other attractions that were being made available to Iraqis by the German authorities, and how political capital was made out of them: [19]

Reduced railway fares and registered marks offer cheap travel and inexpensive living; and the German Legation have made the most of these points in their propaganda among the young generation of Iraqis, who are eager for travel abroad. Many of the tourists are teachers and I have no doubt that they will be well and truly shepherded and imbued with all the best that Nazism has to offer.

However, in spite of these activities, the overall situation was described as not particularly alarming,[20] and German-Iraqi trade, though fluctuating widely, remained proportionately small (about 5 per cent of the Iraqi total import trade).[21] More disturbing to Britain must have been what is often regarded as a modern phenomenon, that is, the truly spectacular rise in Japanese exports to Iraq, which rose from a mere 1.83 per cent of the total in 1930-1 to 20.40 per cent in 1934-5, an increase of more than ten-fold in four years.[22]

To sum up British attitudes to Iraq and its governments during the period under study, Iraq was seen as being of great importance and requiring some sort of connection or presence, and it is only in the light of this background that the creation and development of the Iraqi state can be understood.

The creation of the monarchy

Because of these interests, the British government naturally placed importance on establishing a friendly and co-operative Iraqi government which would be under its control. The alternative – that of ruling Iraq directly – was understood to be impossible for political and financial reasons. Thus, at the Cairo Conference of 1921 it was decided that the best course would be to create a monarchy in Iraq. It was natural that officials coming from a country ruled by a king should regard that as the most satisfactory and stable form of government, and in the particular circumstances of Iraq it was hoped that a monarchy would provide a focus for the unity of the different groups.

It was also decided that Amir Faisal of the Sharifian family would be the monarch. Faisal was the third son of King Husain, the Sharif of Mecca, who, in alliance with the British, had led the Arab revolt of 1916 against the Turks. Sharif Husain was a member of the Hashimite dynasty, which claims direct descendancy from the Prophet Muhammad.

Faisal's political experience was considerable. After receiving his education privately in Istanbul, he had returned to Hijaz, where he was put in charge of the administration of bedouin affairs. In 1913 he had become a member of the Turkish Parliament, during which time he was prominent for his Arab attitude and national zeal.[23] With the outbreak of the Arab revolt, Faisal was entrusted with the leadership of the northern Arab army, and after the capture of Aqaba in July 1917 became Commander-in-Chief of the Arab forces fighting in Palestine alongside the British forces of General Allenby. In October 1918 he entered Damascus at the head of the Arab contingent of the victorious Allied army, and later headed the government that was established in Syria, until his dethronement by the French in July 1920. In addition to his impressive credentials and 'personal courage, and diplomatic skill',[24] Britain hoped, in the opinion of her then Acting Civil Commissioner, that by offering the kingship of Mesopotamia to Faisal she would not only re-establish[25]

> her position in the eyes of the Arab world, but ... might go far to wipe out accusations which would otherwise be made against us [Britain] of bad faith with Faisal and with people of this country [Iraq], and if His Majesty's Government eventually decide drastically to restrict its commitments in this country there would be better prospects of it being done with Faisal here than any other possible arrangement.

The choice of Faisal, therefore, could be explained partly by the sense of guilt that some British officials may have felt towards his unfortunate experience with the French in Syria.[26] Other British diplomats seem to have felt a rather patronising thankfulness to a king who they thought would (and did) serve them 'loyally and well'.[27] But the main reason for the choice of Faisal as monarch must have been his realisation (1) of the weakness of the Hijazi kingdom, and (2) of the wisdom of enjoying close relations with the British government. He appears to have convinced the latter of his 'political realism' by the consistent pressure he tried to apply on his father over the ratification of the Treaty of Versailles. On one occasion, he is believed to have told his father that Britain was 'his only friend',[28] and in a letter to his brother Zaid on the same subject he emphasised the weakness of his father's position and advised an acceptance of the 'bitter reality'.[29]

It was, then, Britain's awareness of her own power and of the relative weakness of the Sharifian dynasty that led to her ultimate choice of Faisal as the first king of Iraq. For Faisal's 'statemanship' was not necessarily known to leading British officials. (It is claimed, for example, that during the discussion of Faisal's candidature, Churchill, then Colonial Secretary, inquired of his officials whether Faisal was a Sunni or a Shi'a.[30]) It was with these considerations in mind, and after ascertaining that Faisal would be prepared to negotiate an Anglo–Iraqi treaty if he were to become king of Iraq, that the British government approved Faisal's candidature. They then came to the question of how Iraqis could be persuaded to choose him. Churchill's disparaging phrase about the dangers of a 'small majority in favour of an unsuitable candidate at elections hardly worthy of the name in so scattered and primitive a community'[31] seems merely to indicate a fear that genuinely free elections might bring success to the candidate of the Iraqis, not of Britain.

Much was done to avert this peril. For example, a vivid candidate, Sayyid Talib al-Naqib, who was apparently received magnificently and who campaigned on the implicitly anti-Sharifian slogan of 'al-'Iraq li'l-'Iraqiyin' (Iraq for the Iraqis), was arrested on a trumped-up charge and deported just before the elections.[32] The actual ballot paper was clearly biased; voters were asked whether they professed allegiance to Amir Faisal or whether they dissented.[33] Nevertheless, 68 out of the 157 votes from Baghdad agreed to support Faisal only if Iraq gained full independence.[34]

With Faisal's coming to the throne in August 1921, the provisional government was dissolved, to be replaced by a Council of Ministers, and an Organic Law passed by the Constituent Assembly assigned legislative powers to the King and Parliament. Faisal's accession was generally acceptable to the nationalist elements in Baghdad, many of whom had served with him in combat and in the government of Syria. In addition, Faisal's claimed descent from the Prophet offered suitable material for religious rhetoric. An open letter in *al-'Iraq* newspaper, for example, hailing the King's arrival in Baghdad, linked the act of obeying him to that of obeying God:[35]

> After welcoming your noble arrival it is our duty to say to you that no King will occupy the throne of Iraq and lead the nation to success but you. May we be your reason. I chose you as King of Iraq and swear service to you in the interests of the nation, obeying the orders of God.

In contrast, the acceptability of Faisal to some tribal shaikhs was based on undisguised political expediency. Thus, when Faisal visited the Euphrates tribal region to receive the oath of allegiance, their paramount shaikhs,[36]

when they learnt that H.M.G. viewed with favour the candidature
of the Emir Faisal to the throne of Iraq, hastened to offer him their
fealty. . . . Both chiefs . . . swore fealty to him 'because you are
acceptable to the British Government'.

Nevertheless, to the Shi'a community as a whole (which formed 56 per
cent of the population), the enthronement of a Sunni prince was all too
reminiscent of the relatively underprivileged position they had endured
under the Sunni Ottomans. Undeterred by the obvious irony, some Shi'a
mujtahids issued a *fatwa* on the conflict between Turkey and the new
Iraqi state over the vilayet of Mosul, prohibiting their members to defend
Iraq against Turkey.[37] Although resident in Iraq, these *mujtahids* were [38]

Persian by birth and nationality . . . they regarded the subservience
of the civil arm to religious leaders . . . as the ideal to be aimed at
in the land of their adoption . . . it was hinted that they wished to
eliminate the King in favour of a republic or even return to direct
British control.

Three years after King Faisal's accession to the throne, his name and
that of his father were still[39]

inserted in the Friday Sermon after that of the Ottoman Sultan and
Caliph who was mentioned by name. . . . King Faisal argued . . .
that it was an insult to himself that the prayers of his people would
be requested for an alien sovereign in the temporal as well as the
spiritual capacity of the latter.

Given these reactions and considerations, the task of governing Iraq
was not an easy one. Nevertheless, Faisal continued to demonstrate a
degree of realism which sometimes verged on resignation. For example,
he is quoted as once having said that 'His Majesty's Government and I
are in the same boat and must sink or swim together.'[40] For their part,
the British were aware of the King's important role in ruling the
kingdom, and also that they could not have a 'contented Iraq without
a reasonably contented Faisal'.[41]

In this way, the Cairo Conference ultimately achieved its primary
aim of safeguarding British interests in Iraq. However, in setting up the
parameters of the system we are examining, the Conference also linked
the Iraqi ruling group so tightly to British political and military power
that force would be needed to break that link and hence to produce
any real change in Iraq's internal structure and external relations.

The Iraqi political system

The first step that the British and the Iraqi monarchy had to take was to establish a political system. In a sense this was done by the promulgation of the Constitution in 1924.

The paper model of the Iraqi state displayed all of the features characterising a functional political system, and in outline strongly resembled any Western democratic state of that period: it had a constitution, a cabinet, a parliament, political parties, free elections, and an impressive number of newspapers and periodicals. However, once light is focused on this model, its internal structure becomes blurred, bearing little resemblance to the propounded image of a viable democratic state. With characteristic clarity, an Iraqi poet of that period depicted the incompatibility of the Iraqi state's image with reality:[42]

A flag, a Constitution, and a National Assembly –
Each one a distortion of the true meaning
Names of which we have only utterances
But as to their true meaning we remain in ignorance
He who reads the Constitution will learn
that it is composed according to the Mandate
He who looks at the flapping banner will find
that it is billowing in the glory of aliens
He who sees our National Assembly will know
that it is constituted by and for the interests of any but the electors
He who enters the Ministries will find
that they are shackled with the chains of foreign advisers.

Seven years later the political system had not fundamentally changed, and another poet of the period expressed similar sentiments:[43]

In the Book of Politics we are a people
Owners of sovereignty: yet we do not even possess wreckage we
could call our own,
In the Book of Politics we are a people
With law and order: yet our lives are ruled by chaos,
In the Book of Politics we are a people
Free: yet we are no more than handicapped orphans.

The really important task, both for the British and for Faisal, was not to create democratic institutions, but to create a ruling elite through whom they could work in order to control the country. As we have seen, Iraq's civil society was divided into three broad groups: (1) the *fallahin*, who were the clear majority of the population; (2) the land-lords (classified as all those referred to in British archives as 'wealthy landlords'), who were mainly tribal shaikhs but also included the *ashraf* and some *'ulama* and city notables; and (3) the city notables, who consisted mostly of merchants (those referred to in the same archives as 'leading merchants'), ex-army officers (their total number in Iraq was 640 in 1920), and the educated elite (anyone with a former higher education). Of these, the tribal shaikhs, who controlled most of the country's agricultural land and vital routes of communication (see map, p. 43), were in a sense the richest and the most powerful, and might therefore have been regarded as strong contenders for the country's leadership. Furthermore, the majority of these shaikhs were sympathetic to British rule, and thus constituted no threat to its continuation.

The economic power of these shaikhs was strengthened even more during the period of British domination. As was seen in chapter 2, the traditional application of Land Regulations in the country was ineffective, and the state was, therefore, left with considerable power to interpret these Regulations as desired. *De facto* ownership of land by certain co-operative shaikhs was thus legalised by the state while that of hostile shaikhs was nullified. In less extreme cases, the magnitude of tax payments made by the shaikhs to the state tended to bear an inverse relation to the degree of their political co-operation. Most importantly, the control of the shaikhs over their peasants could not be secured without the assistance of the state, which promulgated a number of laws in quick succession binding the peasants to the land, and ensuring the ascendancy of the shaikhs over them. Perhaps even more important, incentive was derived by the shaikhs from the fact that the state had, at least in theory, ownership of over four-fifths of the total area of land, and could, therefore, be expected to 'release' land to those favoured among them.

On the other hand, the tribal shaikhs were uneducated, and most of them were illiterate. As was demonstrated during the 1920 revolt, the general naïvety of these shaikhs rendered them susceptible to political agitation, and their traditions and customs[44] made them willing and eager recipients of bribes and favours, which more than one party could manipulate and exploit. Moreover, despite their limited understanding of the art of politics, the tribal shaikhs could claim a significant mass following in their areas, and therefore in the country as a whole; thus there was the risk of their becoming leaders whose co-operation with the British administration could not always be assumed. What the British needed, therefore, was the formulation of a policy that would

Map

Tribal and Communication map of Southern Iraq, 1922
(where most of the tribes of Iraq were concentrated)

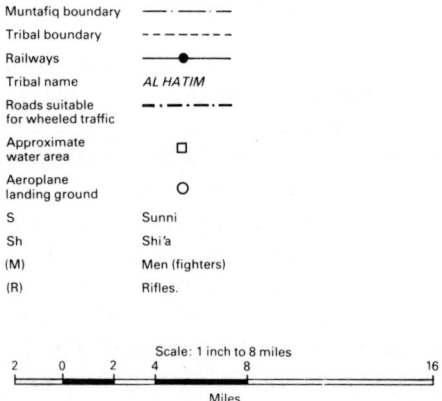

Key

Muntafiq boundary	— · — · —
Tribal boundary	- - - - - - -
Railways	——●——
Tribal name	*AL HATIM*
Roads suitable for wheeled traffic	▬ · ▬ · ▬ · ▬
Approximate water area	☐
Aeroplane landing ground	○
S	Sunni
Sh	Shi'a
(M)	Men (fighters)
(R)	Rifles.

Scale: 1 inch to 8 miles

2　　0　　2　　4　　　8　　　　　　　16

Miles

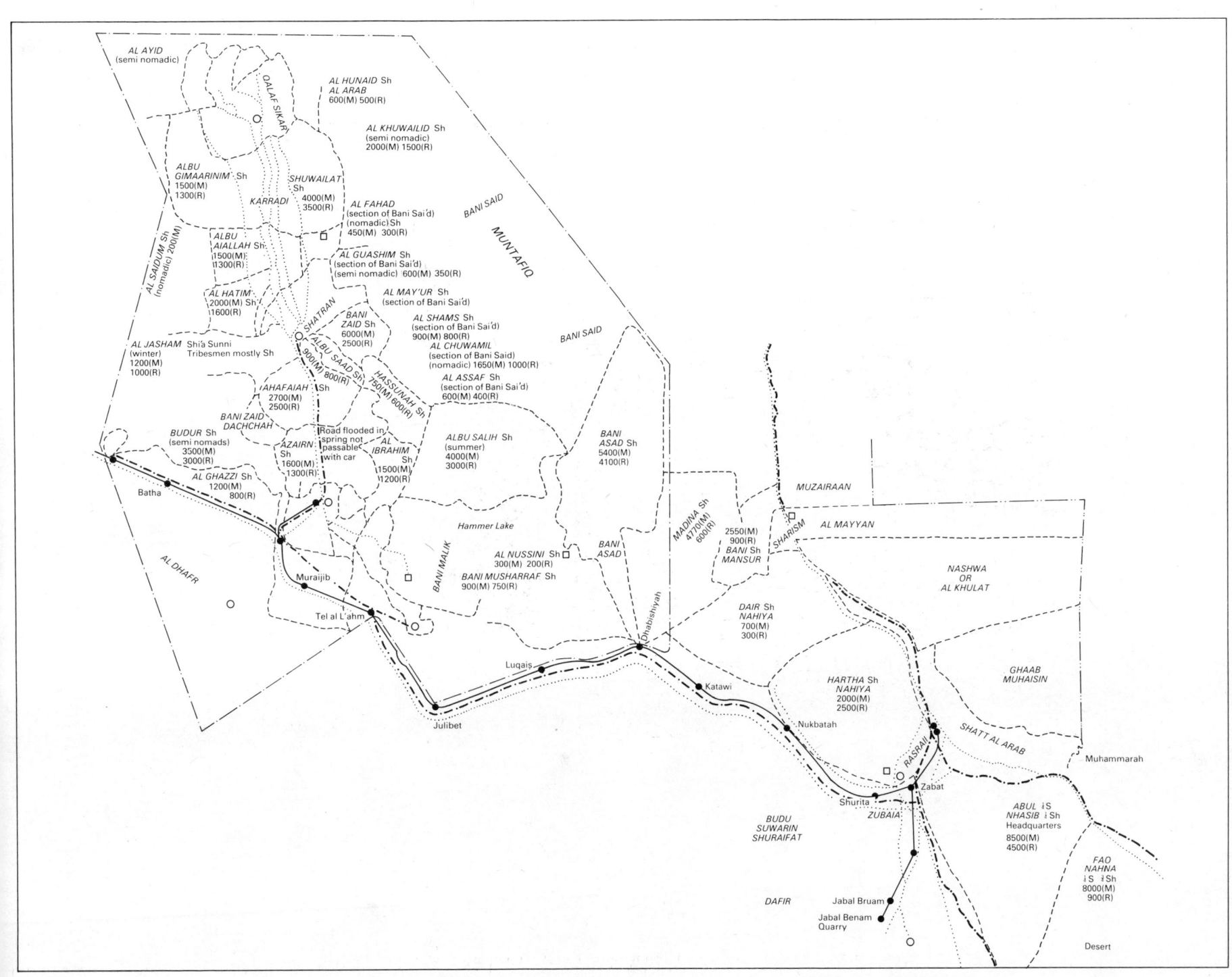

enable the shaikhs to maintain a position of power within the Iraqi socio-political pyramid, while including provisions for checking that power in cases where it exceeded its optimal limits.

But there was an even more important consideration for the British. While they realised the danger from the shaikhs, they were even more aware of the greater danger from the educated nationalists from the cities.

These considerations did not escape Major N. N. Bray, the Special Intelligence Officer of the India Öffice's Political Department, who was assigned to study the political situation in Iraq in the aftermath of the 1920 revolt:[45]

> We must constantly bear in mind one factor of supreme importance in reviewing events in Mesopotamia, namely that the tribesmen, though representing a powerful yet unstable element, do not and cannot of themselves dominate or create a political situation; they are a valuable adjunct or become a serious embarrassment as the case may be, providing a military weapon of no mean order. It is to the educated classes throughout the Jezerat-al-Arab that we look for political trouble or peace. . . . They take the keenest interest in and keep in constant touch with European politics, they are saturated with intrigues, provide a host of valuable speakers and plausible writers – in addition, large numbers of them have had military training both under the Turks and British and have considerable experience of actual warfare. Among them for years has grown up an Arab Nationalist spirit, for the pan-Arab movement is not a thing of recent growth, and before the war broke out preparations were well advanced for severance from Turkey. Independence is with them something very real. They therefore have all the necessary qualifications for being used as instruments by an outside organisation [it seems that Major Bray was here referring to the possible influence of the Bolsheviks] , and it is necessary to thoroughly realise this in order to appreciate the fact that, being imbued with these ideas, and being persuaded, rightly or wrongly, that their ideal was being threatened, they could be easily persuaded to take the most drastic and fanatical action in defence of the same.

In other words, the British needed greater control over the cities than over the countryside. Therefore, their choice of candidates for the political leadership of the new state lay mainly among the urban elite, among the city notables and the former Ottoman officials and officers class, who at least had some education and some knowledge of how modern government should be carried on.

Between city notables and tribal shaikhs there was a vast social and mental difference, but in time, and with British lobbying, the urban elite and the shaikhs both accepted the view that their political and economic interests were interdependent, and an alliance was forged between them. As a result of this alliance, the urban leadership came to constitute the core of what emerged as the country's ruling class, while the landlord class was at its periphery. For the landlord class, particularly the tribal shaikhs, an alliance with the city leadership meant the possibility of evading taxation and of maintaining a powerful position in the social hierarchy of their tribes.

Furthermore, many of the urban politicians had come to acquire large estates of land, and thus developed an additional common interest with the tribal shaikhs. To the city leadership as a whole, the patronage of the shaikhs represented a positive contribution to the pacification of the tribal areas, reinforcing the dubious legitimacy of their political power, attracting the much-needed approval of the British government, and, perhaps most importantly, securing the state's control over those areas that were so vital to the country's economic prosperity.[46] Thus, the government strove to preserve this alliance with the shaikhs by a host of methods, ranging from the offering of prestigious appointments, such as securing the election of tribal shaikhs to Parliament,[47] royal visits[48] and outright bribery,[49] to playing them off against each other.[50] However, as will be seen below, in contrast to the urban elite, the shaikhs' share of political power was considerably less than their economic privileges, a fact that was due mainly to their disadvantageous position *vis-à-vis* the ruling group. This, combined with the erratic economic and ethnic pressures in the tribal areas, constantly threatened an alliance that was growing too weak to withstand the strain. Frequently, the government was forced to deploy its army to reinforce this alliance, either on the *fallahin* when the shaikhs' authority was waning, or on the shaikhs themselves when they violated it. Thus, considerable weaknesses existed within the ruling class itself, and its structure was threatened with collapse in the face of hostile forces both from within and without, including the army. The nature of these forces and their implications for the political system as a whole should emerge from the following discussion.

The structure of the Iraqi cabinet from October 1920 to October 1936

An analysis of the structure of successive Iraqi cabinets shows that tribal shaikhs' share of the cabinet posts that were made available during this period was very small. As shown in table 2, only eight of the 59 people who received at least one cabinet post were tribal shaikhs, and while 70 per cent of the total number of posts during this period went to city notables, only 9 per cent were filled by tribal shaikhs. Taking the landlord class as a whole, we find that only one-third of the people appointed to at least one cabinet post came from this group, and between them they received less than a third of the posts made available during this period.

As shown in table 2, almost three-quarters of members of cabinets formed between 1920 and October 1936 originated from Iraq's three major cities. The proportion of city personalities among those holding the premiership during this period is even more striking: only one prime minister of Iraq during the first sixteen years of the state's existence came from a rural area, while of the remainder, ten were from Baghdad alone (table 3).

The relationship between the composition of the cabinet and place of origin of its members is interesting also when viewed in terms of the distribution of the *total* number of posts. Table 3 shows that 82 per cent of the total number of premierships during the sixteen years in question were held by people with 'city' backgrounds, with 64 per cent going to individuals from Baghdad. The proportion of Baghdadis among those holding other cabinet posts was also large – between them, they occupied 63 per cent of the total number of posts, only 25 per cent of the posts going to people from rural areas.

Taking the city notables alone, we find that only 8 per cent of those holding cabinet posts during the period under study came from a 'commercial' background (in comparison with 54 and 38 per cent from 'professional' and 'military' backgrounds, respectively). This can be explained by the fact that the overriding concern of the commercial section was the maintenance of stability, which would enable them to conduct their commercial business undisturbed. So long as this was achieved, they showed little inclination to seek public office. This overriding concern with their businesses is a reflection of the boom in Iraq's trade and commerce, which was directed mainly by city merchants. Whereas the value of consumption of imports per head of the urban population was ten shillings in the 1860s, it had risen to nearly £3 during the decade before the First World War and to about £4 by 1939.[51] Taking commercial activity in the country as a whole, in spite of the dislocation of Iraqi exports by the First World War and the decline in the army's consumption of grain in the immediate postwar

Table 2   *People holding a cabinet post between 1920 and October 1936*

	Name	Class	Religion	Place of Birth	No. of posts	Remarks
1	'Abd al Rahman al-Kilani	2(a)	Sunni	Baghdad	3	–
2	'Abd al-Latif al-Mandil	2(c)	Sunni	Baghdad	3	–
3	Al-Hajj Ramzi	1(b)	Sunni	Baghdad	1	4
4	'Abd al-Muhsin al-Sa'dun	2(d)	Sunni	3	7	–
5	'Abd al-Husain al-Chalabi	2(c)	Shi'a	Baghdad	9	–
6	'Ali Jaudat al-Ayyubi	1(b)	Sunni	Mosul	3	4
7	'Abd al-Mushin al-Shalash	2(d)	Shi'a	3	3	–
8	Ahmad al-Fakhri	1(a)	Sunni	Mosul	1	–
9	'Abd al-'Aziz al-Qassab	1(a)	Sunni	Baghdad	6	–
10	'Abdallah al-Damluji	1(a)	Sunni	Mosul	2	4
11	'Abdal Qadir Rashid	1(a)	Sunni	Baghdad	1	–
12	'Abbas Mahdi	1(a)	Shi'a	Baghdad	2	–
13	Arshad al-'Umari	2(a)	Sunni	Mosul	1	–
14	Da'ud al-Haidari	2(b)	Sunni	Baghdad	1	–
15	Hasan al-Pachachi	1(b)	Sunni	Baghdad	1	4
16	Hanna Khayyat	1(a)	Christian	Mosul	1	–
17	Hibbat al-Din al-Shahristani	2(b)	Shi'a	3	1	–
18	Hikmat Sulaiman	1(a)	Sunni	Baghdad	4	–
19	Hamdi al-Pachachi	1(a)	Sunni	Baghdad	1	4
20	'Izzat al-Kirkuki	1(b)	Sunni	3	2	4
21	Ibrahim al-Haidari	2(b)	Sunni	Baghdad	1	–
22	Ja'far al-'Askari	1(b)	Sunni	Baghdad	8	4
23	Ja'far abu Timman	2(c)	Shi'a	Baghdad	1	–
24	Jamil al-Madfa'i	1(b)	Sunni	Mosul	5	4
25	Jamal Baban	2(a)	Sunni	3	5	4
26	Jamil al-Rawi	1(b)	Sunni	3	1	4
27	Jamil al-Wadi	1(b)	Sunni	Baghdad	1	4
28	Jalal Baban	2(a)	Sunni	3	3	4
29	Khalid Sulaiman	1(b)	Sunni	Baghdad	1	4
30	Muhammad 'Ali Fadhil	2(b)	Sunni	Mosul	3	–
31	Muhammad Bahr al-'Ulum	2(b)	Shi'a	3	1	–
32	Muhammad Abu'l-Mahasin	2(d)	Shi'a	3	1	–
33	Muzahim al-Pachachi	1(a)	Sunni	Baghdad	1	–
34	Muhammad Ridha al-Shabibi	2(b)	Shi'a	3	2	–
35	Muhammad Amin Zaki	1(b)	Sunni	3	8	4
36	Muhammad Zaki	1(a)	Sunni	Basra	3	–
37	Naji al-Suwaidi	1(a)	Sunni	Baghdad	6	–
38	Nuri al-Sa'id	1(b)	Sunni	Baghdad	14	4
39	Naji Shaukat	1(a)	Sunni	Baghdad	5	4
40	Nasrat al-Farisi	1(a)	Sunni	Baghdad	2	–
41	Rustum Haidar	1(a)	Shi'a	3	5	–
42	Rashid al-Khoja	1(b)	Sunni	Baghdad	3	4
43	Ra'uf al-Bahrani	1(a)	Shi'a	Baghdad	1	4
44	Rashid 'Ali al-Kilani	1(a)	Sunni	Baghdad	6	–
45	Ra'uf al-Chadirchi	1(a)	Sunni	Baghdad	2	–
46	Sadiq al-Bassam	1(a)	Shi'a	Baghdad	1	4
47	Salih Jahr	1(a)	Shi'a	3	1	–
48	Sayyid Talib al-Naqib	2(a)	Sunni	Basra	1	–

Table 2 *continued*

49	Sassun Haskail	1(a)	Jewish	Baghdad	5	–
50	Sayyid Mustafa al-'Alusi	2(c)	Sunni	Baghdad	1	–
51	Sabih Nash'at	1(b)	Sunni	Baghdad	4	4
52	Sayyid 'Abd al-Mahdi	2(d)	Shi'a	3	3	–
53	Salih al-'Abbaasi	2(a)	Sunni	Basra	1	–
54	Salman al-Barrak	2(d)	Shi'a	3	2	–
55	Sayyid Ahmad al-Da'ud	2(b)	Sunni	Baghdad	1	–
56	Taufiq al-Suwaidi	1(a)	Sunni	Baghdad	3	–
57	Taufiq al-Khalidi	1(c)	Sunni	Baghdad	2	–
58	Yasin al-Hashimi	1(b)	Sunni	Baghdad	8	4
59	Yusif Ghanima	1(c)	Christian	Baghdad	4	–

Key to numbers

1(a) City notable from 'professional' background	Social class
1(b) City notable from 'military' background	Social class
1(c) City notable from 'commercial' background	Social class
2(a) Landowner from the Ashraf	Social class
2(b) Landowner from the 'Ulama	Social class
2(c) Landowner from the city notables	Social class
2(d) Landowner from the tribal Shaikhs	Social class
3 In the provinces	Place of birth
4 Served in either or both Turkish or Sharifian army	Remarks

years (owing to the gradual withdrawal of imperial troops from Iraq), the average value of exports rose from £2.9 million per annum in 1912–13 to £3.6 million per annum in 1933–9.[52] During the same period, the total value of imports grew from £3.4 million to £7.5 million.[53]

The distribution of cabinet posts during this period also shows marked inequalities when looked at from the perspective of religion. As can be seen from table 2, the Shi'a who formed 56 per cent of the population of Iraq, provided only 24 per cent of cabinet members, while the proportion of Sunnis in the cabinets (71 per cent) was almost twice their percentage of the total population of Iraq (36 per cent).

A similar analysis of the 'inner circle' of the cabinet[54] shows that only 2 of the 14 members of this group were Shi'a. Between them, these 14 people shared over half (97) of the total number of cabinet posts (179) created during the period under study. Only three of these individuals were drawn from the landlord class, who shared one-fifth of the inner circle posts, while the remaining four-fifths went to city notables, who constituted 79 per cent of the total membership of this

Table 3 *Premiers of Iraq, 1920–36*

Name	Religion	Background	Place of birth	No. of PMs	Total no. of cabinet posts	Total months as PM
'Abd al-Rahman al-Kilani	Sunni	Religious	Baghdad	3	3	23.5
'Abd al-Muhsin al-Sà'dun	Sunni	Military	Muntafiq	4	7	43.0
Ja'far al-'Askari	Sunni	Military	Baghdad	2	8	21.5
Yasin al-Hashimi	Sunni	Military	Baghdad	2	8	30.0
Taufiq Yusif al-Suwaidi	Sunni	Law	Baghdad	1	3	4.0
Naji al-Suwaidi	Sunni	Law	Baghdad	1	6	4.0
Nuri al-Sa'id	Sunni	Military	Baghdad	2	14	31.0
Naji Shaukat	Sunni	Military	Baghdad	1	5	4.5
Rashid 'Ali al-Kilani	Sunni	Law	Baghdad	2	6	7.0
Jamil al-Madfa'i	Sunni	Military	Mosul	3	5	9.5
'Ali Jaudat al-Ayyubi	Sunni	Military	Mosul	1	3	6.0

Table 4 *Cabinets formed from November 1932 until August 1937*

No. of members	of the cabinet holding post for the nth time														Total no. of posts	Total posts held to date	Average experience*	Ratio of newcomers to Experienced members*
	1st	2nd	3rd	4th	5th	6th	7th	8th	9th	10th	11th	12th	13th	14th				
1st cabinet	6	–	–	1	–	–	–	–	–	–	–	–	–	–	7	10	1.4	6:1
2nd cabinet	1	2	2	1	–	1	–	–	1	–	–	–	–	–	8	30	3.7	1:7
3rd cabinet	–	1	2	2	1	–	1	–	–	1	–	–	–	–	8	38	4.7	0:8
4th cabinet	1	2	1	–	2	–	–	–	–	–	1	–	–	–	7	29	4.1	1:6
5th cabinet	–	3	2	–	2	–	–	–	–	–	–	–	–	–	7	22	3.1	0:7
6th cabinet	1	–	2	2	–	–	1	–	–	–	–	1	–	–	7	34	4.8	1:6
7th cabinet	–	–	2	1	2	–	1	1	–	–	–	–	1	–	8	48	6.0	0:8
8th cabinet	1	2	–	–	–	1	–	3	–	–	–	–	–	1	8	49	6.1	1:8
9th cabinet†	4	2	–	–	1	–	–	–	–	–	–	–	–	–	7	13	1.8	4:3
Reshuffled 9th cabinet†	6	–	1	–	1	–	–	–	–	–	–	–	–	–	8	14	1.7	6:2

* Average experience = Total posts held to-date ÷ total no. of posts.
† 9th and 'reshuffled 9th' cabinets are those of the coup government

group. It is interesting that, of the three landlord members of this inner circle, only one – 'Abd al-Muhsin al-Sa'dun – enjoyed a tribal following, while the other two were absentee landlords. In addition, 9 of the 14 members of the inner circle came from Baghdad. Also, over one-third of the members of this inner circle had been officers in either or both the Turkish and Sharifian armies. Viewed individually, we find that the highest number of posts went to Nuri al-Sa'id, a city personality of humble origin; the second highest number went to 'Abd al-Husain al-Chalabi, a wealthy landowner of Kadjimain, while the third place was shared by Ja'far al-'Askari, Yasin al-Hashimi and Muhammad Amin Zaki, all of whom were city people of lower middle-class background.

Twenty-two cabinets were formed in Iraq up to October 1936, giving an average life of eight-and-a-half months. However, an examination of the structure of these cabinets reveals that this high frequency of cabinet change was not matched by a correspondingly high degree of change in the actual members allotted cabinet posts. Table 2 shows that, while the total number of available posts had reached 179 by 1936, the total number of different people who had been cabinet members stood at 59. Over one-third of these served in the cabinet only once. Focusing on the cabinets between the year of independence (November 1932) and the Bakir Sidqi *coup d'état* (October 1936), we find that, while the ratio of newcomers to 'experienced' members was 6:1 in the first post-independence cabinet, it had dropped to 1:6 in the fourth cabinet, reaching 1:8 in the Yasin al-Hashimi cabinet which was overthrown by the *coup d'état* of October 1936 (table 4). During those four post-independence years, there were eight cabinets; thus, each one had an average life of six months.

The low probability of a new person being appointed to the cabinet is perhaps normal or even advantageous in a stable country where the average life of the cabinet is considerably higher than six months. However, in Iraq this comparative lack of newcomers to the cabinet did not symbolise stability, but rather was symptomatic of the intense rivalry and lack of mutual confidence within the ruling elite; and this was the underlying cause of the high rate of cabinet changes. The ruling elite was, in effect, split into a number of factions, the composition and loyalties of which changed almost as frequently as the government itself. It was, for example, not unusual for the king to dissolve the cabinet merely to dismiss the prime minister, should His Majesty consider the latter's popularity to be growing at his own expense (see p. 55 below). Nor was it uncommon for a prime minister to dissolve the cabinet simply in order to leave out a minister he had previously been obliged to include owing to certain pressures that he felt could now be resisted. Nuri al-Sa'id, who had served in 14 of the 22 cabinets, twice as prime minister, was, in the view of a senior British diplomat, 'so clever a schemer that no-one can quite trust him'.[55]

Another leading Iraqi politician of the period who served in six of the 22 cabinets, twice as prime minister, was described to another senior British diplomat by one of his own colleagues as: 'cet imbécile . . . no other word would be strong enough to describe his crazy greed and his general blindness to the wishes of all but himself'.[56]

In a conversation with the same diplomat, Yasin al-Hashimi was sceptical about the loyalty of his former defence and foreign ministers, with one or both of whom he had served in six cabinets. He was[57]

> convinced that neither had been loyal to him. Behind his back they had been long and loud in their criticism of his administration. . . .
> He had never felt completely happy with Ja'far as Minister of Defence and had more than once tried to have him out of that post, but Nuri would have none of it.

This lack of trust seems to have been mutual, and the British Ambassador expressed the view that Nuri al-Sa'id[58]

> disliked Yasin intensely, and would have liked to bring about his downfall. But he was afraid of Rustum [who served in five cabinets and was frequently head of the Royal Diwan]. Rustum would have used all his influence to ensure that Yasin should be called upon again, or alternatively that Jamil Madfa'i or 'Ali Jaudat should succeed. The fall of the cabinet either from the resignation of Nuri and Ja'far, or a revolution or assassination as Ja'far suggested at one meeting of the opposition elements [Ja'far was himself assassinated during the 1936 *coup d'état*] might not necessarily bring Nuri into power or even keep him in office in a cabinet. Nuri, if he has not grabbed land and money like the others, has got used to living at Government expense on perks; it has become a disease.

The King himself played an active role in these personal intrigues. Discussing the formation of a particular new cabinet, a senior British diplomat expressed the opinion that it was not[59]

> beyond the bounds of possibility that the introduction of Yasin Pasha into the cabinet was designed by King Faisal primarily with the object of discrediting him with his supporters. . . . King Faisal used these manoeuvres with great effect in the case of Muzahim al-Pachachi . . . who was a very active and violent member of the

opposition until he was offered and accepted the Ministry of Interior in Nuri Pasha's cabinet. He was allowed to remain in this post sufficiently long to ensure that his connection with the Nationalist Party was definitely broken, and was then forced to leave the cabinet on a trumpery charge. . . . There have been other instances of the fruit of office being used by King Faisal as a carrot to draw inconvenient political opponents to their destruction.

In the view of the British Ambassador, Yasin al-Hashimi was in turn distrustful of the King, and was[66]

suspicious of His Majesty's motives for bringing him back to office. Yasin has seen more than one man with a promising public career discredited and ruined because he had left his friends and broken with his principles for the sake of fickle Palace favour. . . . I had experience of Yasin Pasha as a member of the Cabinet in 1929–30 when he was Minister of Finance in Naji Suwaidi's Administration. On that occasion he dominated the cabinet and was responsible for Naji Suwaidi's downfall. Shortly before my arrival in Baghdad, he had, in the opinion of my predecessor, goaded a former Prime Minister, 'Abdul Muhsin Beg, into suicide.

The King's relations with Nuri al-Sa'id suffered similar strains. Reviewing this relationship in his confidential Annual Report to the Foreign Office, the Ambassador wrote:[61]

Towards the close of the seventh session he began to lose his personal influence with the King. It was as a Palace favourite that he had been called upon in March 1930 to form a Government. . . . King Faisal seems to have little real cause to be displeased with his Prime Minister. . . . The King was possibly a little jealous of his prominence in affairs; and when a serious difference arose between them . . . their old ties became too weak to stand the strain, and snapped. The affair which gave rise to this quarrel between the King and Nuri Pasha had no real national or even political importance. . . . In the summer of 1931 . . . a number of anonymous typewritten letters were circulated accusing the Mayor of Baghdad of having sought to obtain Royal favour by allowing his wife to become the King's mistress. Rumour ascribed responsibility for these letters to several high-placed persons, and the matter attracted much attention in the press. . . . The evidence in the hands of the police also inculpated Muzahim Beg al-Pachachi . . . who had been Minister for the Interior . . . and was still Deputy in the Chamber. The magistrate in charge of the case

asked for a suspension of Muzahim Beg's parliamentary immunities.
... Nuri Pasha did not wish this to be done, but the Minister of
Justice, prompted by the King, supported the magistrate's request.
A quarrel ensued and the Minister of Justice resigned, and at one
time even talked of suicide. ... Jealousy too had begun to poison
his [the King's] old friendship with Nuri. Since taking office in
1930, the latter had, through his visits to Geneva, London, Rome,
Angora and Tehran, become an international figure, and the King
was not pleased to be even partially eclipsed. When he returned to
Baghdad ... his first audience with the King led to his resignation.

Later dispatches from the British Embassy gave even more emphasis to
the role of these 'high-level' personal rivalries in shaping Iraqi political
life. When a new cabinet was formed by Jamil al-Madfa'i in February
1934, the British Ambassador could see no better explanation for the
change of government than that Jamil al-Madfa'i's colleagues in the
former cabinet were 'unable to compose their personal difficulties and
agree to serve together'.[62] By December 1934, the British Ambassador
seems to have formed an even clearer notion of Iraqi politics, which,
he wrote,[63]

> had ceased to be a question of parties or policy, and become entirely
> a matter of personalities ... the futility of talking politics in the
> capital gave rise to a trite if somewhat vulgar Baghdadi proverb
> terminating with the phrase 'Dhart fi suq-as-safafir'. Dhart is a
> breaking of wind, and suq-as-safafir the copper bazaar and the
> noisiest place in Baghdad.

This deep mistrust between members of the Iraqi ruling class must have
generated a feeling of insecurity and an intense fear of losing public
privilege, which may go some way towards explaining the marked
general discrepancy between their public pronouncements and their
actual policies once in office: 'It was well understood in Iraq, that no
politician was obliged to apply, when in office, the principles which he
had advocated when in opposition.'[64] The Ambassador went on to give
an account of an emotional encounter he had had with King Faisal on
attempting to confront him on this subject. 'Was I to report to my
government', he had inquired of the King,[65]

> that Iraq's public men, men who had held the highest positions in
> the State, made speeches on solemn occasions in which they voiced
> opinions which they knew to be false and meaningless? Was I to say
> that the Iraqi Parliament was just a sham, a place where time and

money was wasted by a handful of men, who, while masquerading as statesmen, neither meant what they said, nor said what they believed?

According to the Ambassador, the King 'threw himself into an emotional mood, and bewailed the fate which had made him King of such a "distressful" country as Iraq'.[66]

To be prone to personal rivalry and jealousy is, of course, in no way a unique feature of Iraqis nor of any other people. Given human psychology, it is probably an inevitable feature of political life. However, its effect on the wider political community will vary in accordance with the nature of the state, and the degree of democratisation of its institutions. In Iraq during this period, there were no stable and effective institutions through which legitimate political differences could express themselves and which would have allowed for an easy transfer of power. Therefore, those who were opposed to the government had almost inevitably to look outside the constitutional system.

The nature of opposition between 1920 and October 1936

The examination of the three main possible channels of opposition in the Iraqi state, namely Parliament, political parties and the press, shows that they were understandably underdeveloped; and even when efforts were made to counteract this, the government intervened and nipped such manoeuvres in the bud. Almost invariably, deputies were elected to Parliament primarily on the strength of their personal allegiance to this or that politician, or by their position in the Iraqi social strata. It was thus customary for the British Embassy in Baghdad to refer to various Parliaments by the name of the politician whose supporters occupied the highest number of seats. For example, various dispatches make reference to Nuri's Parliament or Rashid 'Ali's Parliament. They also speak of the deputies having 'been allowed to be elected'.[67]

An analysis of the composition of the five Parliaments that were formed during the period under study shows that their structural characteristics are somewhat different from those of cabinets formed during the same period.[68] Taking the 1925 Parliament as an example, we find that 25 per cent of the deputies were tribal shaikhs, whereas they formed 8 per cent of the aggregate of personalities holding cabinet posts between 1920 and 1936. The proportion of deputies drawn from the landlord class as a whole was also considerably higher than the corresponding figure in cabinets. Whereas 37 per cent of the total members allocated cabinet posts during the period in question were drawn from this class, their share of seats in the 1925 chamber was 57 per cent (table 5). Of the remaining 43 per cent, for reasons already discussed in considering the allocation of cabinet posts, city notables from the 'commercial' sector were the least represented (14 per cent), while the 'professionals' had the highest representation (53 per cent), although city notables with 'military' background still had a considerable share of seats (14 per cent of the general total, and 33 per cent of the share of city notables).

Another considerable difference between the structure of cabinets and Parliaments emerges when numbers of both institutions are viewed in terms of their birthplace. Whereas only a quarter of those appointed to at least one cabinet post during the period under study came from rural areas, almost half of the total number of deputies in the 1925 Parliament had rural origins. It is also noticeable that a slightly higher percentage of parliamentary seats than cabinet posts went to people born in Basra and Mosul. Thus, while their proportion of cabinet posts was 5 and 12 per cent respectively, the corresponding figures in the 1925 Parliament were 7 and 13 per cent.

Only a slight difference is also seen between Parliament and cabinet when their structure is compared in terms of the religious affiliation of their members. The proportion of Sunnis in the 1925 Parliament is almost identical to their proportion of the 59 members allocated cabinet posts between 1920 and 1936, while the ratio of the Shi'as is slightly different, being less than a quarter in the case of cabinet members but one-third in the case of deputies in the 1925 Parliament. The percentage of seats held by Christians and Jews is considerably greater than those in the cabinet, being 3 and 2 per cent respectively in cabinets and 6 and 5 per cent in the 1925 Parliament.

Besides these characteristics of the composition of the 1925 Parliament, the most notable feature is that, with the exception of seven deputies, all were government candidates. In addition, a British intelligence report, analysing the 1925 elections, pointed out the following features:[69]

1. That a private intimation of the candidates preferred by Government was almost always sufficient to secure their return.
2. That the two political parties have exercised no influence whatsoever and have not succeeded in returning their respective Presidents.

Table 5 *Selected characteristics of all members of the 1925 Parliament*

	Name	Class*	Religion	Place of birth	Remarks
1	'Abd al-Razzaq al-Munir	2(c)	Sunni	Baghdad	Independent
2	'Abd al-Hussain al-Chalabi	2(c)	Shi'a	Baghdad	Government candidate
3	'Abdallah Mukhlis	1(b)	Sunni	Mosul	Government candidate
4	Arshad al-'Umari	2(a)	Sunni	Mosul	Government candidate
5	'Ali Effendi al-Imam	2(c)	Sunni	Mosul	Government candidate
6	'Azzam al-Shamdin	1(b)	Sunni	3*	Government candidate
7	Ahmad Mudethar bin Ahmad	2(d)	Sunni	3	Government candidate
8	Amin Zaki	1(b)	Sunni	Baghdad	Government candidate
9	Amir Rabi'a	2(d)	Shi'a	3	Government candidate
10	Ahmad Halat	2(c)	Sunni	3	Government candidate
11	'Abdallah al-Yasin	2(d)	Sunni	3	Government candidate
12	'Abd al-Muhsin al-Sa'dun	2(d)	Sunni	3	Government candidate
13	'Abd al-Latif al-Mandil	2(c)	Sunni	Baghdad	Government candidate
14	'Abbud al-Mallak	2(c)	Sunni	Basrah	Government candidate
15	'Alwan al-Jandil	2(d)	Shi'a	3	Government candidate
16	'Abd al-Ghani Chalabi	2(c)	Shi'a	3	Government candidate
17	'Abd al-Rahman al-Namme	2(c)	Sunni	Basrah	Government candidate
18	'Abdullah Beg al-Falih	2(d)	Sunni	3	Government candidate
19	Da'ud Haidari	2(b)	Sunni	Baghdad	Government candidate
20	Dhia Beg al-Sharif	2(c)	Sunni	Mosul	Government candidate
21	Dr Fai'q Shakir	1(a)	Sunni	Baghdad	Government candidate
22	Fakhri Beg al-Jamil	2(c)	Sunni	Baghdad	Government candidate
23	Hamdi Pachacl	1(a)	Sunni	Baghdad	Government candidate
24	Hikmat Sulaiman	1(a)	Sunni	Baghdad	Government candidate
25	Ibrahim Beg al-Kamal	1(a)	Sunni	Mosul	Government candidate
26	Ishaq Effendi Ifra'im	1(c)	Jewish	Mosul	Government candidate

No.	Name	Code	Religion	Location	Status
27	Isma'il Rawanduzi	2(c)	Sunni	3	Government candidate
28	Ibrahim Yusif	2(c)	Sunni	3	Independent
29	Ja'far al-'Askari†	1(b)	Sunni	Baghdad	Government candidate
30	Khayyun al-'Ubaid	2(d)	Sunni	3	Government candidate
31	Kadhim al-Shamkhani	1(a)	Shi'a	Basrah	Independent
32	Muhammad al-Shimran	2(d)	Sunni	3	Government candidate
33	Muhammad Sa'id 'Abd al-Wahid	1(b)	Sunni	Basrah	Government candidate
34	Muhammad Amin Bash a'yan	2(a)	Shi'a	3	Government candidate
35	Majid al-Khalifa	2(d)	Sunni	3	Government candidate
36	Mahmud Ramiz	1(b)	Sunni	Baghdad	Government candidate
37	Muhan al-Khairallah	2(d)	Shi'a	3	Government candidate
38	Muhammad Baqir al-Shabibi	2(b)	Shi'a	3	Independent
39	Muhammad Ridha al-Shabibi	2(b)	Shi'a	3	Independent
40	Muzahim Pachachi	1(a)	Sunni	Baghdad	Government candidate
41	Majid Beg Shawi	2(c)	Sunni	Baghdad	Government candidate
42	Mahmud Subhi al-Daftari	1(a)	Sunni	Baghdad	Government candidate
43	Muhsin al-Shalash	2(d)	Shi'a	3	Government candidate
44	Muhammad Salih beg	2(c)	Sunni	3	Government candidate
45	Mirza Faraj Salim	1(c)	Sunni	3	Government candidate
46	Nasrat al-Farisi	1(a)	Sunni	Baghdad	Independent
47	Naji Effendi Salih	1(c)	Sunni	3	Government candidate
48	Na'im Zilkha	1(a)	Jewish	Baghdad	Government candidate
49	Naji Suwaidi	1(a)	Sunni	Baghdad	Government candidate
50	Nuri al-Sa'id	1(b)	Sunni	Baghdad	Government candidate
51	Nashat Effendi	1(a)	Sunni	3	Government candidate
52	Rafiq Khaddam Sajjad	2(b)	Sunni	3	Government candidate
53	Rashid 'Ali al-Kilani	1(a)	Sunni	Baghdad	Government candidate
54	Rauf Beg Chadireb	1(a)	Sunni	Baghdad	Government candidate
55	Rashid al-Khoja	1(b)	Sunni	Baghdad	Government candidate
56	Rashid Khattab	1(b)	Sunni	Baghdad	Government candidate
57	Rauf Shammas	1(a)	Christian	Mosul	Government candidate

Table 5 *continued*

	Name	Class*	Religion	Place of birth	Remarks
58	Rubain Sumaikh	1(a)	Jewish	Basrah	Government candidate
59	Salman al-Manshad	2(d)	Shi'a	3	Government candidate
60	Shaikh Habib Talibani	2(d)	Sunni	3	Government candidate
61	Sa'id Affendi	1(a)	Sunni	3	Government candidate
62	Sayyid 'Abd al-Mahdi	2(d)	Shi'a	3	Government candidate
63	Saqban al-'Ali	2(d)	Shi'a	3	Government candidate
64	Sir Sassun Haskail	1(a)	Jewish	Baghdad	Government candidate
65	Salman al-Barrak	2(d)	Shi'a	3	Government candidate
66	Shaikh 'Ali Sulaiman	2(b)	Shi'a	3	Government candidate
67	Shaikh 'Ibadi al-Husain	2(d)	Shi'a	3	Independent
68	Shaikh Salman al-Dhahir	2(d)	Shi'a	3	Government candidate
69	Shaikh Mudhhir al-Saqub	2(d)	Shi'a	3	Government candidate
70	Sayyid 'Alwan al-Yasiki	2(d)	Shi'a	3	Government candidate
71	Sayyid Muhsin Abu-Tabikh	2(d)	Shi'a	3	Government candidate
72	Sayyid Qata 'Awadi	2(d)	Shi'a	3	Government candidate
73	Sayyid Na'if al-Mallak	1(a)	Sunni	Baghdad	Government candidate
74	Sabih Nash'at	1(b)	Sunni	Baghdad	Government candidate
75	Sayyid Khadim 'Ali	2(b)	Shi'a	3	Government candidate

76	Said Chalabi Haji Thabit	1(c)	Sunni	Mosul	Independent
77	Shaikh Nuri Birifqa	2(b)	Sunni	3	Government candidate
78	Sayyid Ilyas	2(a)	Christian	3	Government candidate
79	Thabit 'Abd al-Nur	1(b)	Sunni	Mosul	Government candidate
80	'Umran Haji Sa'dun	2(c)	Sunni	3	Government candidate
81	Yusif Ghanima	1(c)	Christian	Baghdad	Government candidate
82	Yasin al-Hashimi	1(b)	Sunni	Baghdad	Government candidate
83	Yusif Khayyat	2(b)	Christian	Mosul	Government candidate
84	Yasin al-Amir	2(c)	Sunni	Basrah	Government candidate
85	Sayyid Da'ud Kilani	2(a)	Sunni	Baghdad	Government candidate
86	Dr Ghazala	1(a)	Christian	Mosul	Government candidate

* For key numbers see table 2 above.
† Held two seats simultaneously

3. That no candidates or party put forward any political programme. Candidates have been returned on their official backing and their individual merits and position. . . . Meanwhile, members . . . are likely to be divided on purely personal lines, followers of 'Abdul Muhsin al-Sa'dun on the one hand, and followers of Yasin Pasha on the other.

An analysis of the structure of Parliaments in terms of the probability of a new deputy being 'elected' shows that, as in the case of cabinet appointments, the frequency with which new members were drawn into Parliament was low. Taking the 1933 Parliament as an example, we find that, of the 88 deputies in the new chamber, only 21 were entirely new, 44 having sat in the 1928 Parliament and 23 in either the 1925 Parliament or the 1924 Constituent Assembly. In terms of its general characteristics, the 1933 Parliament did not differ significantly from that of 1925. In the view of the British Ambassador,[70]

In general character the new Chamber differs very little from its predecessors. . . . 'Nuri Sa'id tells me privately that too many of Yasin Pasha's personal supporters (about 12) have been allowed to be elected'. . . . I gather that he himself and the Prime Minister have only about three or four nominees each in the Chamber.

Until 1935, the Constitution provided for the election of one deputy for every 20,000 adult males, and each Parliament contained a total of 88 seats. However, owing to the high demand for parliamentary seats [71] and the desire of politicians to increase the number of their supporters in Parliament, the number of parliamentary seats was increased by 20 to 108:[72]

This increase of seats, if it was made with arithmetical accuracy, indicates an increase of 400,000 male adults in the population of the country. It was, however, suggested in many well-informed quarters that the Government had designedly increased the number of Deputies in order that they might be able to reward their supporters without excluding others whose position in tribal or public life made their presence in the Chamber desirable. Everywhere, according to custom, the candidates nominated by the Cabinet were returned. . . . Sixty-eight of those elected had had previous parliamentary experience.

Another British Embassy dispatch was similarly explicit in its description of the alliance existing between politicians and those elected to

Parliament, and the general corruption of the Iraqi parliamentary system:[73]

> Several of the newly-elected members have, however, assured me that they were not pressed at these elections to pledge their allegiance in writing to any given leader or party. . . . Amongst the prominent former Deputies who disappear from the scene are Hikmat Sulaiman, Arshad Umari, 'Ali Jaudat and Jalal Baban. The first mentioned will be remembered as one of the instigators of the revolt in the spring of 'Abdul Wahid, who himself now reappears as one of the Deputies for Diwaniya. . . . Arshad Umari held a ministerial post in the last Government, but his hustling methods, indiscriminate energy, and private peccadilloes made him many enemies. . . . 'Ali Jaudat's incompetence and corruption were mainly responsible for the troubles of last spring, and he is to be kept at a safe distance, for a time at least, as Iraq's minister in London. It can be safely assumed that, so long as the present Government hold together, they will enjoy the confidence of at least two-thirds of the Chamber.

The Iraqi public was well aware of the farce surrounding parliamentary elections and had no illusions about them. To the talented among them, Parliament and deputies provided stimulating subject matters:[74]

> In Baghdad a National Assembly was patched up
> as a ragged garment filled with holes might be patched
> And thus it assembled all defects
> so there is the one-eyed, the blind, and the hairless
> Oh fate how playful you are
> Do you derive pleasures out of these mockeries?

Another poet of the period was no less reproachful:[75]

> Senators they say and a National Assembly
> performing public duties in every way
> But when we tested them we find distortions
> and a game in which a thousand actors played
> Oh Seat are you able to hear me
> for only you do I call and only you reply
> They acquired you without right or merit
> except to spread oppression and receive salaries.

A veteran Iraqi deputy told me that, following a certain parliamentary debate, the cleaner arrived after all the deputies were supposed to have left, and found one deputy still in his seat, snoring. On approaching him, the deputy jumped in the air shouting: 'I agree, . . . I agree'.

The domination of personal over national loyalties in cabinets and Parliaments extended to political parties, and here again, those parties that were allowed to survive would be more accurately referred to by names reflecting their leaders than by their programmes.

Twelve political parties were created in Iraq between 1920 and October 1936. The first two of these, al-Hizb al-Watani al-Iraqi (the Iraq National Party) and Jam'iyat al-Nahda al-'Iraqiya (the Iraq Renaissance Society), emerged almost simultaneously and were to be the only parties founded during our period to have any meaningful, albeit general and undeveloped, programme.[76] Their leaders, Ja'far Abu Timman and Muhammad Husain Charchafchi, respectively, were both Shi'a, and the declared goals of their parties were very similar, including the complete independence of the country, an endeavour to improve public welfare, the expansion and modernisation of agriculture, the improvement of irrigation, and the introduction of compulsory and free elementary education.[77] Less than a month after their formation, the two parties united and organised a demonstration in Baghdad demanding the following:[78]

1 The end of British interference in the administration of the country.
2 The formation of a cabinet consisting of able and reliable men.
3 No negotiation and no treaty [with Britain] until the establishment of a Constituent Assembly.

The government, acting on the advice of the British High Commissioner, reacted to these demands by disbanding the two parties and sending their leaders into exile to Henjam. In the meantime, Mahmud al-Naqib, the son of 'Abd al-Rahman al-Naqib, founded Hizb al-Hurr (the Free Party) to support his father's government. When that particular government fell a month later, however, Hizb al-Hurr disappeared with it.

This trend, whereby political parties failed to outlive the term of office of their leaders, continued throughout our period, the only exceptions being in cases where the new prime minister himself became the new leader of the party of his predecessor. The official inauguration of parliamentary democracy in Iraq in 1925 failed to reverse this trend. Rather than provide an arena for flourishing ideological debate and the emergence of political leadership, these parties continued to function as no more than platforms for cultivating 'followership'. Thus, for example, when 'Abd al-Muhsin al-Sa'dun ceased to be the prime minister in October 1926, Hizb al-Taqaddum (the Progress Party), the party that he had created a year earlier, was handed over to Ja'far al-'Askari, together with the premiership. Having no party of his own, Ja'far al-'Askari went to the headquarters of Hizb al-Taqaddum, and addressed those present: 'I am one of you, so if you throw me out of the door, I will come back through the window. . . . .' 'Welcome, welcome', the audience then applauded.[79]

Of the twelve parties that were created during this period, only three were established as opposition parties: Hizb al-Sha'b (the People's Party), Hizb al-Watani and Hizb al-Ikha al-Watani (the National Brotherhood Party). A close examination of these parties, however, reveals that in neither aims nor structure were they fundamentally different from the government-sponsored parties. Their public pronouncements reflected a deep concern with the country's political independence and prosperity, issues that were similarly adopted publicly by the government parties. The first of these parties, Hizb al-Sha'b, was established by Yasin al-Hashimi in November 1925, and its declared aims were:[80]

Article 3. Improving the well being of the Iraqi people and securing the complete independence of the Iraqi State.

Article 4. The development of national forces in the fields of administration, economy, education and agriculture, and the strengthening of patriotic feeling, and the spread of solidarity and sacrifice among the population.

Article 5. The party will endeavour to secure the admission of Iraq to the League of Nations.

While in opposition, this party published statements in accordance with these aims in its newly established organ, *al-Sha'b* newspaper, while its leader, Yasin al-Hashimi, delivered speeches calling for the revision of the 1924 Anglo–Iraqi Treaty, and generally attacking the government of the day. However, once Yasin al-Hashimi was given a post in the cabinet in November 1926, his party abandoned its formerly critical attitude to the government, and in the spring of 1927 the editor of *al-Sha'b* was given a job in the Council of Ministers, the newspaper closing down two months later in consequence.[81]

In January 1929 Ja'far al-'Askari's cabinet, with Yasin al-Hashimi as its Minister of Finance, resigned, with the result that Yasin al-Hashimi once more retreated to the ranks of opposition in Parliament. Apart from conscription, the prevailing political issue at that time was the revision of the 1926 Agreement with Britain and the negotiations concerning the terms of Iraq's anticipated independence and admission to the League of Nations, which were finally concluded by the government, headed by Nuri al-Sa'id, in the form of a Treaty in June 1930.

Seeking to give their opposition formal expression, Yasin al-Hashimi and other leading politicians outside the government formed a new opposition party called Hizb al-Ikha al-Watani in November 1930. Apart from the additional call for the revision of the 1930 Treaty, the declared aims of this party differed only in expression from those of the disbanded Hizb al-Sha'b. A week later, this party sought and succeeded in establishing an alliance with the Hizb al-Watani al-'Iraqi, Ja'far Abu Timman's party, which had been disbanded in 1922, to be re-licensed in June 1928. The two parties signed a common manifesto which they called Wathiqat al-Ta'akhi (Brotherhood Document), declaring:[82]

1 That the 1930 Treaty is absolute and oppressive and should, therefore, be revised.

2 That parliament does not represent the people and should, therefore, be dissolved.

3 That any government replacing the existing one must work towards achieving the above aims.

The government itself, however, remained unperturbed by this alliance, the deputies in Parliament having, with few exceptions, been nominees of the government.[83] Thus, finding themselves unable to make any impact inside Parliament, the main leaders of opposition, Yasin al-Hashimi, Rashid 'Ali, 'Ali Jaudat al-Ayyubi, and Naji al-Suwaidi, decided to resign (May 1931) and intensify, outside Parliament, their criticism of the Treaty as 'unjust and oppressive by reason of the immense burden of debt which it laid on the shoulders of Iraq, and the foreign forces and advisers which it imposed on the country'.[84]

It is interesting that Yasin al-Hashimi, the most eminent of the government's opponents,[85]

while maintaining his reputation as a disinterested Nationalist, was careful not to commit himself to anything but oracularly vague pronouncements on policy. He left it to the secretary of the Nationalist party, Ja'far Chalabi Abu Timman, to be the spokesman of the extremists, and to declare their intransigent hostility to the Treaty of 1930.

Thus, when the two opposition parties held a meeting in Baghdad on 20 March 1932, it was Ja'far Abu Timman who delivered a long speech criticising Nuri al-Sa'id's government. His chief points were:[86]

> That public funds had been squandered by the Prime Minister on his
> frequent journeys abroad, that admission into the League of Nations
> on the conditions which the Government were accepting, including
> the Treaty of 1930 and the guarantees regarding the minorities,
> would be of no benefit to Iraq, and that the present Government
> had added yet another act of oppression to the long list of their
> violations of the Constitution by applying the Tribal Criminal and
> Civil Disputes Regulations to those who had criticised them in the
> Press.

As will be explained later, in spite of the government's restrictions of
the press, opposition to the 1930 Treaty continued to express itself in
the form of articles and public speeches. This led the government to
resort to a traditionally favoured approach, namely the employment of
'their control of patronage . . . to win over critics and to detach supporters from the opposition parties'.[87]

Thus, in March 1933 King Faisal sounded out the British Ambassador
on the possibility of including Yasin al-Hashimi in a reshuffled cabinet.
The Ambassador reacted by reminding[88]

> His Majesty that his previous efforts to eradicate criticism by giving
> office to Opposition leaders had led to disastrous results. These
> mixed Cabinets had been torn by internal jealousies, and had never
> succeeded in producing any construction programme for the benefit
> of the country. . . . I could not conceive, for instance, that
> harmonious relations would long continue between Nuri Pasha and
> Yasin Pasha, or between either of them and the present Prime
> Minister. . . . Moreover, the Opposition leaders had announced their
> uncompromising hostility to the Anglo-Iraqi Treaty of 1930, and
> were determined, so far as could be deduced from their public
> utterances, to agitate for the drastic amendment of its terms. . . .
> King Faisal . . . said that the opposition of Yasin Pasha and his
> friends towards the Treaty of 1930 had been based entirely on their
> personal hostility to Nuri Pasha. That hostility was now a thing of
> the past, and neither they, nor any other responsible Iraqi, wished
> to alter the terms of the existing alliance with Great Britain.

Subsequently, on 19 March Yasin al-Hashimi was included in the newly
formed cabinet as Minister of Finance, three of his former opposition
colleagues (all from the Brotherhood and none from the National Party)
also being appointed to cabinet posts. Three days later, in a conversation

with the British Ambassador, he confirmed Faisal's analysis of his views and admitted that:[89]

> it was true that he had criticised adversely the Financial Agreement signed by Nuri Pasha and myself [the British Ambassador] in London in August 1930, which had been ratified with the Anglo-Iraqi Treaty of 1930. This did not mean, however, that he had any intention of agitating for the revision of the Financial Agreement, as he realised that his acceptance of office in the new Government implied agreement with the policy of his colleagues . . . he quite realised that the Treaty of 1930 and its annexures . . . had become an international bond which must be honourably observed. . . . He would not urge that complete independence was possible or even beneficial in the present circumstances. . . . Yasin states emphatically that a treaty of alliance was necessary for Iraq until she was strong enough to defend herself without foreign assistance.

These pronouncements of Yasin al-Hashimi were later corroborated by the fact that, at no time during his term of office in that government, did he work towards a revision of the 1930 Treaty with Britain. In the meantime, his alliance with the National Party was dissolved, his partners in the party regarding his joining the government as a betrayal of the cause that had united their parties; and in any case none of the leaders of the National Party had been included in the government.

It should be clear from all this that political parties in Iraq, whether in opposition or government, were in essence no more than one-man concerns, whose support was attracted by personal loyalty rather than by compelling and realistic programmes. In a dispatch informing the Foreign Office of the formation of a new party, the British Ambassador captured this phenomenon most succinctly:[90]

> The formation of a new party, the party of National Unity, was announced. This is intended to be the party of 'Ali Jaudat's Cabinet. Like previous similar parties, it is, in fact, little more than a group of Deputies, and has no organisation outside the Chamber. Its fate will probably be not unlike that of the 'Ahd al-Iraqi, which was founded by Nuri Sa'id when he became Prime Minister in 1930 and ceased to exist when he resigned the premiership in 1932.

The third possible channel of opposition in the country, the press, was noticeably more effective and developed than either of the two already discussed, though it was continually being crippled by censorship laws, and by the inducement of editors into high public offices.

The beginning of the Iraqi press can be traced back to 1869 with the founding by Midhat Pasha of *al-Zawra* newspaper. By the end of the century two more newspapers had been founded, one in Basra (1889) and the other in Mosul (1885).[91] In accordance with the Ottoman Press Regulations of 1863, these publications were under direct government control, and much of what they printed was, therefore, in praise of the Ottoman sultans. However, the 1863 Press Regulations were among those laws that were reformed with the coming to power of the Young Turks in 1908, and were replaced by more liberal regulations. With this relaxation, the following years saw a proliferation in the number of publications in Iraq, the press of Baghdad alone having grown to a total of twenty-five newspapers and journals by 1910.[92] Many of these publications propagated the cause of Arab nationalism, calling for an end to Ottoman rule. This burgeoning of the press was, however, interrupted by the outbreak of the First World War, with the introduction of a number of restrictions by the British and Ottoman authorities in the name of public security. These restrictions were not lifted at the end of the war, and thus one of the demands of the 1920 Iraqi uprising was the 'granting of freedom to the press so that the public can express its wishes and thoughts'.[93] After the suppression of the rebellion, a number of newspapers were licensed, the most notable being *al-Istiqlal*. In its first issue, on 28 September 1920, *al-Istiqlal* described itself as:[94]

an independent patriotic publication serving the Arabs in general and the Iraqis in particular, which says nothing that does not reflect the thoughts of the people and . . . which will endeavour to correct what is warped and reform the corrupt . . . and will listen fully to the call of the patriots.

Al-Istiqlal thus supported the Hashimite family and King Faisal in Syria, and was accordingly viewed with favour by the British authorities. However, when certain nationalist leaders exiled during the Arab Revolt returned to Baghdad in February 1921, a special issue of *al-Istiqlal* welcomed them with an editorial that was to change the British attitude:[95]

We congratulate the Iraqi nation on the return of our honourable exiles and call for the return of all exiles without exception. We also call for the implementation of the following:
1. Freedom of the press. . . .
2. Freedom of assemblies and the setting up of official political unions.
3. An unconditional general amnesty for all political prisoners.

4. The return of the exiles. . . .
5. The lifting of martial laws. . . .
6. Abolition of military courts. . . .
7. The holding of free elections without the interference of the occupation authorities.

The authorities reacted by banning the newspaper and imprisoning its editor together with eleven of his associates.[96] As will be seen later, these repressive measures continued to be applied regularly throughout the period under review.

Soon after the setting up of the state, four newspapers emerged: *al-Fallah*, *Dijla*, *Lisan al-'Arab* and *al-Rafidain*, all supporting the monarchy and Faisal's accession to the throne. *Al-Fallah* showed particular enthusiasm for Faisal:[97]

> The man nominated to the throne must be worthy of the nation's confidence, possessing all the qualities enabling him to be its King. Thus, the nation's overt support to Faisal's candidature is due to its belief that he possesses all of these qualities, and an acknowledgement of his arms outstretched to defend the Arab nation, and its demands for its rights and the resurrection of its glorious past.

A few months later, this newspaper ceased to be published when its editor was called upon by the government to become the Chief of Police.

Other editors were not, however, similarly favoured by the government. The editor of *Lisan al-'Arab*, for example (which changed its name to *al-Mufid* in April 1922), was exiled to Hanjam for publishing a communiqué of Hizb al-Watani al-'Iraqi and Jam'iyat al-Nahda al-'Iraqiya in August 1922. When he returned to Iraq two years later and recommenced the publication of *al-Mufid*, his paper was completely closed down and publication rights were withdrawn by the government in retaliation for the printing by *al-Mufid* of an article criticising the government for not being sufficiently patriotic. The editor of *Dijla* was similarly treated, and his newspaper also closed down for its 'republican sympathies' less than sixteen months after it came into existence. The fourth newspaper, *al-Rafidain*, was suspended six times during its first year of publication until its final closure in August 1922, and its editor was exiled to Henjam for printing communiqués by the political parties mentioned above. On his return a year later, its editor was appointed to the government and no efforts were made to resume publication.

As a result of these respressive measures by the government, some newspapers made a tactical change in their editorial policies, the main brunt of their criticism being directed against Britain and foreign domination rather than against the government itself. Analysing this phenomenon, a British report[98] was to comment later that

> Journalists in Iraq live almost exclusively by purveying political criticism to the literate public. They have learned from experience that circulation varies in direct ratio with the violence of their comments on current affairs, and have not yet discovered the sales value of the Magazine feature. As it is often dangerous to incur the wrath of powerful neighbours with whom they have to live in daily contact, the favourite target for their slings and arrows is the British and all they do in Iraq. The editors can then pose as patriots if successful, and martyrs if suppressed.

This reserve in the criticism of the government by the editors was, however, gradually abandoned during the late 1920s and early 1930s, when the government was conducting the negotiations of the terms of Iraq's independence. During that year,[99]

> Nationalist Press attacked them [the Government] incessantly with bitter articles, and the two affiliated political organisations, the Nationalist party and the party of National Brotherhood, carried on a steady propaganda against the Government in the southern provinces, particularly on the Euphrates. Of the six daily newspapers published in the capital, four were hostile, and the remaining two were subsidised supporters. The most trenchant critics of the Government were two men named Fahmi Beg-al-Mudarris and Raphael Butti. Efforts to deal with them through the Press Law were unavailing, for, as soon as the Minister of the Interior suspended their newspaper they brought it out again under a new name, an elementary device with which the law was unable to contend. At last, in the middle of March, their attacks became so violent that the Government, in desperation, took action against them under Section 40 of the Tribal, Civil and Criminal Disputes Regulations, and deported them both from Baghdad to Arbil. There they were kept out of mischief for a couple of months, and, though Raphael Butti returned to journalism in the autumn, he did so in a chastened spirit.

Despite these measures, some newspapers continued to print articles critical of the government, and according to British reports some editors appeared to be exploiting the independence issue for personal gain.

According to these reports, some articles were 'only thinly-disguised blackmail, and there are many diligent civil servants who won their posts through yellow journalism'.[100] The majority of editors, however, could not have been so motivated. This is borne out by the failure of the government to check their persistent criticism of its policies either by application of clause 40 of the Tribal, Civil and Criminal Disputes Regulations[101] or by the introduction in June 1931 of a Press Law increasing its control over the press.[102] Thus,[103]

> in 1932 Nuri's Government were so persistently attacked that they were obliged to pass an amending law which tightened up very considerably the law of 1931. Their action was bitterly criticised by the extreme nationalist opposition.

The criticism of the government by the opposition over this issue, however, proved to be as shallow as had been their call for a revision of the 1930 Treaty. Their attitude to the freedom of the press was in essence, therefore, no different from that of their colleagues in successive governments, who, while giving 'lip service to the ideal of a free unfettered press . . . are always careful to secure a very tight hold over the "fourth estate" of the realm'.[104]

Thus, when members of the opposition were brought into the government in March 1933, their treatment of the press closely followed that of their predecessors. Reviewing their term in office, the British Ambassador noted that:[105]

> Rashid 'Ali's Cabinet was no exception. Although, in opposition, he and several of his colleagues had championed the freedom of the Press, in office they retained the same close control over it as their predecessors had done. For the sake of window-dressing, the 'oppressive' Press Law of 1931 was repealed, but the new law which took its place in August 1933 reserved for the Government powers just as arbitrary and effective as those which had been exercised under the old law. These powers, moreover, have frequently been used, and the temporary suspension of a newspaper occurs too often to evoke much comment or surprise.

Later cabinets persisted in these efforts to assert governmental control of the press. For example, Jamil al-Madfa'i's government, which followed Rashid 'Ali's cabinet in November 1933, increased these restrictions on the freedom of the press:[106]

> The Madfa'i Government have now found the 1933 law inadequate and full of loopholes which permits local troublemakers to evade

official control and to continue their scurrilous propaganda. Consequently, they have been obliged to strengthen Rashid 'Ali's law by the present amending law, which re-introduces several provisions contained in Nuri Sa'id's law of 1932.

The last cabinet of our period, that of Yasin al-Hashimi, which lasted from March 1935 until its overthrow by the military eighteen months later, introduced amendments that were to strengthen this press law even further.

Conclusions

It has been shown that, numerically, city leaders were predominant in the cabinet during the period under study while the tribal shaikhs were given only a nominal share of cabinet posts. This may be explained, first, by their lack of education, but second by the fact that to add a large measure of political power to the considerable economic and political influence that the tribal shaikhs already enjoyed would have increased the likelihood of their power becoming unmanageable, and thus potentially threatening both to British influence in Iraq and to their ally in Baghdad, the central government. On the other hand, the exclusive allocation of political power to the city notables would have carried similar dangers. Though relatively landless, and therefore lacking an established power base, the more articulate city notables could instigate a more credible opposition to British interests in Iraq than could the landowning class, who would be reluctant to gamble away their already established economic and social privileges in the country. However, by entrusting control of the state machinery to the city notables, this class would seek to safeguard these privileges and would come to rival the tribal shaikhs in striving to acquire for itself large areas of land in the rural areas.

These were the main foundations of Iraq's political structure, clearly undemocratic in character and clearly at odds with Article 2 of the State's Constitution, which proclaimed that 'Iraq is a sovereign State, independent and free . . . with a representative Government.'[107] This undemocratic distribution of political power becomes even more striking when the structure of the cabinet is analysed in terms of rural–urban, ethnic or religious divisions of the population. The lack of democratic representation must have deepened further the ethnic and religious divisions that the new state had inherited, and ultimately the political and economic inequalities that have already been discussed in chapter II.

Moreover, taking the ruling class in isolation from the wider society, we find that, while the forcefulness and constitutional prerogatives of King Faisal stifled the possibility of the emergence of national leadership by politicians and the development of a lasting functional political system, the disunity within the ruling class as a whole and the intense personal rivalries between its members diminished such prospects even further.

It will be shown later that, with Faisal's death, a stabilising force disappeared and the precarious balance within the ruling class was disrupted. There was a resultant power struggle in which the contestants sought to capture the central position, which would again stabilise the structure, and give the winner added prestige and privilege. Almost all of the individual contenders in this classic game of power politics resorted to the army in order to strengthen their own position. Thus, aware of his inexperience and, more importantly, of his unpopularity with British officials and with some of the leading members of the Iraqi ruling class, King Ghazi, Faisal's constitutional successor, sought an alliance with the army. This only increased the antipathy of the British Ambassador towards Ghazi, and barely a week after Faisal's death the Ambassador was noting that:[108]

> What was difficult to a Government presided over by . . . King
> Faisal has become impossible to a Government whose head is the
> youthful champion of the Iraqi army. The cabinet has already
> approached me privately with a view to using my influence to
> control the young King's military enthusiasm and to prevent him
> from turning to his old friends in the army for political advice.

As will be seen later, three prominent members of the cabinet's inner circle also resorted to the army in order to reinforce their own position, both in the country and *vis-à-vis* their political rivals. In this political climate, only the peasant class, which had little to gain by the perpetuation of the status quo, could have effected a radical change in that political system and, by the fact of their numerical majority, laid the foundation of a more representative government. However, given (as has been seen) that the country's Parliament was demonstrably ineffective, that a unity of interest existed between the deputies and the ruling elite, and that the country's political parties were merely one-man concerns, nothing short of a total social revolution could have brought the peasant class to power, and the conditions did not yet exist for this.

Chapter 4

The army

Introduction

In the previous chapters, an attempt was made to show the inherent weaknesses of the Iraqi state, and the virtual absence of the basic prerequisites considered necessary for the maintenance of stability. In the aftermath of the abortive revolt of 1920, Iraq was a country without either an indigenous central authority or any significant structured and functional institutions. Aware of these weaknesses, the British authorities created a puppet government in October 1920 and shortly afterwards proceeded to lay the foundations of what was to become known as the Iraq Arab Army. Military service, the government thought, would encourage the development of a national spirit, and the disciplined and uniformed life of the barracks might succeed in creating some degree of homogeneity among recruits drawn from racially and ethnically diverse backgrounds. In addition, a national army was a significant symbol of national sovereignty, and a vital instrument in the maintenance of internal security and the deterrence of external aggression. It was also essential for upholding the legal rights of merchants and other urban groups that had claims in the countryside, and for enforcing such class-based legislation as the 1933 Agrarian Law.

The formation of the Iraq army

The idea of serving in armed forces was not a new one for the inhabitants of Mesopotamia. From the time when conscription was applied to Iraq in the latter part of the nineteenth century, the Turks normally succeeded in raising a local force of some 16,000 men even in peacetime and in doubling that number in wartime.

By 1914 this force was led by around 1,350 officers who were mainly Turkish; about 60 per cent of the rank and file consisted of Arabs, the rest being Kurds or Turcomans. Those between twenty and forty years of age were liable for military service, recruits being obliged, during the First World War, to serve three years in the regular army (Nizami), six years in the reserve (Ihtiyat), and eleven years in the territorial army (Radif).[1] Recruitment was by conscription, and theoretically applied to all males dwelling in towns and villages. In the tribal areas, the number of eligible males was estimated and each tribe was supposed to pay an annual tax (*badal*) of 50 piastres for every member exempted (the calculated cost of keeping one soldier for one year). A similar tax had to be paid by members of the non-Muslim communities in lieu of military service. In practice, therefore, only Muslims served in the army. These conscription laws provided Constantinople with a source of revenue, and the fact that this was a major incentive led to a lax enforcement of the laws.

The move towards secularism, coupled with the nationalist aspirations of the Young Turks, appear to have had a negative impact on army personnel in Mesopotamia. Whereas before this era of liberal reforms those joining the army may have been encouraged by the promise of ultimate divine rewards, the new emphasis on secularism appears to have resulted in the prevalence of parochial sentiments and tribal loyalties over those traditionally extended to the spiritual leadership in Constantinople. Thus Mesopotamian soldiers, particularly during the First World War, deserted freely and were captured willingly. 'Safely captured', read the telegram sent by a typical soldier to his family soon after being taken prisoner during that war.[2] The officers, on the other hand, reacted to the rising nationalism of the Young Turks by developing their own nationalism and thus, shortly before the war, creating a secret political society, al-'Ahd, calling, *inter alia*, for the secession of Mesopotamia and Syria from the Ottoman Empire. With the setting up of an Arab state in 1920, a political foundation was laid down which could be expected to change the self-image of an army recruit from a mere mercenary to a guardian of the nation. As soon as the state was established, therefore, the process of creating an Arab army was set in motion.

The first step was the setting up of the Ministry of Defence and the appointment of Ja'far Pasha al-'Askari, late Commander-in-Chief of the Hijaz army, as the Minister. Ja'far Pasha's military experience was considerable. He had been born in Baghdad in 1885 to a family that had moved there from the Kurdish village of 'Askar. On graduating from Baghdad Military School in 1904 and joining the army, he was sent to Berlin, where he spent three years training with the German army. On his return he was enrolled in the Staff College in Constantinople. His active involvement in politics started during the First World War, when he met 'Aziz 'Ali al-Masri and other 'politicised' Arab officers who formed the nucleus of the al-'Ahd party. After meeting Amir Faisal in 1916, he had served the Hashimite family and their British allies loyally and was later described by the British Embassy records as a man 'inclined to take the line of least resistance and hope for the best'.[3] Nevertheless, Ja'far Pasha played a not inconsiderable role as a moderniser, and it is perhaps significant that he was among the pioneers discarding the wearing of the tarboush and calling for its abolition. Furthermore, as someone who knew a total of eight languages including German, English and French, Ja'far Pasha must have been influenced by current ideas of militarism and the importance attached in other nations of his time to the armies as symbols of national unity.

Ja'far Pasha's desire to establish a modern army in Iraq could not, therefore, be in question. Two months after al-'Askari's appointment to the Ministry of Defence, his brother-in-law, Nuri Pasha al-Sa'id, another former commander-in-chief of the Hijaz army, arrived from Syria where, until the fall of Damascus, he had been C-in-C. Nuri Pasha had been similarly educated in Turkish military schools, and had served with the Turkish army until 1913 when he was among the founders of the al-'Ahd party. Although less travelled than Ja'far, he nevertheless spoke five languages including German, French and English. His familiarity with modern ideas is indicated by the reference to him in the British Embassy records as a 'modernist with an exceptionally alert intelligence'.[4] Shortly after his arrival in Baghdad, Nuri was appointed Officiating Commander of the General Staff, in spite of the fact that at that time the only army the country could claim was limited to a skeleton Headquarter Staff of ten Iraqi officers. Any expansion of this force would be directly linked with Britain's general policies towards the country as a whole.

At that time, Britain's overriding concern in the Middle East was the maintenance of maximum British influence in the area at the lowest possible cost to the British Treasury. With this in mind, the British Colonial Office arranged a conference for their Middle East officials which was convened at Cairo in 1921 and headed by the Colonial Secretary, Winston Churchill. Regarding Mesopotamia, the main issues on the agenda included the steps to be taken for reduction of expenditure, the treatment of the Kurdish provinces, the claims of the various possible candidates for the throne of Iraq, and the nature of the forces to be created for the defence of the new state.[5]

This last question presented the British with a complex dilemma. They had to formulate a policy that would significantly reduce their defence expenditure in the country without jeopardising its internal and external security. At that time there were two types of armed forces in Iraq, both British-controlled, and costing the British Treasury an annual sum of around £37 million. The first force consisted of thirty-three battalions of British imperial troops and also of detachments of the RAF, whose continued presence in Iraq was considered essential pending the signature of peace with Turkey. The second force was the Iraq Levies, whose rank and file were mostly Assyrians and numbered around 4,000, and whose officers were British.[6] The Levies were known to be loyal to Britain, and had played an important role during the 1920 revolt, performing such essential services to British troops as guidance, scouting and aiding them in combat.[7] The degree of their involvement is indicated by their casualty figure, which amounted to 107 at a time when their total number was a mere 2,000, and by the awarding of fifteen medals by Britain for gallantry performed by members of the Levies.[8]

The expansion of these Levies therefore offered an obvious way for Britain to reduce her own commitment in the country while maintaining an armed force to police it. Another possibility was the transfer of defence responsibilities to the Royal Air Force, whose mobility would enable a relatively small force to deal effectively with any disturbances. Despite these possibilities, however, the political need for raising an indigenous force that would symbolise national sovereignty was overwhelming. Such a force should be of a size and strength to enable it to suppress any anti-government and anti-British activities in the country, as well as protecting it against external aggression. At the same time, its strength should not be permitted to exceed a limit beyond which the central government in Baghdad might feel able to turn its back to Britain and contravene the alliance. The maintenance of the Levies was seen, therefore, as essential, to provide a shock-absorber. Furthermore, as the British High Commissioner was to remark some months later, it was feared that the total disbandment of the Levies might be regarded by the Iraqi public as[9]

a sign that we are expediting termination of our connection with Iraq; it will discourage our friends and moderate elements and will provide extremist agitators with a strong weapon. Also, the mercantile community will be inclined to lose confidence in British intention to maintain effective control, and tribal elements will be encouraged to belittle administration and feel able to refuse payment of revenue.

In addition, should the RAF be assigned the responsibility of maintaining the country's defences, the Levies would provide essential ground forces, guarding its aerodromes and performing general services.

The Conference finally agreed that the Levies should be maintained, while at the same time Britain would work towards the creation of an Arab army to share responsibility for the defence of the country with two detachments of the RAF. Further, it was decided that this army would be organised on British lines and equipped and trained by Britain. In March 1921, the Conference officially decided that:[10]

> Until such time as Iraqi national forces were in being and capable of maintaining internal order and defending the frontiers, Britain would undertake these responsibilities which would be entrusted to the RAF. The strength of the British forces under the scheme of RAF control was to be eight squadrons of aeorplanes, four infantry battalions, one pack battery and other small ancillary units. It was further decided that immediate steps should be taken to raise an Iraqi army of 15,000 and that British forces should be progressively reduced as the army grew.

The strategy to be followed in the raising and organisation of an Arab army was then examined. By June, after it had been decided that this army should be based on a voluntary system, terms of service[11] were agreed upon, and before the end of the month recruiting branches were opened in nineteen towns and cities.

In the meantime, ex-Sharifian and ex-Turkish officers had been arriving in Baghdad, and by this time their combined number had reached 640.[12] Unemployed and imbued with nationalist ideas, these officers constituted a potential threat to the government, which assumed it could be minimised by the promise of regular salaries and swift promotions. Thus, these officers were encouraged to join the army. But their positive response was an indication of economic need rather than an expression of identity with the new state. According to a British intelligence report, many of these officers grew far from satisfied with their new conditions of employment, and sometimes threatened to take employment with the French in Syria or with Mustafa Kamal in Turkey.[13]

Organisation and composition

As had been outlined at the Cairo Conference, the newly created army was to be equipped and trained on British lines. Thus, simultaneously with the creation of the Arab army, a British Military Mission was established and British military advisers attached to the Ministry of Defence. This mission, even during the Mandate, never exceeded fifty officers. However, it would be misleading to draw any conclusions from this relatively small number, since British influence was in the main channelled through the training and instruction of NCOs and officer cadets. When the Iraq Military College opened in July 1921, Britons on the staff included not only its director and his assistant, but also fifteen out of the twenty instructors. English military textbooks and training manuals were translated into Arabic, and even ex-Sharifian and ex-Turkish officers were required to undergo fresh training in order to learn the new system.[14] When the government's austerity measures led to the closure of the college in January 1923 and its replacement by the Iraq Army Training Centre, the director and his assistant in that centre were also British. In June of the next year, the Royal Iraq Military College was opened for the education of military cadets. Its organisation was modelled on that of the Royal Military College, Sandhurst, and it had an annual intake of eighty cadets. It was in 1924 also that a first batch of four cadets was sent to England and India for further training, and this annual flow was augmented until it reached an average of twenty-five during the years 1932–6 (twenty of them going to England). In 1927 it was decided to create an Iraq Royal Air Force (IRAF), and six cadets were sent to the Royal Air Force Cadet College at Cranwell. While in April 1930 Iraq's air force had only five planes, all of them DH Moth light aircraft, by 1936 they had fifty-five planes, all British-made.

As mentioned above, on its creation the army absorbed a total of 640 ex-Turkish and ex-Sharifian officers, but new officer cadets were also recruited, mainly from the towns. Only 25 per cent of the cadets originated from the tribal areas and Kurdistan, and, owing to their relative backwardness, they had to undergo longer courses than their contemporaries from the towns. Despite recruitment, however, the overwhelming majority of high-ranking officers continued to be the ex-Turkish and ex-Sharifian officers. In September 1936, for example, the Iraqi officer corps (comprising officers with the rank of commander and above) numbered 84: a sample of 61 of these officers (table 6) shows that 50 had served in the Turkish army. As over a third of the

Iraqi officers serving in the Turkish army are believed to have joined the Hijaz army during the Arab Revolt, it seems reasonable to assume that approximately that proportion of these 50 officers served in the Sharifian army. A further analysis of our sample shows that only one-tenth of the most senior officers came from the rural areas, while, of the remaining nine-tenths, three-quarters were born in Baghdad.

The most remarkable feature in the character analysis of this officer corps, however, is the fact that only 1 of the 61 officers was a Shi'a and 2 were Christian, while the remaining 58 were all Sunni. This is a reflection of the underprivileged position of the Shi'a community as a whole during the Ottoman rule, with the consequent rarity of members of that sect being elevated to high positions in the army or government; and since, judging from our sample, an experience in the Turkish army was an essential prerequisite for the attainment of a high appointment in the Iraqi army, Shi'a cadets were at a clear disadvantage.

Another phenomenon that might be explained in terms of this exclusiveness of the Iraqi officer corps is the fact that, although Iraqi cadets were being trained at renowned military academies abroad, their superior qualifications were not sufficient to secure them a proportional share of senior appointments, which remained almost exclusively in the hands of the Turkish-trained officers. Out of the fifty cadets trained abroad in 1935 and 1936, for example, only two had been given senior appointments by October 1936. Thus, those officers who were to effect the *coup d'état* later that year belonged almost exclusively to the same stratum from which seven of Iraq's eleven prime ministers since 1920 had come: that is to say, they all shared the common experience of having served in either the Ottoman or the Hijaz army, making the *coup d'état* in effect a horizontal movement within the same arena.

The rank and file, on the other hand, was composed mainly of tribal elements, who in 1924 were estimated to form 70 per cent of the total force.[15] Although no actual figures are given for later years, British Embassy dispatches continued to refer to them as comprising the majority.

The expansion of the army, 1921–36

On Faisal's arrival in Iraq in 1921, the need for a national army was at its most pressing. Externally, Turkey on the north was pressing her claims over the Mosul vilayet; no fixed frontier existed between the two countries, and Turkish penetration into the northern region

Table 6 *Selected characteristics of a sample of the most senior officers in Iraq on the eve of the October 1936 coup*

	Name	Religion	Place of training	Place of birth	Military career prior to 1936	Rank in October 1936	Position in October 1936	Place of appointment
1	'Ali Ghalib bin Isma'il	Sunni	TMC	Sulaimaniya	Turkish army	Major	Commander	1/2 Battalion
2	'Abbas Fadli bin Ahmad Jaudat	Sunni	TMC	Baghdad	Turkish army	Lt Colonel	Commander	HQ, 2nd Infantry Brigade
3	Akram bin Mushtaq	Sunni	Cranwell	Baghdad	–	Snr Captain	Commander	No. 1, (Fighter) Squad. RIAF
4	'Abd al-Majid Hassun	Sunni	TMC	Baghdad	Turkish army	Colonel	Commander	HQ, 1st Infantry Brigade
5	'Abbas bin Muhammad al-Shalchi	Sunni	TMC	Baghdad	Turkish army	Major	Commander	Southern District, Infantry Depot, Hillah
6	'Abd al-Wahhab 'Abd al-Latif	Sunni	TMC	Baghdad	Turkish army	Major	Commander	Southern District, Infantry Depot, Baghdad
7	'Abd al-Razzaq bin Husain	Sunni	TMC	Baghdad	Turkish army	Major	Commander	Royal Iraq Military College
8	'Abd al-Rahman Sharaf	Sunni	TMC	Baghdad	Turkish army	Lt Colonel	Commander	2nd Frontier Battalion
9	Ahmad Fu'ad Muhammad	Sunni	TMC	Baghdad	Turkish army	Captain	Commander	Units, 2nd Field Battery
10	Ahmad Hamdi Zainal	Sunni	TMC	Baghdad	Turkish army	Lt Colonel	Commander	Units, 2nd Cavalry
11	Amin Zaki	Sunni	TMC	Sulaimaniya	Turkish army	Lt Colonel	Commander	HQ, Euphrates Area, Diwaniyah
12	'Abd al-Hamid Nasrat	Sunni	TMC	Baghdad	Turkish army	Lt Colonel	GSOI	HQ, 1st Division, Baghdad
13	'Abd al-Latif Nuri	Sunni	TMC	Baghdad	Turkish army	Major-Gen'l	Commander	HQ, 1st Division, Baghdad
14	'Aziz Mustafa Yamulki	Sunni	TMC	Sulaimaniya	Turkish army	Major	Director (MT) GSOI	HQ, Baghdad
15	Amin al-'Umari	Sunni	TMC	Mosul	Turkish army	Colonel	Commander	HQ, Baghdad
16	Ahmad 'Izzat bin Da'ud	Sunni	TMC	Baghdad	Turkish army	Major	Commander	Units, 2/2 Battalion
17	Bakir Sidqi Shauqi	Sunni	TMC	Askar	Turkish army	Major-Gen'l	Commander	HQ, 2nd Division, Kirkuk
18	Bahjat bin Rauf	Christian	BMC + Cranwell	Mosul	–	Captain	Commander	No. 2 (Bomber Transport) Sqad., RIAF
19	Bashir Sidqi bin Yaqub	Christian	BMC	Mosul	–	Captain	Commander	Aircraft Stores, RIAF
20	Danun Taha	Sunni	TMC	Mosul	Turkish army	Captain	Commander	Units, 5th Mountain Battery

No.	Name	Sect	Training	Place	Army	Rank	Role	Unit
21	Fauzi bin Farajulla	Sunni	TMC	Baghdad	Turkish army	Major	Commander	1/5 Battalion
22	Hifdhi 'Aziz	Sunni	BMC	Baghdad	–	Captain	Commander	Armament, RIAF
23	Hamid Rafat bin Bakir	Sunni	TMC	Baghdad	Turkish army	Major	OC	Units, 2nd Signal Battalion
24	Husain Makki	Sunni	TMC	Baghdad	Turkish army	Snr Captain	OC	Units, Engineer Battalion
25	Husain Jahid 'Ali	Sunni	TMC	Kirkuk	Turkish army	Major	Commander	Motor Machine Gun Company
26	Husain bin 'Alwan	Shi'a	BMC	Diwaniyah	–	Snr Captain	Commander	Units, 1st Field Battery
27	Husain Fauzi	Sunni	TMC	Baghdad	Turkish army	Major-Gen'l	Commander	HQ, Northern District, Mosul
28	Husain Fauzi bin 'Ali Ridha	Sunni	India	Baghdad	–	Major	Director (VS)	HQ, Baghdad
29	Hajji Ramadhan	Sunni	TMC	Baghdad	Turkish army	Colonel	Q-G&M.GO	HQ, Baghdad
30	Isma'il Safwat bin Sa'id	Sunni	TMC	Mosul	Turkish army	Major	Commander	1/3 Battalion
31	Isma'il Namiq	Sunni	TMC	Baghdad	Turkish army	Colonel	Commander	Units, Cavalry Brigade
32	Ibrahim bin Sayyid Hamdi	Sunni	TMC	Baghdad	Turkish army	Colonel	Commander	Units, 3rd Cavalry
33	Isma'il Haqqi bin Khumayyis	Sunni	TMC	Baghdad	Turkish army	Lt Colonel	Commander	Units, Royal Artillery
34	Khalid al-Zahawi	Sunni	TMC	Baghdad	Turkish army	Colonel	Director (RIAF)	HQ, Baghdad
35	Kamil bin Shabib	Sunni	TMC	Baghdad	Turkish army	Major	Commander	2/1 Battalion
36	Khalil Mukhlis	Sunni	TMC	Baghdad	Turkish army	Snr Captain	Commander	Units, 3rd Mountain Battery
37	Musa bin 'Ali	Sunni	BMC + Cranwell	Baghdad	–	Snr Captain	Commander	Flying Training School & Communications Flight
38	Muhammad 'Ali bin Jawad	Sunni	BMC + Cranwell	Baghdad	–	Major	Commander	R.I.A.F.
39	Muhammad Nadhif al-Shawi	Sunni	TMC	Baghdad	Turkish army	Colonel	Commander	Staff school
40	Muhammad 'Ali Sa'id	Sunni	TMC	Mosul	Turkish army	Snr Captain	Commander	2/6 Battalion
41	Mahmud Sirat	Sunni	TMC	Baghdad	Turkish army	Major	Commander	3/5 Battalion
42	Mustafa bin Raghib	Sunni	TMC	Kirkuk	Turkish army	Major	Commander	2/4 Battalion
43	Mahmud Fadhil al-Janabi	Sunni	TMC	Baghdad	Turkish army	Major	Commander	2/7 Battalion
44	Muhammad Nuri bin Ahmad Khairi	Sunni	BMC	Mosul	–	Major	Commander	3/4 Battalion
45	Mustafa Bahjat Yunis	Sunni	TMC	Mosul	Turkish army	Lt Colonel	Commander	1st Frontier Battalion
46	Qasim Maqsud	Sunni	TMC	Baghdad	Turkish army	Lt Colonel	Commander	HQ, 6th Infantry Brigade
46	Rashid bin Ahmad Jaudat	Sunni	TMC	Sulaimaniya	Turkish army	Major	Commander	1/4 Battalion

Table 6 *continued*

	Name	Religion	Place of training	Place of birth	Military career prior to 1936	Rank in October 1936	Position in October 1936	Place of appointment
47	Shakir al-Wadi	Sunni	TMC	Baghdad	Turkish army	Colonel	GSOI	HQ, 2nd Division, Kirkuk
48	Sa'id Yahya	Sunni	TMC	Mosul	Turkish army	Major	Commander	3/1 Battalion
49	Sabah Nuri al-Sa'id	Sunni	Cranwell	Baghdad	—	Lieutenant	Commander	Aircraft Depot, RIAF
50	Shakir 'Abd al-Wahhab	Sunni	TMC	Baghdad	Turkish army	Major-Gen'l	CMA	HQ, Baghdad
51	Sa'id Omar al-Takriti	Sunni	TMC	Baghdad	Turkish army	Colonel	Commander	HQ, 3rd Infantry Brigade
52	Shafiq Qasim	Sunni	TMC	Baghdad	Turkish army	Major	Commander	1/6 Battalion
53	Salih Sa'ib al-Juburi	Sunni	TMC	Baghdad	Turkish army	Lt Colonel	Commander	Small Arms School
54	Shaukat bin 'Ali Yumni	Sunni	TMC	Baghdad	Turkish army	Snr Captain	Commander	Units, 1st Mountain Battery
55	Taha al-Hashimi	Sunni	TMC	Baghdad	Turkish army	General	C-in-C	HQ, Baghdad
56	Taufiq al-Damluji	Sunni	TMC	Mosul	Turkish army	Lt Colonel	Commander	HQ, 5th Infantry Brigade
57	'Umar Muwaffaqi bin Habib	Sunni	TMC	Baghdad	Turkish army	Snr Captain	Commander	Units, 4th Mountain Battery
58	Yusif bin Najmal-Din	Sunni	TMC	Baghdad	Turkish army	Lt Colonel	OC	Units, 1st Signal Battalion
59	Yasin Hasan	Sunni	TMC	Mosul	Turkish army	Major	Commander	3/6 Battalion
60	Zaki Handal	Sunni	TMC	Baghdad	Turkish army	Major	Commander	Northern District Infantry Depot
61	Salih Fauzi	Sunni	BMC	Mosul	—	Captain	Commander	Units, 6th Field Battery
		Sunnis		*Baghdadis*	*Ex-Turkish officers*	*Turkish-trained*		*Ex-Turkish officers*
Total		58		41		50		50
% of grand total		95%		67%		82%		82%

Source: This table was compiled mainly from documents found in the FO 371 series and also from the Arabic and English sources listed in the bibliography.

threatened Iraq's unity. Also in the north, the Kurdish Surchi chiefs of Agra and the tribesmen around Rawanduz were in a state of open revolt. In the south-west of the country the desert tribes were in a state of disorder, while in the west there was constant trouble from the raids by the Syrian tribe of 'Aqaidat. Internally, the Muntafiq, Diwaniya and Karbala *liwas* contained a hostile population, while the *'ulama* of the holy Shi'a cities of Karbala and Najaf were agitating their followers against the government, hoping for a 'weak Government which will allow their ignorant theocracy to rule the tribes and exploit them'.[16] Both the unity and the prosperity of the country were threatened by these divisions, as these northern areas contained not only the principal lines of communication between Baghdad and Tehran, but also the fertile plains of the north-east and the oil areas of Jabal Hamrin.

The government, therefore, saw the need for a mobile force, and the expansion of the young army was given top priority; a policy that was by then agreeable to Britain. Thus the question of defence was discussed by King Faisal's first cabinet, which met on 11 September 1921, and a decision was reached authorising the cabinet to[17]

> persist in its efforts to recruit an army of volunteers from among the people, to carry out the important functions which will be entrusted to it, so that the Kingdom of Iraq may be secure against future troubles and events as well as against internal troubles.

However, although the cabinet was calling for the expansion of the army, the number of recruits offering themselves for service was actually declining. During the first three months of the army's existence, about 2,000 men had enlisted. These included a 'considerable number of undesirable characters',[18] who may have been driven into joining the army by their inability to find alternative employment. Although the monthly rate in the number of recruits averaged 287 during the first seven months of the army's creation, that average had dropped to 204 during the same seven months of the following year, and continued to decline.

This lack of enthusiasm to join the Arab army can be attributed both to the absence of 'national spirit' and to the better rates of pay of the Levies, where a private soldier was earning almost double that of his counterpart in the army. King Faisal's attempts to appeal to the sentiments of the population by giving units of the armed forces names of important figures in the Arab history[19] appear to have had little effect. What does appear to have improved the situation of recruitment, however, was the decision of the British authorities in January 1922 to equalise the rates of pay in the Levies with those of the army and to restrict recruitment to the Levies to non-Arabs. It was further decided that:[20]

> the Iraq army will be increased on the voluntary system from 2,000 to 4,500 by April. The Levies will similarly be increased from 4,500 to 5,500 while the existing force will be reengaged for a year from January 1, except for the Arab element numbering 1,424 which will be reengaged only up to October 1.

In the meantime, a campaign in the national press was calling on the people to respond to the necessity of strengthening the country's armed forces. An article published in the *Iraq Times*, under the title 'Plain Talk' and signed by 'Your sincere friend "Old England"', addressed itself to the[21]

> Younger patriots, why don't you go and form a corps d'élite for the Artillery and other services where intelligence is required? It would be so much more useful than wasting your time [sic] in the coffee shops abusing the Government and the British and the weather and so forth. Moreover, it is so urgently necessary for the defence of your country. We should sleep so much more soundly, if we thought you had a real force capable of standing up to the Turks. . . .

The government also continued its debate about strengthening the army, and the Minister of Defence was already requesting the introduction of some form of conscription if he were to meet the demands made to him to stabilise the interior. At a cabinet meeting held on 9 August 1922, Ja'far al-'Askari, the Minister of Defence, pointed out:[22]

> that the numbers of the Iraq army were insufficient for the defence of the country in cases of emergency and that under these circumstances he would not accept responsibility. He suggested:
> (a) that he should be given a budgetary sanction for another 1,500 men, or
> (b) the introduction of some form of conscription. If neither . . . were accepted he would . . . resign. Jafar's protest has been engendered by the frequent demands made recently by the Interior on the army. Besides a detachment sent to the Jabal Sinjar and another from the Musa Kadhim Battalion to Karbala . . . there has been a request from Yasin Pasha for troops at Nasiriya and another from the Minister of Interior as to whether they could defend the Khaniqin district from Hamawand raiders. . . .

Ja'far's arguments were unsuccessful. Conscription was not introduced, and his threat to resign proved to be a bluff. Meanwhile, however, the recruitment campaign continued in the national press, echoing the views of the Minister of Defence, and by the end of 1922, the *al-'Iraq* newspaper was declaring that[23]

> a big army is now essential . . . we must rely on ourselves . . . compulsory service must be applied. Then in a short time we shall have 20,000 men. Iraqis are accustomed to conscription, it is not a new idea. Volunteer service is new. . . .

However, in spite of these efforts, public apathy towards the army continued. This apathy was explained by a senior British official as follows:[24]

> The Iraqis have not come forward as recruits for their army as one might have expected. This exemplifies the lack of public spirit and the apathy which pervades the whole atmosphere in Iraq. They do not care. . . . Those who have thought about it welcome the date for two reasons, the one because they have complete confidence in the army and look forward to the time when they can use it as they wish, the other because they know the day of our departure spells collapse, the fall of Faisal and the return of the Turks. . . . It is recommended that we tell Faisal that we cannot contemplate the disruption of Iraq. That we consider such an eventuality certain unless military conditions are improved. That the army is inefficient and not likely to meet demands made on it after other forces have withdrawn.

While this absence of national spirit must have been an important reason, it seems that the economic factor remained an overpowering consideration influencing the number of recruits, and a number of cases can be cited as evidence of this. The first is the considerable increase in the number of recruits following the equalisation of rates of pay in the Levies and the army; the second is the immediate drop in the number of recruits following the cabinet decision to reduce the pay of soldiers by 25 per cent in September 1922 as a stringency measure. Subsequent to that decision, the average number of recruits for the last three months of the year was 132, compared with 353 for the first nine months. These reductions in the rate of pay had 'brought recruiting to a standstill and has resulted in numerous desertions and absentees amongst the rank and file to the number of some 200 between 1st and 30th September'.[25]

Finally, when the cabinet reconsidered its decision and sanctioned an increase of 17 per cent in the monthly pay of soldiers, there was an immediate rise in the number of recruits, raising the average to 200 per month for the last six months of the year compared with 80 for the months before the pay rise was implemented. Although Iraqi officers already enjoyed a rate of pay averaging twenty times that of private soldiers and were not affected by these changes of wages, they were offered different types of incentives:[26]

> At a meeting on the 11th June 1923, the Council of Ministers discussed the proposals contained in a letter received from the Minister of Defence suggesting that the Iraq Government should present every officer of the Iraqi army with a sword, to remain with the officer on trust for a period of 10 years at the end of which time it should become the property of the officer. The Council passed a resolution approving this suggestion. . . . On the same day a resolution was passed directing the addition of 2,000 men to the Iraq army and an increase in the budget for defence of £600,000. The question of an increase was brought into urgent prominence by the realisation of the inadequacy of the Iraqi forces.

Owing to the combination of these factors, by the end of 1923 the recruitment situation was improving, and during the subsequent year the size of the army actually expanded by 33 per cent. This trend continued during 1925, reaching a level where the supply was 'far in excess of demand',[27] and forcing the authorities to allot maximum quotas to the various recruiting centres. It is not possible to determine how much of this increase was due to the 'alarming rise' in the cost of living owing to the severity of the weather and the absence of rain.[28]

In spite of this swelling of the army's ranks, and in spite of the fact that a solution of the Mosul dispute was in sight, the government still found it necessary to establish an irregular gendarmerie under the name of the Central Force, composed of tribal volunteers, to protect the Jazira Desert and the right bank of the Tigris from hostile raids. Thus, the need to expand the army was ever-present, and King Faisal, who perhaps was also inspired by the example of the application of conscription in Persia and Turkey, was aware of this need. So were important politicians like Ja'far al-'Askari, Nuri al-Sa'id, Yasin al-Hashimi and Rashid 'Ali, who encouraged the King in these efforts and supported his endeavour to introduce conscription. Apart from wanting to secure the government's dominance over the countryside, these politicians appear to have conceived of conscription as the ultimate commitment to patriotism (and thus a unifying factor), turning the professional army into a levy of all sectors of the population.

Unhappily for the government, a significant proportion of the population did not identify with the state and were, therefore, unwilling to defend it. Thus the question of conscription was basically a political one, and it provides a comprehensive reflection of the fragility and intricacies of the country's socio-political structure. It is with some justification, therefore, that the issue of conscription will be discussed below at some length.

Already in November 1920, less than one month after his appointment to the Ministry of Defence in the provisional government, Ja'far al-'Askari was advocating the adoption of the conscript system, arguing that it had[29]

> started in Iraq some 150 years ago and the people have become
> accustomed to it. It was found in practice that the only way to turn
> the people into satisfactory soldiers was by the control exercised
> by conscription.

However, as will be seen later, from its very inception the notion of conscription contained the seeds of a divisive controversy: it was associated with the Ottoman period, when conscripts could be committed to military service for a total of twenty years and when tribes had to pay heavy taxes to secure the exemption of their tribesmen. It also meant a submission to central authority, which Iraqis, particularly the tribes, were still neither accustomed to nor willing to accept. Not surprisingly, therefore, the question of conscription became the subject of much discussion and heated debate:[30]

> The conscription question continues to be one of the principal
> topics of the day and bids fair to cause considerable dissension
> amongst the Government's party and to a lesser degree amongst the
> opposition. An agent reports that he recently heard Shaikh 'Ali
> Sulaiman, one of the Deputies for the Dulaim, say that the Hizb
> al-Taqaddum is hopelessly divided on the subject and that the future
> attitude of the party is, therefore, quite undecided. The Shaikh
> seemed to be of the opinion that the members of the Hizb . . . would
> ally themselves with other parties. If this comes about it may well
> cause the complete break-up of the Hizb if not the fall of the Govern-
> ment. Curiosity is universal as to what is really the British attitude
> towards the question, and the opinion seems general that any official
> announcement on this subject will have a far-reaching effect.

At this time Britain had not formulated any known policy towards the introduction of conscription in Iraq. British thinking was still influenced more by economic arguments, and in any case a cheap expansion of the army would not have been inconsistent with the policies agreed upon at the Cairo Conference. This almost indifferent attitude to the question of conscription can be seen from the following dispatch sent by the British High Commissioner to London. Discussing the expansion of the army, he wrote:[31]

> The plan which commends itself to the Iraq Government is the conscription of the town populations and the inhabitants of settled villages and although this would be a confession of weakness, so far as the tribesmen are concerned, it would be better than nothing.
> It would provide for rapid expansion within the present revenues of the Iraq Government, whereas an expansion on the present voluntary basis would have to wait for a problematic expansion of revenue.

While the question of conscription continued to be debated (the Constituent Assembly of 1924 discussing it), Britain maintained her reticence until 1926, when the question rapidly came to the fore with the inception of an active campaign by the government and the formation, on the orders of the Prime Minister, of a committee to frame a conscription law. Some members of the Eastern Department in London suggested that the introduction of conscription would be a 'policy which is against all our traditions'[32] while others argued that Britain's approval of conscription might lead some Iraqi politicians to 'accuse Britain of wanting to strengthen the army in order to further its imperialistic end'[33] (since the army would depend on Britain for arms and could also be used by her to crush her political opponents).

Both of these arguments were simplistic. What mattered to Britain most at that time was the internal stability of Iraq, which would enable her to administer the country cheaply and smoothly. The introduction of conscription carried with it the potential of dividing the population [34] and, as it had in Afghanistan, the possible furthering of anti-government activities. In such chaotic conditions, there was no telling who might come to the fore, or what his political colour might be. Moreover, conscription would meet its strongest opposition in the tribal areas, which were Britain's traditional allies and whose support it was essential to keep. Furthermore, it would be morally more difficult for the authorities to prevent a conscript army, with the pretentions of representing the nation, from interfering in the affairs of running the state. As a peripheral issue, it was considered that a conscript army could provide added confidence to ambitious politicians like Nuri al-Sa'id, who, although known for his sympathies to the British alliance, could not be allowed a degree of power beyond which he might contemplate the diminishing of his dependence on the British government.[35] These considerations did not, it seems, escape the British High Commissioner, who communicated to London the following recommendations:[36,37]

> The enforcement of conscription would be a matter entirely for the Iraq Government and that no British forces of any kind could be employed to back them in this matter . . . the British Government should go even further and refuse to allow their forces to suppress disturbances arising in any way out of the policy of conscription.

> If the Iraq army and Police are likely to be strong enough . . . to see through the policy of conscription among the tribes, let them see it through . . . if not, I fear that either the Iraq Government must content itself with abstaining from enforcing the conscription law in tribal areas as the Turks did . . . or they must specifically exempt the more difficult tribal areas from the conscription law, or they must abandon the idea of conscription altogether. . . . All classes of politicians, including the party of the Prime Minister and the opposition, have long set their hearts on conscription and no-one . . . would have the courage to stand up in Parliament and advocate its abandonment.

The settlement of the Mosul dispute with Turkey and the ratification of the Anglo-Iraqi-Turkish agreement in July 1925 gave Iraqi politicians greater confidence and the time to devote more attention to domestic matters. Top priority was given to the question of defence; thus the first meeting of the Iraqi cabinet that was formed in October 1926 declared that:[38]

> The aims which our cabinet hopes to fulfill . . . are the strengthening of the patriotic forces and the reinforcement of our internal and external security and . . . the final drawing-up of the . . . Bills now under review . . . particularly those dealing with National Defence. . . .

Thus the conscription debate continued in Iraq; 'successive cabinets were in doubt whether to drop the project amid the scorn of newspaper patriots and the army[39] itself, or to press it to the point of probable explosion with Shi'a and Kurd'.[40] In March 1927 a draft of the National Defence Act was passed by the Council of Ministers, and in May the government placed the conscription Bill in the programme before the Extraordinary Session of Parliament, expressing their confidence that the delegates[41]

> readily understood the importance of national armies . . . a national army in every nation is its life symbol and the foundation of its independence. . . . Suffice it to refer to what we can now see in our neighbouring countries, Turkey and Persia . . . also look at the National Service Law in France, which in times of need places all the citizens . . . and wealth of the country in the hands of the Government. . . . Our army has gradually expanded since its creation, but so have its responsibilities . . . and every time an effort was made to expand . . . financial problems presented themselves, forcing the Government to accept a decline in the army . . . at a time when it was most needed. . . . This situation continued . . . until the ratification of the 1924 Treaty. . . . Under Article 4, the Iraq Government undertook to allocate 25% of its annual budget to the regular army . . . a proportion which is bigger than that expended by any other nation in the world on defence. Since our neighbours, Turkey and Persia, possess two powerful and well-equipped armies . . . it is essential for Iraq to raise an army capable – albeit for a short time – of facing either of those two armies. . . . The application of national defence would enable us to possess a modern army . . . giving the opportunity to people of all classes to defend the country. . . . All successive Governments as well as the Constituent Assembly and the Military experts were unanimous that there is no way to achieve this other than applying conscription.

This led the Shi'a Minister of Education, Sayyid 'Abbas Mahdi, to resign in protest. Somewhat rhetorically, in his resignation note he wrote: 'to send the draft of the National Defence Bill to Parliament is something my eyes see but my mind cannot see'.[42] His resignation was symbolic of the mounting opposition now spreading in the tribal areas. The Kurdish population too was opposed to conscription, as expressed thus by a Kurdish Deputy:[43]

> I would like to publish the following . . . in order for the public to learn the truth about the attitude of the Kurds to compulsory military service. Some people think that opposition to conscription is confined to our communist brothers. . . . the truth is . . . that all the Kurds are against conscription. . . . We believe that the National Defence Bill does not suit our political position . . . and we believe that this law is useless and would cause . . . considerable harm.

The following day this deputy emphasised that these were the views of 'all the Kurds' and not merely his own.

In an effort to counter these anti-conscription sentiments, both King Faisal and his Minister of Interior, Rashid 'Ali, conducted various tours of those areas known to be hostile to conscription, meeting leaders and trying to win them over to the government's side. The King also tried to win the support of leading Shi'a personalities by tempting them with promises of cabinet posts. All these vigorous attempts to secure support, however, ended in vain. One prominent Shi'a politician who was approached by Faisal on this matter warned his party, Hizb al-Nahda, against supporting the conscription law unless and until it met with Britain's approval.[44] His party echoed his views, threatening any Shi'a supporting the cabinet with dire consequences.[45]

In spite of these failures, canvassing for conscription continued in various forms. Nuri al-Sa'id, for example, suggested that[46]

> conscription could be enforced by the infliction of increased
> taxation on those who opposed it . . . the tribal deputies replied to
> this suggestion that if it was applied these tribes in the Euphrates
> area would secede to Najd and those of the Tigris area to Persia.

In the meantime, officers of the King's bodyguard were reported to be writing threatening letters to the anti-conscription deputies,[47] and urban politicians, including some Shi'a such as Ja'far Abu al-Timman, were expressing their support:[48]

> Rashid 'Ali wrote on behalf of the opposition . . . to Samawi
> al-Challub [Hindiya], 'Alwan al-Haji Sa'dun [Shaikh of the Bani
> Hasan], Sayid Muhsin Abu Tabikh and others. The letters urged the
> addressees to come to Baghdad and state to the King and other
> authorities that the anti-conscription tribal deputies were not
> correctly representing the opinions of their constituents and that
> they had been 'got at' by the British.

These diverse methods of campaigning continued, and in September 1928, at a gathering attended by the most prominent Iraqi politicians of that period,[49] it was decided to circulate letters to the tribal leaders in the Euphrates areas, Ba'quba and the northern *liwas*, proposing that the national defence law would be[50]

> applicable to the towns and settled areas only; that it is intended,
> when the Iraq Government had become sufficiently powerful through
> the adoption of conscription, to throw off the yoke of the Mandate
> and to make Iraq a completely independent country. The writers

added that if necessary they would arrange to seize Hinaidi and that they would certainly destroy the Maude Statue which was a disgrace to the capital.

These efforts failed as dismally as their predecessors. In October the Shaikhs and leaders of the Shi'a tribes reacted to the call of politicians by issuing their own appeal:[51]

> To all the Shi'as and especially to the deputies, chiefs and leaders who should beware of this great catastrophe, namely conscription. Our co-religionists should call back to mind that during the Mesopotamian wars none of the other sects were killed, deported or hanged except the Shi'as. When the war was over and you entered into negotiations with the ally you decided that cooperation with Britain and its Mandate was necessary. But you all know that since then the others [the Sunnis] occupied Government seats and positions and you remained to suffer miseries and misfortunes. . . . The Conscription Bill was distributed among the deputies for study and will be submitted to the Majlis during its next session for decision. We therefore enjoin you to put party views aside and know well that conscription is only meant for reasons such as these: Kurdistan will not come under conscription law because it is on the frontier; the Dulaim and Diala liwas likewise, there remains therefore only the districts inhabited by Shi'as on the Tigris and Euphrates. . . . So our sect only is to bear the burden.

The influential *'ulama* took up a similar position, although according to a British agent the introduction of conscription would be accepted by them were it to have the support of Britain.[52]

In addition, it was stated that the townspeople were carefully observing the attitude of the tribes towards conscription and would doubtless be much influenced by it.[53]

Unknown to the general public, though perhaps not to the tribal leaders, Britain had already communicated her views to the Iraqi government, reiterating the recommendations made by their High Commissioner in 1926 and confirming that:[54]

> If the Iraqi Government desire to press on with the project of conscription, H.M.G. will not oppose it, although fully aware of the great difficulties which lie in its way. But in their judgement conscription is not in present circumstances essential and it should be possible for the Iraqi Government to maintain and pay for a sufficiently efficient army on the voluntary system. If the Iraqi

Government nevertheless insist on attempting to apply conscription, British forces will not be available for the purpose and Iraq must rely on her own forces.

In terms of Anglo–Iraqi relations, the question of conscription was, in any case, not the most urgent, the two governments having been pre-occupied since the summer of 1927 with negotiations for the revision of the 1926 Agreement. Details of the negotiations and the circumstances surrounding them are amply dealt with elsewhere.[55] Suffice it to say that this proved to be an era characterised by government crises, violent spurts of anti-government and anti-British activities, and the intro-duction of a host of repressive measures. The climate was not right for the introduction of conscription. This situation continued unchecked until the final signing of the Anglo–Iraqi Treaty of 1930, and the admission of Iraq into the League of Nations in October 1932. Shortly afterwards, the government renewed its campaign for the introduction of conscription:[56]

> It now seems certain that when King Faisal visited the Diwaniya and Karbala liwas last November, his chief object was to endeavour to obtain the support of the 'Ulama and the tribal Shaikhs for con-scription. The 'Ulama are said to have refused to take sides on a political question, but, in return for undertakings touching their personal and material interest, the King succeeded in obtaining from a number of tribal leaders a promise that they would not oppose the introduction of a system of compulsory service. . . . Among these were al-Wahid [sic], al-Haji Sikkar of the powerful Fatlah tribe, Muhammad al-Abtan and 'Ajja al-Dalli. These three have now become deputies for the Diwaniya liwa, evidently on pro-conscription coupons.

Back in Baghdad, the Iraq cabinet met on 10 April and reiterated previous cabinet decisions to strengthen the army by the introduction of the system of national service. Again, the same pattern of opposition unfolded, with the majority of *'ulama* now openly against conscription, setting up a new political party (Hizb al-Ahrar) and intensifying their anti-government propaganda. However, the government persisted despite the loss of a forceful ally of the pro-conscription group with King Faisal's death in September 1933.

To those advocating the introduction of conscription, the loss of Faisal's support was more than compensated by the well publicised suc-cesses of the Iraqi army in its first major confrontation: the suppression of the Assyrian revolt of August 1933. As will be seen later, this victory enhanced the image of the armed forces in public estimation, bringing fame and promotion to the commanders of the expedition. This undoubtedly encouraged the government; thus, the first cabinet formed after Faisal's death opened its parliamentary session with the first reading of the National Service Law, which was greeted with 'acclamation'.[57] By early 1934 this law had been passed, and, after the necessary arrangements had been made and a census taken, a royal *iradah* (decree) was issued, making it operative from 12 June 1935. Active measures were soon taken to register eligible males between the ages of eighteen and twenty-one, and it was expected that by the end of the year the influx of conscripts to training depots would have reached 5,000.[58]

By the end of 1935 the army's total strength, which had stood at less than 12,000 in 1933, had risen to 15,300; and on the eve of the first successful military *coup d'état* in Iraq its strength was 20,000. At that time, the army was organised into three regiments of cavalry, six field batteries of artillery, five mountain batteries of artillery and seven infantry brigades. It is significant that the main concentration of the armed forces was in the Euphrates area (the main tribal areas), although there was a virtual absence of external threat in that region. Before the settlement of the Mosul dispute, almost 50 per cent of the army's strength had been concentrated in the Mosul *liwa*, the rest being nearly equally divided between the areas of Baghdad and the Euphrates. In 1936, shortly before the *coup d'état*, with no significant external threat in the north and only the Kurdish unrest to deal with there, the army's northern strength was reduced to 24 per cent of the total armed forces while 66 per cent, including all of the Iraqi Royal Air Force, were stationed in the Euphrates district.

Chapter 5

First ventures of the army into politics

Thus far, it should be clear that the Iraqi political system – the state – was created by an external power, acting mainly in its own interests and working primarily through the monarchy that it had established. The internal structure of this system was controlled and maintained largely by coercion but also by intrigue and bribery. However, the interaction of contradictory forces within this system constituted a constant challenge to its superstructure. During 1935 and 1936 these forces threatened radically to change the main characteristics of the system until the intervention of the army in October 1936 averted that danger. The nature and degree of these internal contradictions will become clear by a close examination of three crucial events: the Assyrian question, King Faisal's death, and the tribal uprising of 1935-6.

The Assyrian question

The settling of the Assyrian community in Iraq dates back to the First World War. These Assyrians – Nestorian Christians claiming descent from the ancient Assyrian Empire – had until 1915 lived in the Hakkiari district of the highlands of what is now Turkish Kurdistan. At the outbreak of the war, their resentment of Turkish rule, reinforced by the existing strong relations between the Nestorian and certain Western churches, led to the Assyrians identifying with the Allied cause and rebelling against the Turks. Thus, in the spring of 1915 they joined the advancing Russian troops. During the ensuing hostilities the Assyrians found their position in Hakkiari untenable and had to withdraw to Persian Kurdistan. Even after the cessation of hostilities, despite strenuous efforts by the Allies, particularly Britain, to secure their

95

return to Hakkiari, Turkey refused to give way, and by 1919 Britain had managed to transfer 35,000 Assyrians to camps around Ba'quba in Mesopotamia. There they remained for two years, at a cost to the British Treasury of about £3 million.

During this time, some able-bodied Assyrians were used by Britain for building roads, while others were recruited into the British-controlled Iraq Levies, which were used mainly for garrison duties in Kurdistan.[1] Also during this time, the first attempts were made to settle them on land expropriated from Kurdish rebels,[2] but these efforts had to be shelved in the wake of the popular uprising of 1920, during which, as has been mentioned earlier, the Assyrians rendered valuable services to Britain.[3]

Soon after the suppression of the 1920 Iraqi revolt, Britain renewed her efforts to settle the Assyrians, either by repatriating them to Hakkiari or by finding them permanent homes in Iraq, spending another £450,000 on the upkeep of the camps between August 1920 and August 1921. This British attitude was later reinforced by the recommendations of the Frontier Commission assigned by the League of Nations to examine the Mosul dispute and demarcate the borders between Iraq and Turkey. In its September 1925 report to the League, this Commission recommended that:[4]

> the Assyrians should be guaranteed the re-establishment of the ancient privileges which they possessed in practice if not officially before the war. Whichever may be the Sovereign State, it ought to grant these Assyrians a certain local autonomy, recognising their right to appoint their own officials and contenting itself with a tribute from them to be paid through the agency of their Patriarch. (4)

However, in spite of this implicit assumption by the Commission that the Assyrians should ultimately return to their Hakkiari enclave, the Assyrians themselves were 'determined not to have anything further to do with the Turks, and remained of their own volition in Iraq'.[5]

Efforts to settle the Assyrians in Iraq thus continued in earnest, and by the end of 1928 1,700 families had been permanently settled, while the remainder were accommodated in government-owned villages or possessing land freehold.[6] By 1930, observing that only 300–400 families were still waiting to be moved into suitable homes, the British High Commissioner felt able to report that the 'Assyrians ceased to be refugees in fact as well as theory'.[7] At the same time, the Assyrians were until 1931 granted remission of taxation by the Iraqi government, and were extended other auxiliary privileges, such as being charged only one-fifth of the rifle licence fee paid by the Kurds.[8] In addition to these material concessions, they were allowed to settle all personal matters through their own ecclesiastical authorities.

In spite of these privileges, however, the Assyrians refused to acquire Iraqi citizenship, scarcely learnt Arabic, and remained 'tactless and aloof' in their dealing with the Iraqis.[9] They also continued to show a marked preference for short-term leases, with the implication that they did not regard their settlement in Iraq as permanent. In public matters, they short-circuited the Iraqi authorities, dealing directly with the British High Commissioner. In time, these attitudes, combined with the Assyrians' close economic and military association with Britain,[10] gave rise to an atmosphere of mutual distrust and antagonism between the Iraqis and Assyrians, with the latter being increasingly regarded as a symbol of foreign domination. As K. Husry expressed it,[11]

> The swaggering Assyrian levies with their slouch hats and red or white hackles, who stood guard at the Homes of the High Commissioner, and Hinaidi, the British Air Force Headquarters, situated in a suburb of Baghdad, became the symbol of British domination.

This tension became particularly marked between 1930 and 1932, while Iraq's application for membership of the League of Nations was being considered by the Council. A series of petitions were sent to the Permanent Mandates Commission by the Assyrians, calling for either their complete transfer from Iraq, or the granting of their virtual independence from the Iraqi state. King Faisal's visit to the Assyrian district during this period failed, as did that of his prime minister, to secure any significant change in their attitude. As the date of Iraq's admission to the League of Nations drew nearer, Assyrian demands became more and more extreme.

It is possible that Assyrian nationalist feeling was given a boost at this particular time by the fact that they now had as their spokesman an ambitious man with all the traditional credentials for political leadership. This potential leader was Eshai, the Mar Shimun or Patriarch of the East, whose family had been holding the office of Patriarch for over 500 years, and who had now himself come of age and was being given the total backing of his aunt Surma Khanum, described as 'formidable' by the British High Commissioner.[12] On 18 June 1932, Mar Shimun presented to the Permanent Mandates Commission a petition in which he demanded, *inter alia*, 'administrative autonomy, the creation of a special sub-district in an area predominantly Kurdish . . . and the rendition of the Sanjak of Hakkiari by the Turks'.[13] If these demands were not accepted by the League of Nations and embodied in the Iraq constitution by 28 June, the Assyrians serving in the Iraq Levies would withdraw their services.

To Britain, these demands represented a threat not only to the future position of the Assyrians in Iraq, but also to Britain's own standing in the country. An anti-Assyrian movement in reaction to these demands might well take on an anti-foreign and hence anti-British colouring. Thus, by a combination of gentle persuasion and a dramatic demonstration of force (such as the sudden arrival of a British battalion from Egypt), the British succeeded in getting the Assyrians to withdraw their threats and to agree to wait for the decision of the Permanent Mandates Commission. On 15 December, acting on the recommendations of that Commission, the Council of the League of Nations rejected the Assyrian demand for administrative autonomy and passed a resolution stating that it had:[14]

1 Adopted the Permanent Mandates Commission's view that administrative autonomy for the Assyrians was impossible within Iraq;
2 Noted with satisfaction the readiness of the Iraqi Government to select a foreign expert to assist them in the settlement of all landless inhabitants of Iraq, including Assyrians, under suitable conditions so far as may be possible in homogeneous units; and
3 Expressed confidence that, if necessary, the Iraqi Government would facilitate the settlement outside Iraq of Assyrians unwilling to settle in the country.

In accordance with this resolution, the Iraqi government set up a Settlement Committee headed by Major Thomson, a British officer. However, when Mar Shimun returned from Geneva in January, he refused to co-operate with this committee and continued to show 'uncompromising opposition' to the work of resettlement, while pressing for the establishment of the Assyrians as a compact national group.[15] This attitude encouraged extremism on both sides, and the rapid deterioration of Assyrian–Iraqi relations during the spring of 1933 culminated in a major confrontation between the Assyrians and the Iraqi army in August 1933, from which the army emerged victorious. The sequence of events in this confrontation has been dealt with adequately by K. Husry.[16] Our main concern is with its consequences, particularly its role in the revival of nationalist feeling throughout the country. Almost three months before the Assyrian uprising, the British Ambassador had noted that 'The Arabic Press had adopted an increasingly anti-British attitude since the beginning of June. . . . It is alleged that H.M.G. are deliberately fomenting unrest among the Assyrians.'[17] When the revolt actually took place, it provided, in the view of the same British Ambassador,[18]

> a splendid subject for impassioned journalism, and dark allusions to a plot by the British colonisers to enslave the country with Christian mercenaries were the favourite ornament of the 'leader' of the day. The Government did not, however, permit the campaign to continue for long, and several of the worst offenders were soon suspended.

Not surprisingly, therefore, the immediate result of the revolt was that 'the British became as unpopular as the Assyrians; not even during the rebellion of 1920 had there been such a fierce wave of anti-British feeling in the country'.[19]

The deployment of the Iraqi army against the Assyrian rebels was applauded throughout Iraq. In Mosul and Kirkuk, where memories of Assyrians' wrongdoings still rankled, the high degree of public excitement was particularly in evidence.[20] Thus, when the revolt was crushed and news of the army victory reached Mosul,[21]

> few of the inhabitants displayed the least regret for what had occurred. On August 18th the troops which had taken part in the Dairadun fighting returned to Mosul. They were given an enthusiastic reception. Triumphal arches had been erected. Some of the arches had been decorated with melons stained with blood and with daggers stuck into them. This delicate representation of the heads of slain Assyrians was in keeping with the prevailing sentiment in the town. . . . There was much firing of revolvers and rifles in the air to mark their joy at the deliverance from the menace of the Assyrians. There were loud cheers for the Army and Bakir Sidqi.

This popular reaction came as no surprise to British officials working in Iraq. According to a typical report by General Rowan-Robinson, the head of the British Military Mission in Baghdad, the Iraqis[22]

> have always feared as well as hated the Assyrians. They have continually heard the British broadcast the superiority of the latter over the Arabs as soldiers. Consequently, their victory over the Assyrians has increased national pride enormously; to the extent in fact that the uneducated masses now feel they require no outside support.

However, perhaps the most significant feature of this popular enthusiasm was that it was directed not towards the government but towards the armed forces. For the army, the Assyrian revolt had been the first major test of its strength and organisation, and its widely acclaimed victory elevated it to a position commanding public respect. A hitherto little known senior officer, Bakir Sidqi, wasted no time in capitalising on the army's newly acquired prestige. 'O, liberal sons of the "Hadba"',* he addressed the mob that greeted his unit in Mosul,[23]

> Your display of the noble Arab character and your enthusiasm in honouring the Iraqi Army, which has disciplined the rebel Assyrians, and your great welcome to it in appreciation of the small duty it has performed, has brought back to mind those immortal episodes, the true patriotism and the noble deeds, in which the people of Mosul were prominent under the most trying and difficult of times, when the sword of occupation was upon your necks. Thanks to you, O sons of the Hadba thanks added to admiration and esteem, thanks which I offer as a pledge of what the Army is about to perform in the future, in accomplishment of the great duty, which the Army has felt and is still feeling that it must be prepared to perform. Therefore, let us, with Army and Nation, await that day.

The tumultuous welcome that greeted units of the army on their return to Baghdad could have only reinforced the morale of officers like Bakir Sidqi. K. Husry, who was an eye-witness to this event, has described it vividly:[24]

> On 26 August practically the entire city turned out to welcome the army units returning after completion of their operations against the Assyrians. Thousands upon thousands of men, women, and children filled the streets, the squares, the rooftops of the city, bringing everything to a standstill for hours. The immense crowds cheered deliriously as the troops marched throughout the capital. Men, women, and children showered flowers and rose water on them from rooftops. The writer well remembers that on that day he and his sister were allowed to pick all the roses and flowers of their garden, filling every available basket and container at home, then scattering their contents on the heads of marching troops from the balcony of a doctor's clinic overlooking Rashid Street. Planes of the Iraqi Air Force flew over the city, raining coloured leaflets that carried the following words. . . . 'Welcome, Protectors of the Fatherland. . . . Stand up to

*The Arabic word means 'learning', and is used to refer to Mosul in reference to its characteristically tilted minaret.

Your Enemies the Tools and the Creatures of Imperialism'. The army and Crown Prince Ghazi, whose openly displayed approval of the campaign against the Assyrians had made him the darling of the masses, were cheered to heavens.

K. Husry also recalls meeting Bakir Sidqi a few days after this:[25]

He patted me on the shoulder and asked me what I wanted to be when I finished school. I said: an army officer. (So popular was the army then that probably no boy of the writer's age could think at the time of taking any other profession.)

The significance of King Faisal's death

Less than a fortnight after the Assyrian revolt, King Faisal died suddenly in Switzerland, in mysterious circumstances which gave rise to speculation and which the British Foreign Office deemed worthy of further investigation, though that decision was later reversed.[26] Whatever its cause, the King's death created a power vacuum in Iraq which the country was ill-equipped to fill. His powerful figure had been essential to a country still searching for a viable political system. In the words of the British Ambassador,[27]

It was King Faisal's skill and political subtlety which enabled him to hold the delicate balance between Sunni and Shi'ah, and through his profound understanding of the Arab mind he was able to deal with his turbulent tribal chieftains with a marked degree of success.

Faisal's noble birth and personal involvement in the struggle for Arab independence from Turkey had made him uniquely qualified to appeal to the nationalist sentiments of the people. Above all, perhaps, he had been acceptable to the British, and the working relationship he had succeeded in developing with them was essential to the political and therefore economic stability of the country.

However, while Faisal's acknowledged ability in handling his opponents[28] gave the country the unity it so badly needed, this same vigour and idiosyncratic style of rule had a detrimental effect in contributing to the colossal obstacles in the way of developing a viable political system. The suppression of the 1920 revolt had brought an end not only to active hostilities, but also to the possibility of developing indigenous political machinery which might be capable of threatening British hegemony in Iraq. Had Faisal been of lesser calibre, it is doubtful that Britain could have maintained her influence in the country with such relative ease, and probable that a more representative leadership would have emerged. Faisal had indeed lived up to British expectations, and proved, as Mr Churchill had predicted thirteen years earlier, to be 'the best chance of saving our money'.[29]

Even when the British government was subjected to major waves of criticism both at home and abroad over the handling of the Assyrian revolt by the Iraqi government, the importance the British Ambassador had attached to a continuation of Faisal's rule over Iraq was not adversely affected:[30]

> If intervention were forced on Iraq, King Faisal and Nuri Pasha would go and an extreme nationalist Government would come to power; there would be an outburst of xenophobia throughout the country and lives and property of foreigners would not be safe.

In the event, although Britain did not actually intervene, the sequence of events that was to follow Faisal's death a week later did not deviate significantly from that feared by the British Ambassador. As will be seen later, less than a year after Faisal's death Iraq stood once again on the brink of total revolution, and its political structure would be threatened with total collapse until the final intervention of the army prevented both the outbreak of revolution and the collapse of the existing political system.

Revolt and containment: the tribal uprising of 1935–6

The relative political lull and sense of national unity produced by the Assyrian crisis did not last for long. In this section it will be shown how, from the end of 1934 onwards, the established political system began to crumble under the impact of three factors. First came the effects of continued bouts of rebellion and disorder in tribal areas. Second, the growing divisions within the political elite between rival factions and personalities exacerbated rather than mitigated the tribal problem and weakened the authority of the state. Third, the new King, Ghazi, was weak and politically inexperienced, with the result that the monarchy was unable to play as successfully a stabilising role as it had the reign of Faisal. In the light of the mounting political crisis throughout 1935 and 1936, it will then be shown how conditions favoured the emergence of the army as an active and crucial force within Iraqi politics.

In 1934, as had been customary, the government of the day (led by 'Ali Jaudat al-'Ayyubi and his Wahda party), had come to power by its success in the continuing game of high-level intrigue and personal rivalry. Consistently with the pattern established by their predecessors, they awarded their supporters by the usual endowments of parliamentary seats and lucrative posts. Although, as has been argued in previous chapters, parliamentary elections in Iraq habitually contained their farcical elements, with deputies being elected, at best, because of their loyalties to individual politicians rather than to constituencies, it appears that 'Ali Jaudat's government had overplayed its hand. Thus it was claimed, during the parliamentary elections of December 1934, that in certain constituencies not even a nominal vote was taken, and that the ballot boxes were directly filled by the scrutineers.[31] In other districts, voting slips were deposited in the ballot boxes only after verifying that they carried the names of the government candidates.[32] Consequently, the majority of those elected were government officials or municipal employees known for their sympathies with the government. Moreover, in order to pre-empt any criticism by the press, the editors of three main daily newspapers were also given parliamentary seats.[33]

By conducting the elections in this manner, the government inevitably deprived men of local standing of their seats. Unhappily for the government, most of those excluded came in fact from the tribal areas. The cabal of Baghdad, led by Yasin al-Hashimi's al-Ikha al-Watani Party and supported by Rashid 'Ali al-Kilani and Hikmat Sulaiman, quickly recognised the promising opportunity offered by this error of judgment by the government. Provoked and bitterly resentful at not having succeeded in getting their own men in the Chamber, they wasted little time in launching their campaign against the government. At first they directed their criticism through the Chamber, but their efforts were soon thwarted by the huge government bloc. Success awaited them, however, in the Senate, where nine out of the twenty senators were supporters of the Ikha al-Watani Party.[34] Their attack was pressed with great vigour, and, in the view of the then British Ambassador, their criticism of the 'way in which the election had been conducted . . . were tantamount to a vote of censure on the cabinet'.[35]

Nevertheless, success in the Senate proved to be insufficient to bring down the government, and, thus frustrated, Yasin al-Hashimi and his followers decided to look for more support among the public. They started their campaign in the north of Iraq, where the underprivileged Kurdish population was always eager to air its racial and linguistic grievances against the central government in Baghdad. In the south, they found a common cause with the powerful Shi'a shaikh of the

Fatlah tribe, 'Abd al-Wahid al-Hajji Sukkar, whom the government had unwisely not included in its Parliament.

The government reacted by mobilising their own supporters in the tribal areas;[36] these later toured the mid-Euphrates canvassing support for the government and calling on the tribes to send in telegrams and messages of solidarity to the cabinet. The opposition counteracted by intensifying their political activities among the same tribal areas, pointing to the discourtesy with which tribal dignitaries were often treated by government officials and to the latter's general greed and maladministration. More ominously, they addressed themselves to the Shi'a *'ulama* of the Holy Cities, whose followers were the oppressed majority of the population; and they succeeded, without any apparent difficulty, in persuading their paramount *'alim*, Shaikh Kashif al-Ghita, to issue a *fatwa* implicitly criticising the government and directly appealing to the tribes not to fight each other.[37] In the towns, Yasin al-Hashimi's supporters were swiftly backed by disgruntled would-be deputies and government officials who were kept out of lucrative employment by 'Ali Jaudat's cabinet.[38]

It is perhaps symptomatic of this general atmosphere of defiance that the communists, hitherto virtually unnoticed in Iraq, were now issuing a number of pamphlets and leaflets calling for the overthrow of the government and the eviction of the imperialist despoilers.[39] The government reacted by rounding up a number of suspects, mainly writers and lawyers, and putting them in prison.[40]

Back in Baghdad, the cabinet itself was riddled by intrigues from within. According to confidential dispatches from the British Embassy, Jamil al-Madfa'i, then Minister of Defence, constantly disagreed with his chief on important issues.[41] Also, the then Minister of Economics and Communication, Arshad al-'Umari, was a source of embarrassment to his colleagues on account of his summary dismissals of a large number of senior officials and for his reckless disregard of all experienced advice in the conduct of the work of his ministry.[42]

This generally unfavourable situation was made even worse by a devastating flood of the Tigris, which swept away whole villages in the northern district and drowned large areas of the city of Baghdad, bringing commercial and agricultural activities in the affected areas to a standstill. In this adverse environment, the tasks of government became too burdensome, and the 'Ali Jaudat government had to abandon, for the time being, their ambition to remain the rulers of Iraq. Grudgingly, they submitted their resignation to the King on 23 February 1935. As was expected, the King invited Yasin al-Hashimi to form a government, but stipulated that, since Rashid 'Ali and Hikmat Sulaiman had been strongly associated with the 'lawless' tribes of the mid-Euphrates, they should not be included in the government. His Majesty also added that there should be no dissolution of Parliament. Faced with this prospect of failing to reward his 'men', Yasin al-Hashimi declined to form a cabinet, and the King had to look elsewhere for a new prime minister. Some days later, His Majesty approached Jamil al-Madfa'i, who formed a cabinet on 3 March.

This change of government did nothing to appease the opposition, who continued unabated their intrigues among the tribes of the mid-Euphrates, making rich promises and persuading malcontents everywhere that the moment had come to right their wrongs. Less than a week after the formation of the Madfa'i cabinet, encouraged by his supporters in Baghdad, 'Abd al-Wahid mobilised his tribesmen and, after destroying three bridges twelve miles south-east of Kufa, occupied the strategically important Abu Sukhair district of the Diwaniya *liwa*.[43]

This act of open hostility against the authority of the government sowed the seeds of lawlessness in an area that was too prone to such stimuli. Traditional feuds among the tribes came to the surface, and the tribes were now seeking to reinforce their supplies of arms and ammunition.[44]

Rifles stored away for years were being bought and sold, Faisaliya have replenished their stocks from Najaf and Daghghara from Mamamiya, and I am also informed that the Kuwait market also provides a supply of arms and ammunition to the mid-Euphrates. The cost of a British rifle is double that of a month ago and is now about ID 4–5.

Inspired by the Fatlah's defiance of central authority, another important tribe, the 'Aqrab tribe led by Shaikh Sha'alan al-'Atiya, took control of an important irrigation regulator at Daghghara, while their rivals joined camp with other tribes favoured by the government. Armed tribal demonstration became so frequent in the Shamiya, Daghghara and Diwaniya districts that Sir Kinahan Cornwallis, the adviser to the Ministry of Interior, reported that the 'situation was graver than any he had known since his arrival in the country in 1921'.[45] Those tribal shaikhs who supported the government were now appealing to the cabinet to let them attack the insurgent elements.[46] Their proposals presented the government with a bewildering dilemma. Were they to encourage their tribal supporters to attack their opponents, the whole tribal region could plunge into uncontrollable chaos and there was no telling what the outcome would be. Their decision could, perhaps, have been made more easily had they been confident of their authority over the state's national army. Not only was the army then headed by Taha al-Hashimi, Yasin al-Hashimi's brother, but the majority of the rank and file originated from the tribal areas, and there was no certainty that their allegiance to the state superseded their tribal loyalties.[47] Nevertheless, on 13 March the government dispatched a military force southwards from Hilla to Diwaniya, while the Minister of Interior had already commenced his plea with the tribes. Acting on the advice of Rashid 'Ali and other opposition leaders in Baghdad, 'Abd al-Wahid refused to discuss the situation with the government's envoy; thus, faced with certain defeat, Jamil al-Madfa'i opted for the easy way out, and he and his cabinet submitted their resignation to the King on 15 March. Predictably, the King invited Yasin Pasha to form a government, and this time made no conditions.

Yasin al-Hashimi's acquisition of power in this instance marked a novel departure in Iraqi politics. Until now, cabinets came and went almost entirely owing to dissensions within the urban political elite, to the influence of King Faisal or to the British Embassy. Now, for the first time in the history of modern Iraq, a government came to power owing to what was indeed a popular movement or even, as the then British Ambassador described it, a revolution.[48] The activities of Yasin al-Hashimi and his companions, the tribes, had awakened a political consciousness hitherto dormant or at least suppressed. The grounds for this are not hard to seek. At that time, almost everyone in Iraq had a grievance to redress. Therefore, while in opposition, the mission of Yasin al-Hashimi and his followers was hardly an impossible one. They toured the tribal areas pointing out the existing injustices that were a daily reality to the majority of the Iraqi populace. The popular support given to those new saviours of people's civil and political rights, therefore, could only have been born out of conviction. Given the existing political structure, now that Yasin al-Hashimi and his al-Ikha al-Watani Party were again in power, could they fulfil their promises? With the ultimate success of his mission, and with the way now open to him to form a representative popular government, would Yasin al-Hashimi break away from the political elite that had been largely responsible for the existence of the glaring injustices he himself fought against while in opposition? Would he even treat the opposition any differently?

Unhappily for Iraq, even before forming his cabinet, Yasin al-Hashimi's political allies were locked in a battle of the type by now too familiar in Iraqi politics. His two main allies, Rashid 'Ali and

Hikmat Sulaiman, were now both bidding for the post of minister of interior. To the bitter resentment of Hikmat Sulaiman, Yasin al-Hashimi sided with Rashid 'Ali and offered him the post. Hikmat Sulaiman reacted by resigning from the al-Ikha al-Watani Party and joining Kamil al-Chadirchi's group, Jama'at al-Ahali.[49] More striking evidence of Yasin's intention to perpetuate the political system that had hitherto obtained in Iraq was his inclusion of two members of the defeated Jamil al-Madfa'i's government in his cabinet.[50]

Viewed as a whole, the main characteristics of Yasin al-Hashim's cabinet did not differ significantly from those of the average cabinet created in Iraq since the inception of the state.[51] The only slight deviation from the pattern was the fact that, out of the eight members of the new cabinet, two were Shi'a. The first was Shaikh Muhammad Ridha al-Shabibi, a Shi'a of Baghdad and a long associate of Yasin al-Hashimi, and the other was Rauf al-Bahrani, another Baghdadi Shi'a whose appointment to the Ministry of Finance, according to the British Ambassador, 'caused some surprise, since he is reported to be stupid and has hitherto played no role in public life.' It appears that his inclusion in the Cabinet is due to the Government's desire to placate the Shia's.[52]

Having thus formed the cabinet, Yasin al-Hashimi was now confronted with the mammoth task of fulfilling the generous promises made to his supporters, without isolating those two cabinet members who had been part of the previous government, either for reasons of political expediency or because they were habitually antagonistic to 'Abd al-Wahid. He was quick to issue a communiqué proclaiming the government's intention to govern justly. Rather prudently, this was followed by a dissolution of Parliament, with a promise that in the forthcoming election the number of seats allotted would be increased by 20 to 108.[53]

The exclusion from Parliament of some tribal shaikhs had been one of the direct reasons for the revolt against 'Ali Jaudat's government. But in the political environment now prevailing, promises for parliamentary privileges could have placated only a handful of the tribal dissidents. Having realised their real strength and the fact that there was no omnipotence in government, the tribes were naturally unwilling to lose their newly acquired momentum, and were now making their political excursions to Baghdad. Soon after Yasin's coming to power, therefore, Kurdish and Shi'a dignitaries came to the capital in some numbers.[54]

At about the same time, 'Abd al-Wahid arrived in Baghdad with a train of thirty cars and was acclaimed by the press as a great leader. He too had an account to settle with the government, which was now faced with the task of persuading him to be patient.[55] Aware of 'Abd al-Wahid's value in lobbying the government, the Shi'a *'ulama* were now endeavouring to convert him to their cause. At first they seemed to succeed, and had in fact induced him to visit them at Najaf. However, they failed to persuade him to sign their manifesto containing a list of demands calling for fuller Shi'a participation in public life and for greater degree of religious autonomy. This is significant, since it clearly shows that political allegiances in Iraq were not based on purely religious or ethnic grounds. Though himself a Shi'a, 'Abd al-Wahid's main reason for supporting Yasin al-Hashimi, in opposition and in government, was primarily due to the longstanding disputes he had with the Muntafiq Sunni tribes of mid-Euphrates (supporters of the 'Ali Jaudat and Madfa'i governments and now anti-government), over land settlements. 'Abd al-Wahid's conflict with the Muntafiq Sunni tribes should thus be viewed as a striking example of the recurring hostility that existed within the tribes themselves, and of the fact that tribal revolts were not always directed against the government.

Disappointed by 'Abd al-Wahid's indifference to Shi'a affairs, the paramount *'alim*, Shaikh Kashif al-Ghita, was now talking of issuing a *fatwa* condemning him as an infidel. In the meantime, he opened negotiations with the anti-'Abd al-Wahid (and anti-government) shaikhs, who, for reasons of political expediency, soon agreed to forge an alliance with him, nominating him as their spokesman.[56] By thus securing their signature, Shaikh Kashif al-Ghita then submitted his list of demands to the government, mainly calling for free elections and proportionate Shi'a representation in Parliament, government and civil service.[57] More significantly, in order to secure the full support of their *afrad* (members of the tribes), the Muntafiq shaikhs were now promising them full exemption from *sarkal* duties in exchange for their armed uprising against the government.[58]

These moves signalled an ominous development in tribal politics which the government could hardly fail to see. In an attempt to forestall its escalation, they hurried Mr Ditchburn, a British official known for his 'popularity' among tribal shaikhs, to the restless areas. After spending some days talking to the shaikhs, Mr Ditchburn returned to Baghdad and reported that 'all the shaikhs were pledged to support the demands put forward by Kashif al-Ghita and must continue to struggle for their acceptance by the Government unless told by the 'Ulema to desist'.[59]

The government then decided to send Rashid 'Ali, the Minister of

Interior, to discuss the situation with the shaikhs and *'ulama*. Complex and strenuous negotiations continued for most of the month of April; but, sensing their futility, Shaikh Ahmad Asadullah, a Shi'a divine and follower of Shaikh Kashif al-Ghita, incited his tribal followers in the Rumaitha district into open rebellion against the government. The government took an ill-advised step and arrested him. The reaction to his arrest was as immediate as it was violent. On the same evening, the local tribes of Abu Hassan, Bani Zuraij and the Duweilim revolted. Led by Shaikh Khawwam al-'Abbas, they tore up the railway lines running through these areas, burnt the government buildings and police station and looted the bazaar. Consequently, the communication system within those areas was brought to a halt and no trains could run south of Diwaniya or north of Samawa. On the following day, an RAF plane flying over the area was brought down and both its pilot and mechanic were killed. Two days later (9 May) handbills were scattered over the area from Iraqi planes, warning the tribes that 'unless they disappeared to their homes within twenty-four hours and resumed their normal lives, the Government would be forced to take punitive action against them'.[60] The tribes ignored the warning, and the government followed its ultimatum by authorising aerial bombing of the area, while arrangements were made for the concentration at Diwaniya of five infantry battalions, one field battery, one mountain battery and one company of motor machine-guns with auxiliary troops. The government also appointed General Bakir Sidqi, well known for his ruthless handling of the Assyrians in 1933, as Commander of all troops between Hilla and Basra.

In the meantime, martial law was declared in the Rumaitha district. The following day, by a combination of air and ground attacks, the government forces actually began to make a headway against the tribes. However, before the benefits of this advance could be reaped, the Muntafiq tribes declared a state of open revolt in Nasiriya while the tribes in the neighbourhood of Suq al-Shuyukh were attacking the local government offices and police station at 'Aqiqa and Qarma Bani Sa'id. In the ensuing hostilities, it is claimed that a total of 600 people were killed or injured on both sides.

The government reacted by imposing martial law on the area and ordering the immediate advance of a battalion of infantry from Baghdad to Nasiriya, and the IRAF were called upon to take down supplies. Unfortunately, for the government, the aircraft not already engaged in active raids against Rumaitha were bogged down in the waterlogged aerodrome at Diwaniya. Deprived of air cover, the government's expedition against Nasiriya and Suq al-Shuyukh was thus ineffective, and the tribes continued their military success, tearing up the railway line between Basra and Nasiriya and occupying the town of Suq al-Shuyukh, while in Nasiriya itself they forced 300 armed policemen to surrender.[61] By the third week of May, however, after a massive reinforcement of troops and with the IRAF now in action, the government forces were able to make decisive military gains against the rebels. They overran the towns of Rumaitha and Nasiriya successively, and, although no figures are available for the casualties sustained during this operation, it is known that Shaikh Khawwam al-'Abbas and his brother were both wounded and captured by the government troops. Shaikh Khawwam was later tried by a military court, which sentenced him to penal servitude for life, ordered the confiscation of all his movable property, deprived him of the unalienated *miri* land in his position, and transferred its *'tasarruf'* to one of his rivals, Shaikh Shanshal.[62] Fines of money and rifles were also imposed on the tribes, several summary executions were carried out, and an estimated 100 prisoners were taken and later sentenced to terms of imprisonment varying from one to twenty years.[63] In the meantime, General Bakir Sidqi was once again proclaimed a national saviour and hero. As further demonstration of his loyalty to the system he fought for, he was now calling on the government to agree to execute a number of shaikhs and to inflict heavy punishment on the tribes guilty of taking up arms against the government.[64]

After this initial military success against the tribes, the government delegated Ja'far al-'Askari, the Minister of Defence, to the tribal areas in order to negotiate a ceasefire. On his promising to open discussions at once regarding the Shi'a demands, both conflicting parties agreed on a truce. However, just as Yasin Pasha had discovered that controlling the shaikhs was not as easy as instigating them, the shaikhs were themselves now unable to control the third politically relevant group, the *afrad*, whom they had incited into rebellion. Thus, in spite of Shaikh Kashif al-Ghita's personal appeals to the rebels to observe the truce, skirmishes with police patrols continued and attacks were made on railway tracks while telephone and telegraph lines were pulled down or cut.[65]

Though on a smaller scale than they had been during the month of May, armed flare-ups continued to be a daily reality in the tribal areas. In such a state of national fragmentation, and with its urgent need for a strong army, the government seems to have decided that this was an opportune time to introduce conscription.[66] Thus, on 12 June, a royal *iradah* was issued for the application of the National Defence Law of 1934.

It is not possible to discern singularly the impact that the introduction of this law must have had on the tribes, for its effect must have been mixed with the other adverse forces then at work against the government. But even if it were not the sole reason for their disaffection, conscription was used by some tribal and ethnic groups as a pretext for their rising against the state. In the Qurna *liwa*, for example, the local tribes of al-Makin revolted against the registration of conscripts.[67] The government reacted by sending an expeditionary force, and after some fighting, in which casualties were sustained on both sides, order was restored. In the north, led by Da'ud Da'ud, the Yazidi tribes, never known for their identification with the Iraqi state and strongly opposed to conscription, were reported to be[68]

> selling their property, buying . . . rifles and ammunition from
> Shammar Arabs, and retreating into the mountains where there are
> caves known to be capable of holding thousands of men. Other
> Arab tribes, notably the Juaish, are also arming, in the hope of
> profiting by any disorder that may occur by looting Yazidi villages.

A combined punitive force of police, troops and the IRAF was dispatched to the area, and in the ensuing hostilities the government troops suffered 40 casualties, killed and wounded, while the Yazidi's losses were estimated to be 200 killed and 120 wounded.[69] Martial law was then declared in the area, and a military court was set up which later sentenced Yazidis to death and 328 people to terms of imprisonment varying from one year to life.[70]

In spite of the government's success in suppressing the Yazidis, a combination of pressure from the British Embassy and reasons of expediency persuaded them to be very elastic in their application of conscription in those areas considered difficult. Perhaps resentful of this display of favouritism towards some tribes, and eager to exploit the general disorder to their economic advantage, some tribes were now invading Yazidi villages and occupying their land:[71]

> Shaikh 'Ajil is continuing to encroach on Yazidi lands. . . . Shaikh 'Ajil
> has now built a village to accommodate twenty families and con-
> structed four wells on land owned by Quhbal village and is said to be
> intending to build a second village on the same land for occupation
> by Jubu tribesmen from the Hawi Nimrud area.

Such quarrels between the Yazidi tribes and their neighbours weighed heavily on the enormous difficulties that the government was already encountering in its administration of the northern regions, particularly

111

in the Kurdish areas. United by common language, land and tradition, and aware of the underprivileged position they occupied in the country's political and economic structure, the Kurds were a recurring source of trouble to the state. The different terrain and severe weather conditions of Kurdistan rendered effective counter-measures against the Kurdish tribes impossible. A comprehensive account of these recurring uprisings is outside the scope of our survey, but the following is typical of the descriptive memoranda that British officials in Iraq had dispatched to the Foreign Office:[72]

> Late in June, Khalil Khoshawi was once more raiding and pillaging villages in Iraq. The Iraqi Government again strengthened their forces, and the Turkish Government reinforced their frontier troops with two battalions of infantry and 200 cavalry. Martial law was proclaimed and a number of villages were evacuated. The concerned operations were somewhat successful. . . . at the beginning of September, Khalil Khoshawi was reported to have fled to Iran, and during the last week of October the reign of martial law was terminated. Some 63 of Khalil's followers were tried by the military courts and sentenced to varying terms of imprisonment, and eight were hanged, but as soon as the winter fell Khalil returned, and about the middle of November he was again harassing the north of Barosh and Baradost districts. The tribesmen and villagers of the whole of the Barazan area have now been reduced to great poverty and want. The depredations of Khoshawi have interrupted their agricultural and pastoral routine, and the presence in their country for several months of large bodies of troops and police has denuded it of supplies.

These, then, were the general conditions prevailing in Iraq during 1935. By the time the year had come to an end, the IRAF alone had made 700 flying hours over the rebellious areas, in the process dropping a total of 5,678 bombs and incendiary devices.

The dissension of the tribes and the emergence of radical 'propaganda', which characterised 1935,[73] continued into the following year. As the following chronology should show, 1936 was a year when attacks and counter-attacks by tribesmen and government forces were a frequent occurrence. About the middle of February, a serious outbreak of disorder broke out among the Hatim, the Bani Rikab and the Khafaja tribes of the Muntafiq Confederation. As had been the case in 1935, the causes of this unrest were mixed and varied, and land disputes figured prominently among them. The Hatim had a longstanding grievance against a local landowner, Zamil al-Manna, who had 'acquired by dubious means title deeds to a large part'[74] of the Hatim lands, while the destruction of the Khafaja's irrigation canals by the army had caused them acute poverty. Moreover, the government's reinstating of an 'unpopular shaikh'[75] in the Chamber intensified their anti-government feeling. Economic factors were also prominent among the causes of the revolt of Bani Rikabs, who had longstanding land disputes with their powerful landlords, the Sa'dun shaikhs.

The revolt of these tribes took the by now familiar form of armed demonstrations, war dances, refusal to obey government orders to disperse, and general negligence of daily duties. The government response was the usual one of authorising aerial bombing of the area and dispatching troops and police units, whose combined forces succeeded in pacifying the tribes. However, about the same time, inspired by this abortive revolt or perhaps because of it, the neighbouring Gharraf tribes of Suq al-Shuyukh made an attack on the local police station but were successfully driven back later by a government counter-force. In the Rumaitha and Samawa districts, still embittered by their defeat at the hands of government force, the tribes were antagonised further by the appointment of 'Abd al-Hamid al-Shalchi, a military officer, as Mutasarrif of the Diwaniya *liwa*. Moreover, they too were now (April) suffering acute hardship as a result of serious, and possibly avoidable flooding of their land. According to British reports, much loss was caused by these floods which, 'many believed, could have been avoided if the Government had agreed to allow the surplus water to flow into the Habaniya lake'.[76] On the 20 April, members of these Duweilim tribes (who had supported Shaikh Khawwam al-'Abbas in 1935) fired on a train passing near Rumaitha. The government summoned their leaders, but the latter refused to obey unless the government agreed to undertake (a) to restore Shaikh Khawwam's confiscated lands, (b) to exempt the Duweilim tribes from conscription, and (c) to declare that it would not enforce the wearing of the Pahlavi hats.[77] (This is added evidence to the fact that economic and religious grievances were mixed together. The Pahlavi hat, which, together with abolition of the veil, had been introduced in Persia as a measure of secularism, represented to the tribes an interference in their religious affairs by the state.) The government refused to meet those demands while the shaikhs persisted in their refusal to comply with the government's orders. Subsequently, aerial raids against those tribes were carried out and 'incendiary bombs were used and several villages destroyed'.[78] On the same day,[79] the unrest spread to the north of Rumaitha, and the Bani Aridh and the Aajib tribes attacked a small police post at Aridhat. They also tore up a section of the railway line a few miles north of Rumaitha. On the 2nd of May the police at Rumaitha, supported by a battalion of infantry, . . . claim to have inflicted heavy casualties on the tribesmen. At the same time planes bombed appropriate targets in the Aridh and Aajib tribal areas. . . . On 5th May . . . two army columns, together with two flights of the Iraqi Air Force, dispersed a large gathering of tribesmen astride the railway five miles north of Rumaitha. The enemy were estimated to number about 1,200 armed men, including contingents from the Duweilim, the Bani Aridh and the Aajib, and the army claim to have inflicted about 200 casualties. . . . The losses sustained by the Government forces were two officers and eight other ranks killed and forty wounded. On the same day an Irada was issued proclaiming martial law in the Rumaitha area.

Hostilities continued throughout the month of May. During the second week of May, the army sustained a further thirty casualties and two aircraft were shot down by the tribesmen, the pilot and mechanic of one of them perishing in the explosion while the crew of the other were killed on reaching the ground after parachuting successfully. According to British reports, this incident caused a loss of morale among Iraqi pilots and seems to have led to the government's decision to withdraw its air force from Diwaniya to Baghdad.[80] Encouraged by this sign of government defeat, the tribes followed their temporary success by attempting to cut off land and rail communication to their area through flooding the railway near Wawiya. Although this operation ended in failure, the area was cut off to outside communication all the same by the general lawlessness of the tribes. Thus, for example, when a train ventured into the area on 10 May in an attempt to reach Basra, it was fired on and forced to return.[81] Naturally in these circumstances, the government decided to recommence its aerial raids and intensify its land attack. Subsequently, between the 14 and 21 May,[82]

Numerous villages [were] destroyed and large areas of crops burned. Some stories of brutality on the part of the troops are now beginning to reach Baghdad. Few prisoners have it seems been taken and there are the usual rumours of the shooting out of hand of parties of surrendering tribesmen with their womenfolk. . . . The Minister of Interior returned to Baghdad on the 14th May from Diwaniya and . . . worked hard to keep other neighbouring tribes from joining the revolt and also told me that the Government were working out a plan for scattering the rebel tribesmen amongst less turbulent elements, and giving their lands to others whose loyalty could be better counted upon.

Such counter-measures by the government naturally further incensed the Duwailim tribes, who were now receiving support from other tribal shaikhs. During the last week,[83] for example, Shaikh Sha'lan al-'Atiya,[84] chief of the Shibana section of the Akra confederation, together with other neighbouring shaikhs, declared their support for the Duwailim. Their solidarity was manifested by their expelling a tax collector, sniping at police patrols, and cutting off the telephone line between Diwaniya and Daghghara.[85] Moreover, they issued a list of demands, mainly calling on the government to issue an immediate amnesty for all the Rumaitha insurgents, to suspend conscription 'until work on a local canal had been finished',[86] and to undertake to respect religious customs. Rejecting these demands, the government issued an ultimatum calling on the shaikhs to report to Diwaniya, and when twenty-four hours lapsed without a positive response from the shaikhs, the government followed its ultimatum by sending in the IRAF and the troops:[87]

On June 5th, a total of six infantry battalions, one cavalry regiment and two batteries of artillery began operations against the new insurgents. A force of about 100 tribesmen was dispersed as soon as the advanced guard deployed. . . . By noon Daghgara was occupied and Shaikh Sha'lan's fort destroyed. . . . The Prime Minister estimates the total tribal casualties at about 300. Amongst the killed were Sha'lan's brother and his eldest son. Another son was wounded and made prisoner. The army's losses were two other ranks killed and two officers and nine other ranks wounded.

This frequent use of force against the anti-government tribes was accompanied by similarly stringent suppression of political opposition. Although it is claimed that King Faisal sometimes used to encourage opponents to his rule in order to use them as a bargaining force in his negotiations with the British,[88] it was the general practice of Iraqi governments not to tolerate open criticism of their conduct of affairs. When Yasin al-Hashimi's cabinet banned political parties and censored publications that took a critical view of the government,[89] it was therefore following established practice. Thus, when *Sawt al-Ahali* (the organ of the Ahali group), for example, emerged from a year's enforced silence in August 1936 and, under the direction of Hikmat Sulaiman and Ja'far Abu Timman, printed an article critical of, among other things, the government's handling of the Anglo–Iraqi railway agreement,[90] the offices of the newspaper were raided by the police and all existing issues were confiscated.[91] (It is claimed that Hikmat Sulaiman managed to salvage a number of copies and was himself selling them later that morning in the bazaar at one shilling each.)[92] Also on the same day, the government issued a ruling suspending *Sawt al-Ahali* for another year. Incensed by this action, both Hikmat Sulaiman and Ja'far Abu Timman secured an audience with the King and protested vigorously about the suppression of what 'they considered to be legitimate criticism'.[93]

Although, as stated above, such action by the government was not a unique characteristic of al-Hashimi's cabinet, what must have posed a real threat to the government's political opponents was the fact that Yasin al-Hashimi's rule was expected to be long. For example, during a speech delivered at Basra on 7 September, the Prime Minister expressed the hope that he would be spared for another ten years to devote himself to the welfare of Iraq.[94] Commenting on this speech, the British Ambassador informed the Foreign Office that[95]

> the passage caused a mild sensation in Baghdad where the spectre of Yasin as dictator again reared its head and gave his opponents an excuse for contending that he was usurping the King's place. Hikmat Sulaiman was heard to make a caustic comment to the effect that, from now on, he presumed that the mot d'ordre would be changed, so far as the Prime Minister was concerned, from 'Vive le Roi' to 'Vive le moi'.

For Yasin al-Hashimi to be 'dreaming' of absolute power would have been neither out of character nor out of reach, and it appears that his opponents were aware of this. In addition to the fact that the monarchy was a recent innovation in Iraq and had no deep roots in the country's traditions, it is very likely that Yasin al-Hashimi was influenced by the spirit of his time. Mustapha Kamal, Mussolini, Reza Shah and Hitler had all in their different ways been nationalist/patriotic leaders who succeeded in rising to positions of absolute power, and it does not seem so extraordinary that their success may have fired his imagination. Moreover, right from his early days, Yasin al-Hashimi was clearly a domineering and highly ambitious person.

Born and educated in Baghdad, where his father was a Mukhtar, Yasin joined the Turkish army and served in Constantinople. In 1917 he was already commanding a Turkish division on the Rumanian front in Galicia, where his success in that campaign won him the rank of Major General. In 1918 he was made commander of the Turkish troops fighting against the Allies at Salt and Amman. There he was wounded and later transported to Damascus, where he remained until joining the Arab movement some months later. During his stay in Damascus, he was[96]

> suspected of having been the instigator of anti-French propaganda in Syria and of anti-British propaganda in Mesopotamia.[97] He was also in touch with Mustafa Kamal, and at that time was also a professed adherent to Bolshevism. He was also believed to be preparing a coup against King Faisal [The Arab Government in Syria], whose views he considered too moderate.

Also while in Syria, it is claimed that he made an attempt to re-join the Turkish army but was refused on the ground that no officer could be re-admitted who had not applied within a year of the Armistice.[98] In March 1922, he returned to Baghdad, and three months later was appointed by King Faisal as Mutasarrif of the Muntafiq *liwa*. Six months later the King invited him to join the cabinet, but later withdrew that offer owing to Yasin's refusal to give 'assurances that he would support the Treaty with Britain'.[99] However, a month later Yasin changed his mind, and, promising to support the Treaty, he joined the cabinet in November 1922. During this time, he was believed by the British to be 'intriguing against the existing order with the general idea of replacing the Monarchy by a Republic'.[100] These British fears were later tempered by Yasin's general pragmatism and manifestations of realism once in office.[101]

It seems to be on these bases that the British Ambassador felt able to offer the Foreign Office the following assessment of Yasin's premiership in 1935:[102]

> The name of Yassin Pasha Al-Hashimi is one which, in the past, has awakened misgivings in the minds of some of my predecessors in Baghdad. An atrabiliar (sic) man, stiffnecked, suspicious and xenophobe. A narrow and all too tenacious Moslem, holding in hatred outselves and, above all, the 1930 treaty. A clever and an uncomfortable enemy. All this, and more, has been believed of Yassin. . . . But of late a metamorphosis has taken him. . . . It has not only left him frank enough to confess, with some sadness, his old mistakes and to declare his faith in a hand-to-hand association of his country with ours; it has also brought with it something not far

off confidence in the disinterestedness of the policy of His Majesty's
Government.... It is enough to put it on record that we have, I
think, in Iraq a new friend who was an old enemy.

In addition to Yasin's having succeeded in developing such a good
rapport with Britain and having come to office through a phenomenon
novel in Iraqi politics, he also possessed the personal advantages of
having his brother as CGS of the Iraqi army, and the Director of Police
'completely under his influence'.[103]

Given these advantages, and the fact that, through continuous use of
force, the tribal areas were now relatively calm, the only force that could
have constituted an obstacle between Yasin and the fulfilment of his possible ambition to become a dictator of Iraq could have been the King.But,
unlike his father, King Ghazi was too weak and too indulgent in his
personal hobbies to form a real obstacle. King Faisal, while not averse to
the more immediate forms of personal gratifications, had pursued them
discreetly and moderately. His political skill both added to and gained
from the strength of the political system whose first head he had been.
His son, on the other hand, was the archetypal playboy prince, living
and acting in a way which, while by no means unusual among his peers
in the Europe of the period, was deeply shocking in a conservative
Muslim society. As the British Ambassador expressed it,[104]

His [King Ghazi's] absorption in his private hobbies had led him
into a heedlessness of the welfare and the susceptibilities of his
subjects and indifference to affairs of State which had become
notorious. And, still more, even amongst a people by no means and
by no right (sic) queasy about human frailties, ... his mode of life
had long been a cause for whispered scandal and had served to make
the Iraqis hold him in aversion. What had been whispered about him
before now became the subject of the common talk of the coffee
shops, and of talk of such a kind as to bring His Majesty into
contempt.

The Ambassador was here referring to an event that had occurred with
a classic mixture of tragedy and comedy: King Ghazi's sister, Princess
'Azza, had eloped with, married, and adopted the faith of a waiter of
Greek birth and Italian nationality. As a reaction to this unfortunate
incident, Nuri al-Sa'id (then Foreign Minister) argued that 'the Royal
Family had been so disgraced that there was nothing for it but to depose
King Ghazi'.[105] Yasin al-Hashimi, on the other hand, told the British
Ambassador that[106]

public feeling was running so high that it might be difficult for King Ghazi to hold his own unless his honour were speedily retrieved. It was his Majesty's first and obvious duty to kill his sister with his own hand. His lost honour could not properly be regained by means of a hired assassin. If King Ghazi killed the princess promptly, he could hold up his head again and look people in the face. Otherwise, as time went on, his position might become so shaken as to be beyond saving.

The Ambassador replied that such an act, while doubtless sanctioned by old Arab custom, would hardly be well received in the outside world. Unlike Nuri al-Sa'id, who made proposals to the same British Ambassador to 'rid' the country of King Ghazi,[107] it seems that Yasin's scheme was to rule Iraq with the King remaining as a figure-head. It is possible that in this case Yasin had feared that Nuri, himself a dreamer of having absolute power in Iraq, might prove a formidable would-be rival to him in attaining supreme power in the event of the King being deposed. Thus, in this same encounter with the Ambassador, Yasin went on to declare his belief that 'a Prime Minister could discharge most of the duties of the Crown. . . . There was, therefore, nothing to be gained by Nuri's scheme.'[108] Driven by this spirit, Yasin al-Hashimi continued to interfere with the affairs of the King, and since he enjoyed the support of the British and the King did not,[109] he achieved a measure of success in controlling him.[110]

Aware of Yasin's expanding power, it was natural that his political opponents would resort to the only force in the country capable of containing it: the army, which, through its frequent use against the tribes, had in any case become an extension of the civilian government. Already in 1930, a British intelligence officer had warned that, within the armed forces,[111]

most of the senior appointments are held not so much through soldierly qualifications as through political graft and knowing the people in high places. Intrigue is to be found everywhere and is not confined to army matters; officers mix freely with the local politicians and are prepared to follow anyone who they think will benefit them. Officers only see their men on parade and are not in close sympathy with them. The men as a whole however are stupid and dull in intellect. At present there is no reason to suppose that they would refuse to do what they were ordered providing it was not too dangerous.

Loyalty within the armed forces was based on neither national nor professional grounds; soldiers and officers carried their class, ethnic and cultural differences with them in the army. 'Feeling often runs high between these various elements', commented another intelligence report:[112]

> The Arabs consider the Kurds treacherous and say they never know whether they will not be shot in the back by the Kurds in action. They treat the Kurdish soldiers with opprobrium. This the Kurds resent in their turn and the whole force is full of mutual jealousy and hatred and mistrust.

Inevitably, while giving army officers added importance, the increasing reliance of the government on the armed forces led to a gradual weakening of its control over them. The administration of King Faisal, with the general support it received from Britain, succeeded in maintaining a delicate balance between the government and the army, and the existence of imperial troops[113] and Assyrian Levies[114] in the country reduced the Iraqi army's virtual monopoly over the use of force. After King Faisal's death, however, the army's role took a new turn. The fact that the Levies were finally either disbanded or assimilated into the Iraqi army in 1932, coupled with Faisal's death in 1933, resulted in a power vacuum in the country which, as will be seen later, Iraqi officers were eager to fill. As seen above, during 1935-6 the country was, as the British Ambassador described it, 'drifting into something not far off civil war',[115] while the introduction of conscription in 1935 led to a considerable improvement in the army's numerical strength, and the exploitation of this power for political ends was now contemplated by politicians of all shades, the most extreme case being Ja'far al-'Askari's reported plans to effect a *coup d'état*.[116] When a *coup d'état* was actually executed in October 1936, its architects lost no time in drawing maximum gain from the fact that the army was a conscript one. Thus, their first communiqué opened with the following statement:[117]

> The army which is composed of your sons has lost patience with the present Government, who have been concerned only with their own personal interest, disregarding the public welfare. . . .

In the post-Faisal era, therefore, no longer contented, and perhaps not even feeling able to guard the nation, army officers abandoned their barracks and sought to govern.

Chapter 6

The Bakir Sidqi *coup d'état* of October 1936

There was nothing left for us except the Army; the Army is also from and for the nation – the soldiers are brothers to the oppressed millions, and the majority of the officers felt the strains of repression and bemoaned the death of freedoms; so we resorted to the Army.[1]

It was, apparently a perfect October morning in Baghdad. But, for the Iraqi state and the people of Baghdad, Thursday the twenty-ninth of October was to be a day with a difference; a day when Iraqi generals would overtly and decisively enter politics – marking the beginning of an era that at the time of writing has not yet ended.

While members of the Iraqi cabinet were making their way to the *serai* (Government building) shortly after 7 a.m., the state's army was supposedly performing its duties in various parts of the country. According to plan, one army battalion was stationed in the troubled area of the mid-Euphrates, another was at Mosul, while the remaining two were gathering in the neighbourhood of Qaraghan, on the road to the Persian frontier, for their annual training. Also at Qaraghan were al-Fariq Bakir Sidqi, who, in the absence of General Taha al-Hashimi abroad,[2] was now Acting General Commander of the Iraqi army, and 'Abd al-Latif Nuri, Commander of the First Division. At about 7.30 a.m. they instructed Muhammad Jawad, the Commander of the IRAF, along with ten other pilots, to be ready for the eleventh hour. There was nothing remarkable about such orders, except that this time their destination was to be not the tribal areas, but the centre of state power.

Less than an hour later, eleven planes were in the air, flying low over the capital and dropping handfuls of leaflets appealing to the King to dismiss the government and replace it by one headed by Hikmat Sulaiman.[3] This advice was backed by a none-too-subtle hint as to the

121

possible use of force and signed by General Bakir Sidqi as Commander of the National Forces of Reform:[4]

> The army, which is composed of your sons, has lost patience with the present Government, who have been concerned only with their own personal interests, disregarding the public welfare. The army has therefore appealed to His Majesty the King to dismiss the present cabinet and to replace it by another composed of sincere citizens under the leadership of Sayid Hikmat Sulaiman, who is held in the greatest esteem and respect by the public. By this appeal we have no desire except to improve your condition and the country's welfare, and we have therefore no doubt that you will cooperate with your brothers, the personnel of the army and their officers, with all your power – as the power of the people is always supreme. To our brother officials we say: We are only your brothers and colleagues in the service of the State, which we all wish to be one having regard for the interests of the public. We expect you to do your duty by non-co-operation with the oppressive Government, and by leaving your offices until a new cabinet, of which you will be proud, is formed. It is possible that the army may be compelled to take certain forcible measures, through which harm might unavoidably come to those who do not conform with this sincere appeal.

While these leaflets were being scattered over Baghdad, Hikmat Sulaiman arrived at the Royal Palace and delivered a letter[5] signed by Bakir Sidqi and 'Abd al-Latif Nuri, making the same points contained in the leaflets and adding that, should His Majesty fail to meet the generals' demands, 'Baghdad would be bombed from the air in three hours time'.[6] King Ghazi then sent for the British Ambassador for consultations (the latter, as far as can be established, was taken completely by surprise by the army's move). On arrival at the Palace, His Excellency advised the King against resisting the generals' ultimatum, only adding that they should be discouraged from making a triumphal entry into the capital.[7] Shortly afterwards (about 10 a.m.), Yasin al-Hashimi and his Foreign Minister (Nuri al-Sa'id) arrived at the Palace; both in their different ways were surprised, and the Prime Minister caused further confusion by stating that he had had a telephone conversation with Bakir Sidqi who had assured him that the army's move had the support of the King – a claim naturally vehemently denied by His Majesty.[8] The Prime Minister added that he was willing to resign provided that Hikmat Sulaiman assured him of his 'honourable' intentions.

While this dialogue was in progress, Bakir Sidqi was approaching the capital at the head of eighty lorries packed with troops, including the field and company officers of the two divisions that were stationed at Qaraghan.[9] In order to show his serious intentions, he authorised a demonstration of force over Baghdad; thus, at about 11 a.m., a flight of five planes dropped four bombs in the neighbourhood of the *serai*, three falling near the Prime Minister's office and the Ministry of Interior and injuring a number of people.[10]

The government was thus faced with a hopeless situation; even the city's police force could not have been mobilised for its defence, owing to the fact that large numbers of them had been drafted to the tribal areas of the mid-Euphrates. Any ideas of resistance that Yasin al-Hashimi and some of his ministers seem to have considered[11] were soon abandoned, therefore, and less than an hour later they, together with the rest of the cabinet, submitted their resignation to the King. The King then called upon Hikmat Sulaiman to form a cabinet, which he did by the end of the day. This was shortly followed by a message from the latter to the British Ambassador, which was perhaps the first clear intimation that *plus ça change, plus c'est la même chose*, given that it conveyed the desire of the new government to maintain the existing friendly relations with His Majesty's Government and to have the support of the British Embassy.[12]

Given the circumstances, this would have been a relatively smooth transition of power, had it not been for one event. Later in the day, Nuri al-Sa'id crept into the British Embassy via the water gate (some would say an appropriate entrance for one of his political style), informing the Ambassador that the King had sent the former Defence Minister, Ja'far al-'Askari, to the two generals in an apparent attempt to dissuade them from advancing, with the result that the unfortunate Ja'far had been shot dead, and that the same fate had been planned for himself (Nuri), the former prime minister, and Rashid 'Ali. Nuri was successfully hidden in the Embassy and later left for Egypt, and his two erstwhile colleagues similarly got to Syria.

Thus, for the first time the constitutional system of government had been undermined by an open intervention of the armed forces. We must ask, however, how far this event effected a real change in Iraqi politics; and this makes it necessary to look into the causes of the coup.

The possible causes of the coup and the ideology and social characteristics of its leaders

As the title of this section suggests, the true causes of the Bakir Sidqi

123

coup are not known. The clandestine nature of the army's plan and the premature death of both Bakir Sadqi and his foremost ally, Muhammad Jawad, make it inevitable that an analysis of the causes of the coup be largely speculative interpretations (even confidential reports and analyses that were written at the time suffer the same constraints).

Quite naturally, in this context a number of guidelines can be discerned. As was seen earlier, the first communiqué issued by the National Force of Reform, for example, made a direct reference to the latter's belief that the Hashimi cabinet had neglected the welfare of the Iraqi populace and, instead, had striven to further the personal interests of its own members. However, as will be discussed below, at least in terms of internal policy, the new regime did not make a significant shift from the patterns adopted by its predecessors, and this must surely throw doubt on whether their initial move against the government was motivated by a genuine concern for the welfare of the public at large. More likely, it seems that the shortcomings of the Hashimi government provided a suitable climate[13] for ambitious men in the army and political elite to, as it were, ride the storm. The government that they brought to power consisted essentially of three elements: Bakir Sidqi, who had led the coup and now become C-in-C; Hikmat Sulaiman, who became prime minister; and a number of politicians of whom the most important was associated with the group known as Jama'at al-Ahali. This was in fact a coalition of elements whose nature and motives were, in the final analysis, very different.

Hikmat Sulaiman himself, like most of the political elite, was a Sunni. He had been Director of Education in Baghdad during the Ottoman period and a member of the Young Turk movement, which was looked on with disfavour by most Arabs because of its desire to stress the Turkish nature of the Empire. He had remained in Constantinople until the British occupation of 1920–1, when he returned to Iraq where he served in four of the twenty-two cabinets created between 1920 and 1936. Although, like Yasin al-Hashimi, he played a prominent part in organising opposition to 'Ali Jaudat's government in 1935, he was not offered the post he desired in the subsequent administration. His exclusion from the government may have intensified the feeling of animosity he seems to have already harboured towards Yasin al-Hashimi. Shortly after taking office, for example, he complained bitterly to the British Ambassador about the contrast between his apparently dwindling financial situation and the considerable wealth that Yasin al-Hashimi and former members of his cabinet had accumulated.[14] In the view of the same Ambassador, 'the stimulus afforded by these reflections may have stirred him [Hikmat Sulaiman] as much as his zeal for public welfare'.[15] The Ambassador went on to point out that:[16]

> Rashid 'Ali, as Minister of the Interior and Justice, controlled immense patronage, which he had turned to personal profit, and his nomination of himself as trustee of the Qadriyal Waqf provoked appropriate comment. By a number of clever devices Yasin had become possessed of large areas of Government land. . . . Nuri had not acquired land, but he had built a large house, and the lavish expenditure of public money on the medical treatment of his son after an aeroplane accident at the beginning of the year had become something of a scandal.

In another report, the same Ambassador continued to document the way in which members of the former cabinet had acquired wealth:[17]

> Yasin Pasha had taken over 50,000 masharas [about 15,000 hectares] of Government land and 5 shaikhs were living at the moment in Hikmat Sulaiman's garden pleading for their land to be restored to them. Rashid 'Ali has also appropriated land and abused his position at the Quadiriya waqf. Nuri has squandered public funds with his tours abroad, etc., and also the journey to England with his son; huge palace in Baghdad probably built from payments from B.O.D. [British Oil Development Company]. Enormous wedding ceremonies. . . .

Bakir Sidqi, on the other hand, had a forceful and domineering personality. He had studied at Turkish, German and British staff schools, and besides Arabic he spoke Turkish, English, German and some French. Though 'heavy and rather stout', he is reported to have been very active and to have travelled widely.[18] Being 'very ambitious', 'ruthless', 'very vindictive' and 'rather jealous',[19] he must have strongly resented those standing, or appearing to stand, between him and the fulfilment of his ambitions. He was also regarded as being possessed of great intelligence, determination and self-control. His private life was as disreputable as his public views were stern and strict. In the months preceeding the coup, Bakir Sidqi had been annoyed that his applications to visit England had been twice rejected by the British Embassy. His disappointment was turned against his superior, Taha al-Hashimi, when the latter disregarded Bakir Sidqi's pleas with him to cancel his own visit to Britain as an expression of solidarity with the now humiliated general.[20]

At first, Bakir Sidqi showed his dissatisfaction with his chief by submitting his resignation from the army; this was, perhaps naturally, rejected. According to Taha al-Hashimi, it was only after this exhibition of anger failed to impress him, and thereby to lead him to reverse his decision concerning his planned visit to England, that Bakir Sidqi decided to organise a coup against the government.[21] Sidqi seems to have also resented the elevation of some personalities (particularly Ja'far al-'Askari, who was his 'village compatriot') to relatively more important positions than his own. He apparently complained to Taha al-Hashimi about the misbehaviour of Nuri al-Sa'id and Ja'far al-'Askari and inquired whether it was not time to 'rid the country of them',[22] and when Taha asked him to elaborate and explain what exactly he had in mind, Sidqi replied that 'there were in the army patriotic men . . . who included amongst them . . . reliable young officers . . . who were ready to give any sacrifices demanded of them'.[23]

More clearly, the ambitious Bakir Sidqi must have felt that he had reached a dead end in his career and that the chances of him becoming CGS were, at best, very slight, especially in view of the fact that Taha al-Hashimi had been CGS for the preceeding seven years. Similarly, Bakir Sidqi's ally, 'Abd al-Latif Nuri, was embittered by the government's refusal to pay for medical treatment he had hoped to undergo in England. This feeling of bitterness against the government emerges very clearly from a rather passionate letter that he sent to Ja'far al-'Askari, the Minister of Defence, less than two weeks before the coup:[24]

To his Honour, the Minister of Defence, (1) Neither in the Hijaz, the Syrian, or the Iraqi army, have I gambled, drank alcohol [obviously, in a Moslem context, these were signs of virtuous behaviour] ; nor have I committed any dishonest act. I have reason to believe that, thank God, my record is white. I have performed my military duties conscientiously and never in my life have I been a member of a political party. (2) While in the service, as is well documented, I fell ill, and for the last three years I have been seeking and receiving medical treatment at my own expense. The only person who had helped me in that matter was Yasin al-Hashimi, may God endow him with the best of rewards. Last year, he had given me 100 I.D. and this year he gave me another 40 I.D. (these payments were made through Nuri al-Sa'id and Jafar al-'Askari respectively). (3) My huge expenses during the last three years exceeded 1,000 I.D. and I had hoped that I would be able to . . . be granted an offer to pursue my medical treatment at the Government's expense. (4) Finally, Yasin al-Hashimi made a promise, and my hope was that His Honour [Yasin al-Hashimi] would undoubtedly fulfil that promise. *Otherwise, overwhelming desperation might have its hold on me resulting in dire consequences* [my emphasis] . (5) I pray that God will inspire those in charge of the people's destiny to benefit from the endeavours of the faithful amongst the people who are striving to perform their sacred duties to the country.

These arguments are quite serious, especially when reviewed in the light of the government's lavish expenditure on the medical treatment of Sabah, Nuri al-Sa'id's son.[25]

But that these embittered generals succeeded in mobilising what seems to have been a significant section of the army behind them must surely be explained by two factors: first, the hostility many officers were reported to have felt towards the government for its tough handling of tribal dissidents;[26] and, secondly, the frustration they must have felt at the government's failure to supply the army with the arms and equipment it needed. According to the 1930 Treaty with Britain, His Majesty's Government undertook, among other things, to:[27]

grant whenever they may be required by His Majesty the King of Iraq all possible facilities in the following matters. . . . The provision of arms, ammunition, equipment, ships and aeroplanes of the latest available pattern for the forces of His Majesty the King of Iraq. . . .

However, Britain's success in fulfilling these obligations was not consistent, and all too often the British munitions industry responded in a way that has, perhaps, since become familiar. For example, in February 1936 the Iraqi Defence Ministry complained to their London legation about delays on the part of the British War Office in the delivery and shipment of arms. They pointed out that:[28]

About 750 rifles should have been delivered in the United Kingdom in October and November, 1935, and 800 in December 1935. Allowing a period of 15 days for inspection, 750 rifles ought to have been shipped in December 1935, and 800 in January, 1936, but not a single rifle was shipped on these dates. . . . The Ministry having some time ago proceeded with the calling up of conscripts for military service, the delay in the delivery and shipment of the rifles will hamper the training of the first quota of conscripts owing to the fact that the Army does not at present possess adequate quantities of arms.

After making seven other references to similar delays or complete failure in arms delivery, the Defence Ministry requested their legation to remind the British authorities concerned of their pressing needs for these arms, and concluded their letter by expressing their[29]

> fear that we shall not be able to carry out the expansion of the army within the scheduled time. You are therefore earnestly requested to approach the authorities concerned at the British War Office with a request for the delivery, examination and shipment of the arms in question with all possible expedition.

To a government facing serious tribal dissidence, and to an army assigned the task of enforcing that government's authority, such delay was damaging to more than just their sense of self-importance. While bewailing their inability to supply as many arms as the Iraqis required in a world that was rapidly re-arming, the Foreign Office concurred that it was proper to 'frankly admit that . . . the Iraqi Government have justification for complaining . . . the delay in the supply of automatics . . . has been due to the failure of Vickers-Armstrong to keep to their contract dates'.[30]

As the tribal uprising continued to spread in the course of 1936, the Iraqi government persisted with their appeals to Britain to supply them with the arms needed. Thus, during the May uprising in Rumaitha, Yasin al-Hashimi himself wrote to the British Ambassador, complaining that the forces used to quell that revolt simply did not have a total of 200 machine-guns ordered from Britain, the first fifty of which should have arrived by October 1935.[31] After informing the Ambassador of the existence of 'much bitterness in the Army at the possibility of having to go into action without the proper number of machine-guns',[32] he proceeded to argue that the arrangements established under the provisions of the Treaty had proved a failure, and that he hoped that His Excellency would understand how he (Yasin al-Hashimi) had been obliged to authorise[33]

> the Ministry of Defence to obtain the machine-guns required for the Army from Czechoslovakian factories. Your Excellency will no doubt appreciate the evil effect of this delay in circumstances in which the Army is compelled to undertake punitive operations.

Following this letter, the Iraqi government went ahead and placed an order with the Skoda factory for the supply of 200 light automatics, with the usual proportion of spares.[34] Delivery, however, was promised only for December 1936 at the earliest, and thus this source of dissatisfaction was not eliminated by the government's initiative. It seems quite conceivable that some army officers were appalled by the government's dragging of feet before turning to Czechoslovakia (and then, only on such a small scale). This is particularly probable since some army leaders seem to have had a vested interest in ordering arms from Czechoslovakia. It is claimed, for example, that the Baghdad agent of the Skoda factory, who was 'a very industrious Jew', had secured a 'mysterious holiday in Europe' for Bakir Sidqi[35]

> between July and September [1936]. It is known for certain that he [Bakir Sidqi] was in Prague (like other army leaders he has been taking bribes from the Jewish agents of Czechoslovak armament firms who abound in the Middle East). . . . At the same time it is quite possible that this rather sinister person has established a secret *liaison* with the German army through the assistance of the German Minister in Baghdad.

Apart from harbouring such feelings of animosity towards the government, there is no evidence that either the generals who led the coup or their followers in the armed forces had any thought-out ideology which could have inspired their movement. In the final analysis, their alliance was a negative one, whose foundation was consolidated by common grievance rather than a vision for the future. The same is not however true of the third element, the Ahali group, who supported the coup and who, in view of their later attempts to implement some of the reforms advocated by their programme, clearly had patriotic motives in seeking the downfall of the Hashimi government.

The nucleus of Jama'at al-Ahali was formed in the 1920s, when a number of Iraqi students studying at the American University of Beirut set up an Iraqi Cultural Society. Because of the short stay of these students in Beirut, however, and the fact that some of them had left for Europe in pursuit of higher education, the Iraqi Cultural Society soon faded away. Some years later, in 1930, when some of these pioneers returned to Baghdad, they decided to revive the Iraqi Cultural Society, and in fact succeeded in establishing a 'group' (*jama'at*) which they later called Jama'at al-Ahali. By now this group included a selection of the better educated Iraqis like 'Abd al-Qadir Isma'il, 'Abd al-Fatah Ibrahim, Husain Jamil, Khalil Kanna and Muhammad Hadid; later (in 1934) they succeeded in attracting Kamil al-Chadirchi, then a member of the Executive Committee of the Ikha al-Watani Party, to join their group.

From the very beginning of their movement Jama'at al-Ahali directed their attention to ideas of social reform. As reformers, they endeavoured to work for the accomplishment of their ideas in a constitutional manner within the state system. They believed in religion, traditions

129

and the re-distribution of wealth. Until 1935 the most radical statements they made were two that were published in their *Sawt al-Ahali*
newspaper (which first appeared in January 1932 but, like its contemporaries, had often been subjected to censorship or complete closure
by the government). The first statement called upon the government
to nationalise the Baghdad Electricity Company, and the second was
an article criticising the Law Governing the Rights and Duties of Cultivators and the Tribal Criminal and Civil Disputes Regulations, and
calling for their abolition.

By the mid-1930s the ideas of Jama'at al-Ahali had acquired a scope
and consistency that made it possible for the founders to view them as
a political doctrine which they called *al-Sha'biya* (popularism). As
Muhammad Hadid described this doctrine, '*al-Sha'biya* can be summed
up as an ideology which in the main advocates the adoption of the
principles of liberal parliamentary democracy.'[36]

The Ahali decision to resort finally to the army in order to achieve
this aim has been explained by some veteran members of this group,
and appears to be quite plausible. Emphasising how notorious Yasin
al-Hashimi's government was in suppressing any opposition, they
claimed that [37]

> even articles which we [the Ahali] managed to send to some news-
> papers in Beirut were censored by Yasin al-Hashimi who made
> generous payments to the editors concerned in order to induce them
> to suppress such articles. In the absence of any democratic channels
> through which a repressive Government could be pushed out of
> office, we, quite simply, had to look to the only force capable of
> achieving that goal, and thus we resorted to the Army.

That the army was both a possible and an effective channel for the
acquisition of political power had been adequately demonstrated in
other parts of the world at that time, and the Iraqi intelligentsia must
have been aware of that trend.[38] As a leader in *The Times* was to
express it:[39]

> the example of other countries has certainly whetted their ambitions.
> In Greece, Paraguay, and Spain – and these names do not exhaust
> the list – the soldiers have seized, or attempted to seize, power. In
> Japan they have the last word in the policy of a great Empire. Young
> armies are naturally imitative.

This group, Jama'at al-Ahali, were the main force behind the Popular
Reform League, the new party that was formed in November 1936 in

order to support the Sulaiman government. The programme[40] of this party called for far-reaching reforms, ranging from the nationalisation of the means of transport and re-distribution of land to the restriction of working hours; altogether it had, as the British Ambassador expressed it, a 'Red tinge about it'.[41] After the programme was announced and a broadcast made by Ja'far Abu Timman undertaking to fulfil the promises made in it, 'giant demonstrations were arranged in Baghdad, and the capital's main streets were a stage for the dancing and singing of crowds and of tribesmen and workers. The outgoing Ministry was everywhere denigrated'.[42]

However, it is interesting that, although members of the Ahali group occupied nearly half the posts in the new cabinet,[43] and although the Popular Reform League was created specifically to support the government, the government did not pledge themselves to adopt the full programme of the League;[44] and until his fall, Hikmat Sulaiman had in fact persistently refused to join the party. Thus, eight months after its publication, the only proposal in the programme that had actually been implemented was the restriction of conditions and hours of work in Iraq. Otherwise, unhappily for the people of Iraq, the building of the egalitarian society towards which the adoption of the League's programme would have been a major step was not to be. In fact, no sooner was the programme published in the press than members of the government started making determined efforts to dispel any possible misinterpretation of their intentions, particularly any conceivable association with communism.[45] In an interview with a leading Lebanese journalist, for example, Hikmat Sulaiman, while admitting the necessity for social reform, was, quite rightly, unequivocal in his denial of any association with communism. 'I beg you, Sir,' he told Mr Yazbak,[46]

they accuse me of being a Communist. Do you know why? Because although I had been a Deputy and a Minister many times, I remained poor; because I say that these luxurious palaces should not be built alongside the hovels in which the poor live; because I say that our country is wretched due to its appalling feudal traditions . . . ; because I say that *miri* land should be distributed on the fallahin and the poor, not on the rich and the Ministers. . . . Who protects the country and insures its independence Sir? Is it the rich, the Ministers, or the Politicians? Nay, by God it is not so. . . . It is the Army, and the Army alone, which protects the homeland and defends its dignity. But how can we demand of the soldier to expose himself to danger in order to protect us, when he does not feel that this land is not his

131

but the Ministers', the Pashas', and the notables' . . . . This is what I
have been saying and this is what led them to accuse me of being
a Communist.

With similar forcefulness, Ja'far Abu Timman, Minister of Finance and
himself member of the Ahali group, explained to the correspondent of
the Egyptian newspaper, *al-Muqattam*, how and why neither he nor his
colleagues could have been supporters of communism, and how the
League's programme was dictated solely by social necessities. He
pointed out how severely the[47]

Iraqi fallah was oppressed and downtrodden and is treated by the
feudal lords and notables of this country in a way which should be
reserved for non-humans. The same is also true in the case of
employers who make their labourers work for a period which varies
between 9 and 16 hours per day and at the end pay them meagerly
in return for their labour.

Since it has been my nature to side with and support the oppressed
. . . I wanted that working hours should be limited to 8–9 per day.
I also wanted an augmentation of wages and altogether wanted to
work for a just treatment of the fallahin and to put an end to the
arbitrary powers of their lords. That was considered excessive by
some who strove to distort the truth by classifying these inclinations
of mine and those of my colleagues . . . as being communist. It is
nothing of the sort. If an endeavour to reform, to support the weak
and oppressed, to see that justice reigns supreme amongst the people
of this country (and all of these principles are in accordance with the
Shar'a and are principles of Islam which I am proud of adopting);
if all these are considered communistic, then I pray to God to make
us all communists. . . .

It has escaped those people that, by being myself engaged in
commerce and financial matters, and since I am a landowner, it is
unthinkable that I would have communist leanings. The same is
true also in the case of the Prime Minister, who is the owner of
large estates, and also of Kamil al-Chadirchi, the Minister of
Economics and Communications. Given these circumstances, it is
not possible that they would be communists.

These views were also echoed by Bakir Sidqi, who gave his own reasons
as to why Iraq could not adhere to communist notions. In an interview
with the same Lebanese journalist, he emphasised how deeply traditional
Iraqi society was, and how it had[48]

not reached the standard which would enable it to accept extremist ideas. . . . Besides, Communism contradicts the Monarchy and there is no one in Iraq who wishes to see a system in existence other than the Monarchy, and as the Commander of the National Forces of Reform, I would like to remind you that . . . the Army rose against the previous Government . . . in defence of the Throne of our beloved King . . . and as the highest ranking officer in the Army after His Majesty, I would like to declare that the Army is ready to fight until the end any movement which aims at harming, no matter how slightly, our great Monarch . . . and would suppress such a movement ruthlessly, whether it was a Communist movement or any other.

In the light of these declarations, and in view of the government's failure to implement any of the reforms envisaged by the Reform League, it seems justifiable to conclude that both the original programme of the League and the diluted version of it that was adopted by the government as its policy programme were in fact little more than a list of visionary hopes designed to appeal to the sentiments of the people. Nevertheless, it is possible that the authors of the programme had hoped that it would also give the government a sense of orientation coupled with a greater degree of unity. Given the background of the principal leaders, such a unifying factor would have been not only desirable but indispensible for the very survival of the government.

This coalition, flimsy as it was, did not last. However, the threat to it did not come, as might have been expected, from outside. The fact that this government had come to power through military intervention posed a problem to the forces that held ultimate power in the country: the monarchy and the British. In the event, they both reconciled themselves to its existence, and it is important to ask why this was so.

The attitude of the King

As referred to in the previous chapter, King Ghazi's position during the Hashimi term of office was becoming increasingly precarious. He was known to be chafing under Yasin's efforts to control his private life and that of his associates. More importantly, the King's relations with British diplomats, though outwardly cordial, involved a degree of mutual mistrust, and Foreign Office documents reveal an open hostility to His Majesty. In July 1936, for example, the Foreign Office calmly discussed the possible necessity of forcing King Ghazi to abdicate,[49] and

133

grimly analysed the objections to any alternative. There were supposedly no suitable Iraqi families, and the Iraqi's dislike of foreigners militated against a foreign princeling – the Shi'as would object particularly strongly to one of the Saudi royal house (who, most probably, would have tried to unite the country with Saudi Arabia anyway); the low standards of public life[50] made a republic undesirable; and, finally, the succession of King Ghazi by his infant son, Faisal, would involve a very long regency.[51]

Thus, we see a king deprived of the crucial support of Britain, his prestige with his people in tatters and fighting against attempts such as that of Yasin al-Hashimi and Nuri Sa'id to control his life.[52] Is it not highly likely, therefore, that the weakened and annoyed monarch would look for a change; would in fact be casting thoughtful glances at the armed forces, the only factor that would effect such a change to a government which, while allowing him greater freedom, could rule the country with a firmness that would reduce his dependence on Britain?

There was indeed a general impression at the time that the King had been privy to the coup in advance.[53] The evidence is inconclusive, but some of it does point in this direction, and in particular the King's instructions to Ja'far al-'Askari. It should be fairly clear that insurgent army officers, faced with their responsible minister (Minister of Defence) asking them to desist, are quite likely to use violence.[54] It is evident, therefore, that, by delegating Ja'far al-'Askari (against whom the officers were ultimately rebelling) to negotiate with the rebellious officers, the King might not have considered the Minister's survival to be of great consequence. It is also curious how Rustum Haidar, the President of the Royal Court, who presumably also acted as an aide to His Majesty, is alleged to have advised leaders of the opposition that only by force could they realistically hope to undermine the position of the Hashimi government. It will be remembered that Hikmat Sulaiman had not been invited to join the Hashimi cabinet, and hence had led a group of politicians in opposition to the government. It will also be remembered that, during the summer of 1936, these opposition leaders were making a habit of delivering petitions to the King appealing to His Majesty against the repressive measures of the cabinet. On one such occasion it is claimed that, on delivering a petition, Hikmat Sulaiman and Kamil Chadirchi were met by Rustum Haidar, who told them: 'What is the use of these scraps of paper which you bring now and then? The Government relies on force, so if you are in a possession of a counter-force, produce it; otherwise what is the use?'[55] Following this encounter with Rustum Haidar, it is claimed that Hikmat Sulaiman went immediately to Bakir Sidqi, and pleaded for his support. 'O Bakir Sidqi,' he is reported to have said,[56]

'the security and future of the Kingdom, the freedom of Iraq and the dignity of its people, the honour of its womenfolk and every-thing which is dear in this homeland: all of these things are at your mercy. The situation, as you see, has become unbearable, and the final say has become the monopoly of the powerful; that is, the army, and that is you. So, your ancestors are calling you from their graves that the time has come.'

It is claimed that Bakir Sidqi was moved by this appeal and decided to respond favourably by organising the overthrow of the government.[57]

The King's involvement cannot be definitely established. Nevertheless, there is sufficient evidence to suggest that, once it succeeded, the coup received the open support of His Majesty. It seems highly probable that this *expost facto* attitude of the King towards the overthrow of the Hashimi government had been expected by the generals and urban politicians who had engineered the coup and who had, therefore, felt encouraged by it to effect their plans.

The attitude of Britain

Inevitably, in discussing the attitude of the King, some aspects of this topic have been covered. Britain's relationship with Iraq was ambiguous in that it partook of the characteristics of both international relations and a metropolitan–colonial connection. This is well summed up in a report on conditions of life in Baghdad, which firmly states that:[58]

the work of the Embassy at Baghdad differs from that of other posts in that remnants of the High Commission (i.e. mandate) days still remain. . . . The presence of the Royal Air Force and the British Advisory Military Mission, and the fact that His Majesty's Govern-ment have the *right* to be consulted and are consulted in *all* major matters affecting the foreign policy of Iraq. . . . [my emphasis]

This British hegemony over Iraq meant that Britain was also inevitably concerned about internal changes for a number of reasons: because they might affect the foreign policy of Iraq and hence its strategic and economic value to Britain; because certain changes could reflect un-favourably on Britain's prestige abroad and on public opinion at home; and, perhaps more importantly, because a state of internal chaos or a radical change might endanger the operation of British commercial and strategic activities, notably oil production and RAF bases or staging posts.

The architects of the coup were naturally aware of the importance Britain attached to Iraq and of the possibility, therefore, that their efforts to overthrow the government might be frustrated either by Britain's use of counter-force or by simply her denying them her crucial support once in office. This is why, on the eve of the coup, Hikmat Sulaiman made several determined attempts to see Edmonds, a senior British adviser to the Ministry of Interior, and apparently had[59]

intended, without divulging either the time or the instrument . . . , to warn me [Edmonds] that a subversive movement against the Government was imminent and that it was serious, so that as soon as I [Edmonds] should hear of the dropping of the warning leaflets I should recognise that it was not a case of silly intrigue and prevent any waste of time . . . and the consequent dangers.

It seems very doubtful that Hikmat Sulaiman would have risked exposing his plans and that of his colleagues simply in order to warn Edmonds against not taking them seriously. What appears more likely is that he, on behalf of his collaborators, was very anxious to know which way the British would react to their movement. In fact, it was considered so unlikely for a coup that did not receive British support to succeed that the first reaction of a number of Syrian and Lebanese newspapers was to point a finger at Britain as being a possible party to the army's move.[60] The Russian press seemed to have reached the same conclusion. For example, *Zarya Vostoka*, a Tiflis newspaper, rejected the[61]

facile assumption . . . that the change of Government in Iraq came as a surprise to His Majesty's Government and will be damaging to British imperial interests: on the contrary, the new Government, whose position is inevitably shaky, may find the prospect of using British aid to strengthen its hold very tempting. . . . The British military advisers, who are known to have a decisive influence in the Iraq army, placed no obstacles in the way of the revolt.

I have not, however, found any evidence that would support this claim, and this view was unanimously accepted by all of the Iraqi notables that I interviewed.

But at least Britain did not oppose the coup, and once the army made its move on Baghdad, the British Ambassador was in fact very keen for the Sulaiman government to be formed as soon as possible. One reason for this reaction from Britain may have been the fact that the coup was[62]

> so immediately successful. Had the struggle been prolonged, with echoes of strife in Mosul (where many would have supported Yasin), the minorities would certainly have suffered at the hands of mischievous elements exploiting disorder for their own ends.

However, the main reasons why Britain did not oppose the coup must be the fact that the personalities involved came exclusively from the same elite that had been ruling the state since its formation in 1920, and, as mentioned above, that Hikmat Sulaiman was quick to make his intentions of respecting the spirit and letter of the 1930 Treaty known to the British Ambassador. Thus, to Britain, although the overt intervention of the army in politics marked a significant and quite obviously dangerous development in the internal affairs of the Iraqi state, this 'departure' could be tolerated so long as it had no adverse effects on the country's foreign policy and hence on its relations with Britain.

At that time, Britain had worries about two possible changes in Iraq's foreign policy. One was that Iraq would develop an enthusiasm for pan-Arabism; the other, that she would seek a closer connection with Turkey and perhaps Persia.

Bakir Sidqi's attitude to the Arabs emerges from an interview that he gave to the *New York Times* shortly after the coup. After giving the ritual expression of sympathy for the Arab cause, he emphasised categorically that he felt compelled, first, 'to establish my [Bakir Sidqi's] own country on a firm footing. How can we endeavour to establish an All-Arabia empire before we have first ensured for each component section of such an empire a good, strong and independent Government?'[63] Similarly, Hikmat Sulaiman (who, in fact, was the brother of General Mahmud Shaukat Pasha, who had served in the first Young Turk reformist government of the Ottoman Empire until his murder in 1913) was, in the view of the British Ambassador, 'less disposed than his predecessors to foster pan-Arab ambitions'.[64]

But Sulaiman's room for manoeuvre must have been severely limited by the attitude of large sections of his people to an area of the Arab world of extreme importance to Britain, namely Palestine. Particularly during 1936, when a general strike was successfully organised in Palestine, the Iraqis' support of the Palestinians was manifested in a variety of ways.

It is not within the scope of our present survey to document this with any great detail. A few examples are, however, called for. First of all, frequent references were made by British Embassy dispatches describing meetings and strikes that were organised in various parts of the country in support of the Palestinians. For example, the Foreign Office was informed of a day of mourning for Palestine which was observed in Baghdad on 22 May 1936, and of a telegram that was sent by a number of Mosul notables protesting against the policy of HMG in Palestine, copies of which had been delivered to the British Embassy and to the heads of other foreign missions in Baghdad.[65] Also, the British Embassy refers to several meetings which were held by the Nadi al-Muthanna, the principal Arab nationalist society in Baghdad, which were normally 'well attended' and which were sometimes addressed by Palestinian delegates, who inflamed the nationalist feelings of the audience by relating to them stories of the heroic struggle of the people of Palestine.[66] At one such meeting, for example, Mu'in al-Mahdi, a Palestinian nationalist, told his audience how widespread the strike in Palestine was by relating to them the following incident:[67]

> 'A little girl entered the premises of a shop-keeper who had opened his shop regardless of public feeling. Being asked by the shop-keeper whether she wanted anything, she replied: "I just want one thing of which you have none". He replied: "I have everything here". She retorted: "No. I cannot find that you have a single yard of honour". This word of retort sufficed for the closing of the shop.'

It is true that, in real terms, Hikmat's predecessors' backing of the Palestinian cause was insignificant; and although, on occasions,[68] they made strong verbal statements in support of the Palestinians, they were always quick to explain apologetically to the British Ambassador the political need for such a concession to public pressure,[69] while continuing to cripple the activities of Arab nationalists in Iraq who made several abortive attempts to dispatch volunteers and ammunition to the Palestinians.[70]

Nevertheless, through their efforts to mediate with Britain over the Palestinian problem, Yasin al-Hashimi and Nuri al-Sa'id were perceived by the Palestinians, and more importantly by the Iraqi nationalist societies, as strong allies, and their fall was thus viewed with dismay by the Palestinian nationalists.[71]

By contrast, the Sulaiman government was enthusiastically welcomed by the Iraqi Jewish community who, as a result of the tendency to associate some of their members with the Zionist movement, had been having a difficult time during the latter months of the Hashimi

government.[72] As a result of the Sulaiman government's general atti-
tude to pan-Arabism and, more specifically, to their suppression of
Arab nationalists such as Fauzi al-Qawuqji and Sa'id Haji Thabit, the
position of the Iraqi Jewish community improved noticeably; by
February 1937 the Prime Minister felt able to point out to the British
Ambassador[73]

> how secure the Jews now felt and how ardently they supported the
> new regime. He [Hikmat Sulaiman] had banished Fauzi [Qawuqji]
> to Kirkuk. Sa'id Haji Thabit was trembling with fear and know [sic]
> that he had only to raise his head to get a hard knock.

However, there was a limit to the extent to which the Sulaimani government could deviate from the nationalist line, and events in Palestine
were always bound to have repurcussions in Iraq. It was thus a matter
of dire political expediency for the government to maintain an overt
interest in the Palestinian problem. Perhaps this is what motivated
Hikmat Sulaiman to come out with a proposal that could be seen as a
constructive development of an idea of Nuri al-Sa'id, that is, a federation
of Iraq, Palestine and Transjordan, but with the added incentive of
unlimited Jewish immigration.[74]

In retrospect, it seems that Hikmat Sulaiman had a worthwhile
scheme which was worthy of very full consideration and might have
avoided a veritable torrent of later human misery and disruption. But
although the British Foreign Office were initially attracted by the idea,
they soon pointed out a number of obvious objections, such as that the
scheme might fully satisfy neither the Jews (who wanted a sovereign
state) nor the Palestinian Arabs (who would still be overwhelmed
politically).[75] Other objections raised were that the difficulties of
linking countries with differing degrees of political autonomy (as was
later seen with the ill-fated Central African Federation) were formidable;
that it was strategically impossible for Britain to give up the Mandates
for Palestine and Transjordan;[76] that the League of Nations might
withold its consent to such a scheme;[77] and, finally, that rivalry between
Amir 'Abdullah and King Ghazi, and the jealousy of Ibn Sa'ud of
whoever might succeed to the throne, could lead to complications.[78]

As the Prime Minister put it, his government's desire to 'dispel the
widespread (and quite true) impression that [they] did not care a hang
for Pan-Arabs [sic], which [they] saw as damaging',[79] thus ended in
failure. Nevertheless, the Sulaiman government's attitude towards pan-
Arabism remained unenthusiastic, and their cool attitude is reflected
very clearly in their 'Programme of Policy',[80] where inter-Arab relations
came last in their list of priorities.

On the other hand, it is perhaps significant that their second priority in foreign relations (after relations with Britain) was:[81]

to strengthen the ties of friendship and co-operation between Iraq and the Turkish Republic, and to use every endeavour to hasten the conclusion of a non-aggression pact between Iraq, Turkey, Iran and Afghanistan.

This may be viewed as a remarkable precursor of the Cento Pact signed between these countries (less Afghanistan but plus Pakistan and the two main Western powers) some twenty years later. It is interesting to note that, unlike most of the other plans of the Sulaiman cabinet, this item was actually put into practice by the signing of both a treaty of friendship with Turkey, and a non-aggression pact with Turkey, Iran and Afghanistan.[82]

Apart from this, it was never clearly discovered how pro-Turkish Hikmat Sulaiman and Bakir Sidqi really were. Quite naturally, they, like other Middle Eastern politicians of that period including the 'average Iraqi nationalist',[83] must have been influenced by Mustafa Kemal, and by the Turkish example in building a republic. Their admiration for Turkey must have also been strengthened by the fact that:[84]

General Bakir Sidqi was a pure Turk [he was in fact born in 'Askar, a small village in Kurdistan, to a Turkish family], and has always had an unbounded admiration for M. Ataturk. Sayid Hikmat Sulaiman is a Turkish Arab [a member of a Turkish family domiciled in Mesopotamia], and had for long held similar views about M. Ataturk.

These reasons, combined with the new regime's evident indifference to pan-Arabism, make it understandable that Iraqi nationalists were convinced of Bakir Sidqi's and Hikmat Sulaiman's Turkish inclination; a view that was initially shared also by the Foreign Office, which, as we shall see, refers to General Amin al-'Umari, the main organiser of the former's assassination, as 'the champion of the Arab element in the army, who had felt themselves slighted by Bakır Sidqi'.[85]

In addition, it is perhaps significant that the first two telegrams of condolence on Bakir Sidqi's death came from the Turkish and Persian governments.[86] It is also interesting that, according to Taha al-Hashimi, the Turkish press strongly and unanimously condemned the assassination of Bakir Sidqi, declaring him as the 'greatest Iraqi personality in the history of modern Iraq'.[87] The official Turkish reaction was similarly one of deep sorrow. According to Naji Shaukat, then Iraqi's Minister in the Turkish capital, the Turkish Foreign Minister was 'not only very disturbed by the news, but also expressed fears that this incident might lead to Hikmat Sulaiman being forced out of office, and by consequence to the worsening of relations between Iraq and Turkey'.[88]

In conclusion, however, it has to be said that there is no definite evidence to establish that the new regime had more than 'romantic' sentiments towards effecting a radical change in Iraq's relations with Turkey, and it seems probable that Britain had become aware of this at an early stage. The first reaction of the Foreign Office to the coup did indeed express concern about the Turkish inclinations of the new rulers. Thus, the Eastern Department argued that[89]

Bakir Sidqi and Hikmat Sulaiman are pro-Turks, and it is to be feared that they may strive after a re-alignment away from Arab influence like Ibn Sa'ud and towards Turkey, and even attempt to re-cast the essentially Arab-Moslem country on modern Turkish lines.

Two months later, the Foreign Office again hypothesised that[90]

with a weak Government in Iraq, dependent on a pro-Turkish section of the army, and faced with the possible development of chaotic conditions at any moment if things should go wrong, the risk of Turkish intervention in Northern Iraq if a suitable opportunity offers can no longer be absolutely ruled out.

As it happened, Turkey's actual actions were in fact in the other direction. Ismet Inönü, the Turkish Prime Minister, advised Hikmat Sulaiman[91]

(1) To do nothing to spoil Iraq's good relations with His Majesty's Government.
(2) To go slow with his social reforms and not to try to follow the pace of Turkey.

It might also be relevant here to point out that Turkey showed no inclination to intervene in Iraq during the very troubled period of 1940-1, when Britain's ability to repel such a move appeared at least limited.

Finally, in considering the foreign policy attitudes of the coup government, which were of primary importance to Britain, we must of course consider their attitude to Britain herself. The first official comment by Hikmat Sulaiman to the British Ambassador amounted to 'no change'. He wished to maintain the existing friendly relations with

His Majesty's Government and hoped that he and his cabinet would have the support of the British Embassy.[92] Thus, in his first post-coup dispatch, the British Ambassador offered the Foreign Office a lengthy analysis which reflected very clearly his satisfaction with the new regime. Concluding his report, he wrote:[93]

> So far as we are concerned, his [Hikmat Sulaiman's] attitude has been *more* than correct. *He has gone out of his way* to give satisfaction and to declare his friendship. He has accepted and acted upon *every* suggestion I have made to him. He has assured me that he will honour the treaty of 1930, the railway convention and all other agreements concluded between His Majesty's Government and Iraq. [my emphasis]

Bakir Sidqi's known attitude to Britain was also friendly. The British discovered – rather to their surprise, it seems – that it was thanks to their efforts that Bakir Sidqi was secured, first, his post as an intelligence agent of the British military forces, which were stationed in the sort of no-man's-land that then existed between Iraq and Turkey,[94] and, then, his commission, by 'special recommendation of the British General Staff',[95] in the Iraqi army in January 1921. Bakir Sidqi's attitude to Britain was summed up by the Foreign Office as one of 'respect, probably sincere, for Great Britain'; but his admiration may have been soured by the British government's rejection of visits he had planned to England in 1934 and again in 1936.[96] Bakir Sidqi himself declared, in an interview with the *New York Times*, that his policy[97]

> towards the English is friendly. Our [Iraq's] connection with them is now 20 years old, and we have come to know them and they to know us. A friend already known is preferable to one not yet known. Were the English to abandon us, we would follow them seeking recovery of their friendship.

It was clearly in Bakir Sidqi's interest to say this, but it also appears that he was almost the archetype of the hard-working, hard-drinking military man without the kind of subtlety that would lead him to think in this way.

In spite of these statements, Bakir Sidqi was vaguely suspected by the British of having pro-German sympathies.[98] The Foreign Office does not provide any possible explanation of these suspicions, but it is known that Bakir Sidqi was in close touch with the German legation in Baghdad, and that he was in fact visiting Dr Grobba, the head of that legation, 'almost daily'.[99] Dr Grobba claims that, during these visits,

Bakir Sidqi persistently wanted to discuss the possibility of purchasing arms from Germany, and that he later succeeded in arranging for two representatives of German arms factories to visit Baghdad who were then handed an application from the Ministry of Defence for the purchase of five million marks' worth of arms.[100] More curious, perhaps, Bakir Sidqi is reported to have sought the advice of the Germans for the drawing up of a defence plan for Kurdistan; and in fact, General Heinz, a retired army general, arrived in Iraq later for such a purpose.[101] Other evidence relating to Bakir Sidqi's possible links with Germany appears to be lacking in substance.[102]

But given events in Spain at the time, it was perhaps natural that a military take-over would be suspected of having some links with Germany and/or Italy. Even harder to substantiate is the claim that, on the day of his assassination, Bakir Sidqi was in fact on his way to Berlin, via Turkey, in response to an invitation that he had received from Hitler; and it was a leak of this information that had caused the British to plan his assassination.[103]

Owing to the short life of the regime, we shall never know the nature and degree of Bakir Sidqi's German sympathies and whether he intended to bring Iraq closer to Germany. Had there been any clear proof of it, it would have been of extreme importance to Britain.[104] But since the suspicions were only vague, she was prepared to give him the benefit of the doubt.

The end of the coup government

Just as the coming to power of the new government did not alter the relationship between Iraq and Britain, so it did not make any changes in Iraqi political behaviour. It soon became clear that the new rulers of Iraq were not any different from the old ones, that each element in the government was pursuing its own interests, and that there were no strong bonds between them. Hikmat Sulaiman was widely respected for his intelligence, but some suspected that his cynicism verged on weakness. The British Ambassador relates an encounter with him which, in addition to clearly showing the immense degree of British influence in Iraq, also reflects the weakness of the Prime Minister's character. The Ambassador informed the Foreign Office how he told Hikmat Suliaman[105]

very sharply that his manners were bad ... when ... the time came to tell him what was thought about it [the Government's desire to buy arms from non-British sources] by all in London, I was in some difficulty because I had, as it were, to hold him up with one hand and hit him with the other. I hit him, nevertheless, and the blow was harder because it took him by surprise. . . . Hikmat was very near resignation and we came to the verge of a complete break when he dined with me a few nights later and I had to give him a jolt about the way the Ministry of Defence was behaving. . . . When he called on me the next day, he told the Oriental Secretary that, if I meant to hit him again, he would walk out and not come back.

In fact, there was much debate as to whether Sulaiman had the strength or the desire to stand up to Bakir Sidqi, who like himself had a Turkish background, although his parents were domiciled in Kurdistan. It was generally accepted that Hikmat Sulaiman was horrified at the murder of Ja'far al-'Askari, both because it was a deplorable act and because it made it impossible for him to fulfil his intention of asking Nuri al-Sa'id, al-'Askari's brother-in-law, to join the new government.[106] He seems to have been a negative character; indifferent to religion and pan-Arabism, and contemptuous of the fanaticism and peculation of Yasin al-Hashimi and his colleagues.[107] There is perhaps something in Yasin al-Hashimi's comment that Hikmat Sulaiman was possessed of very few original ideas and had no capacity at all for accomplishing them once they had been formulated.[108] Even people who saw him as rather a 'strong' man, such as Shaikh Hafiz Wahba, the Saudi Arabian Ambassador in London, were prepared to agree that the relationship between him and Bakir Sidqi was reminiscent of that between Reza Pahlevi and Sayyid Zia al-Din.[109] In the early stages of the coup government, comment on Hikmat Sulaiman varied from a claim that he was 'pretty obviously . . . merely a stalking-horse for Bakir Sidqi'[110] to a suggestion that he was sailing with a composure and determination above the immediate post-coup problems and might yet gather enough strength to be dominant over Bakir Sidqi.[111]

As for Bakir Sidqi, no doubts as to the strength of his character existed. But although he was respected, he was not loved. In the view of a member of the British Military Mission, 100 per cent of his army feared him, 75 per cent respected him, and 60 per cent loathed him.[112] This would seem to be confirmed by the lack of public demonstration at his death.[113] His undoubted ambition was thought to be quite possibly for his country as much as for himself, and it was suggested that 'for years signs had not been lacking that he had some deep game in mind'.[114] It was hotly disputed how much this led him to exceed the literal demands of his post as CGS and influence the Hikmat Sulaiman government. As late as June 1937, Hikmat Sulaiman claimed to be working in harmony with him, and that Bakir Sidqi was in full sympathy with the policy that he was trying to pursue. On the other hand, Naji Shaukat claimed that Bakir Sidqi's influence on policy was greater than that of the Prime Minister himself,[115] a view naturally shared by Jama'at al-Ahali. As already mentioned, the Ahali group, which formed the third 'component' of the new government, was represented in the cabinet by Ja'far Abu Timman, Kamil Chadirchi and Yusif 'Izz al-Din. Ja'far Abu Timman, who had served in one cabinet before, was a Baghdadi Shi'a merchant. He had always been an active nationalist, taking part in the 1920 rebellion and later organising the Hizb al-Watani. He was described as being well educated, and as the only person other than Hikmat Sulaiman in the cabinet who was 'in the least out-standing'.[116] However, another report throws doubts on Ja'far's ability, and referred to him as being[117]

> clearly unfitted for his present office [Minister of Finance]. His understanding of finance is that of a small merchant and restricted to the ordinary 'kambiala' - . . . Mr Hogg [his British advisor] has difficulty in getting him to grasp the first beginnings of Government finance. . . . Mr Hogg has been obliged to wrap up his loan proposals in a form calculated to appeal to Abu Timman's untutored intelligence.

But given that the only reference to Abu Timman's alleged failings is connected with Mr Hogg, it is possible that such unfavourable opinion was a reflection of a personal or political disagreement rather than lack of ability.

The second Ahali minister was Kamil Chadirchi. Unlike Abu Timman, Kamil Chadirchi was a Sunni and had never been a member of the pre-coup governments. But like Abu Timman, he was a Baghdadi notable, whose father had been the Mayor of Baghdad during the Ottoman period. He was also related to Mahmud Subhi al-Daftari, who was the Mayor of Baghdad in 1931 and was married to Kamil's sister. Kamil Chadirchi was reported to be perturbed by the anonymous letter which circulated at that time in connection with his sister's conduct and her unusual visits to King Faisal's estate (see chapter 3 above). In the early 1930s he had become active in the Ikha al-Watani party, and by 1933-4 succeeded in becoming a member of its executive com-mittee where he served alongside Yasin al-Hashimi and Rashid 'Ali. In 1934, however, he was persuaded to leave the Ikha al-Watani and join the Ahali group, where he became a prominent member of the opposition until the October coup when he became the Minister of Economics and Communications.

The third Ahali minister was Yusif 'Izz al-Din, a Sunni Kurd who was born in Baghdad, where he later held several official posts, including Director of Finance in 1930 and Director General of Land Settlement in 1934. His first cabinet appointment was in the coup government, where he served as Minister of Education.

A fourth minister, Salih Jabr, though not a member of the Ahali, shared the three ministers' opinion of the government's policy. Salih Jabr was born to a Shi'a family in Nasiriya where his father was a local dignitary. From Nasiriya he went to Baghdad, where he studied law and later worked as a political bureaucrat. In 1933 he served as the Minister of Education in the Madfa'i cabinet, a post he later held in the Sulaimani government.

The remaining two ministers in the original cabinet were 'Abd al-Latif Nuri, a Baghdadi Sunni, thought to be a relatively colourless personality, who had been a close friend of Nuri al-Sa'id and who was appointed because, as Minister of Defence, he would be no rival to Bakir Sidqi; and finally, we have Naji al-Asil, also Baghdadi Sunni, who had been the Hashimite semi-official representative in London until 1925, and who on his return to Iraq was offered a variety of official posts including the Director-General in the Ministry for Foreign Affairs.

To sum up, a review of the Sulaimani cabinet would show that, although its members were of remarkably similar social characteristics to their predecessors, they were relatively 'deprived' politicians, who seem to have resented their comparatively small share of political power. It should also be pointed out that the only ministers who could possibly be regarded as ideological resigned before the final collapse of the cabinet; that dissensions with other politicians can be seen essentially in terms of personal rivalry; and, finally, therefore, that the cabinet's refusal to take a different stand on external or internal affairs is comprehensible because of these facts.

It soon became clear that the alliance was dissolving, and that its ultimate collapse could not be long delayed. Bakir Sidqi's and Hikmat Sulaiman's public denials of having any communistic inclination themselves were soon turned into a hostile campaign against people who either did or were thought to have them, including members of Jama'at al-Ahali itself.[118] Furthermore, the government soon revived the maladministrative practices of their predecessors, against which they had claimed to have rebelled, and for the termination of which they

146

had made generous promises. For example, the freedom of the press, which the government had pledged to allow, was soon withdrawn from those newspapers daring to be critical of the government's policies.[119] Similarly, the parliamentary elections that they held were no different from the farce that parliamentary elections had always been in Iraq. Quite naturally, these elections brought the results desired by the government, more particularly, by Bakir Sidqi himself.[120] Moreover, not only was the armed suppression of tribal dissidents, for which the Hashimi cabinet had been so categorically condemned, soon revived, but it was now accompanied by a campaign of terror against the government's real or alleged political opponents. This wave of terror was carried into Baghdad itself, and among the personalities who were to lose their lives in this way was Dhia Yunis, a native of Mosul who had often been a deputy and had been a secretary to the Hashimi cabinet.[121] As to be expected, the Ahali ministers, angry at the government's exacerbation of problems it was supposed to have come to redress, resigned *en bloc* in June 1937. Fearing for their lives, Kamil Chadirchi and Ja'far Abu Timman initially left for Beirut; but on hearing that Bakir Sidqi had hired gangs to kill them, they proceeded north-westwards to Cyprus, where they remained in exile until the final fall of the government.

Following the resignation of the Ahali ministers just mentioned, 'Abbas Mahdi, Ja'far Hamandi, Muhammad 'Ali Mahmud and 'Ali Mahmud al-Shaikh 'Ali were appointed to the cabinet. In addition, Hikmat Sulaiman gave up the post of Minister of Interior, which he had held, in favour of Mustafa al-'Umari. Of these five, three were Sunnis, two Shi'a and, with the exception of 'Abbas Mahdi, who had held two cabinet appointments before, none had served in the government previously. Apart from 'Ali Mahmud al-Shaikh 'Ali, who was described as an 'extreme and often violent nationalist' (who was however thought to be mellowed by time and was further tamed by office),[122] the newcomers were thought to be 'dependable if undistinguished men',[123] but unimpressive, and offering little prospect of permanence.[124]

In the meantime, Bakir Sidqi, never failing in his capacity to be ruthless,[125] was pressing for even harsher treatment of the government's opponents, and his interference in the running of the state had become more blatant.[126] Added to this, his decadent behaviour was restrained by only a minimum of self-control. A very heavy drinker and notorious womaniser, his very name soon became a by-word for debauchery. Perhaps inevitably, even his supposedly professional relations with his own officers suffered from his immoral behaviour. According to a British report, there were[127] officers who are his bitter enemies by reason of his interfering with their womenfolk. There are complacent officers who have been given appointments to keep them – and their wives – near him. The better sort of his countrymen are reluctant to have their wives near him.

These pastime indulgences of Bakir Sidqi were shared by the Prime Minister himself, who is reported to have been a frequent visitor to the many nightclubs that had mushroomed in Baghdad during his reign.[128]

These immoral pursuits brought on the government the condemnation of the more conservative (and considerably more numerous) elements of society, while their indifference to pan-Arabism united the nationalist forces within the armed forces and the public at large.[129] Perhaps more important, although the non-implementation of the government's Policy Programme failed to gain them lasting popular support, its very publication had, nevertheless, frightened certain sectors of the population who viewed it as a potential threat to their traditionally privileged positions in the Iraqi social structure. As the British Ambassador expressed it, the government's programme[131]

in itself did much to disturb those (landowners, merchants and the like) who saw in it a possible threat to property. These may be said to represent a not unformidable body of opinion which, . . . would be ready enough to rally to anyone who seemed likely to shake the position of the Prime Minister. To them should be added the men who were driven from lucrative posts when he first came to power.

As will be seen below, by the beginning of August these opposition forces, which had been forming on many fronts, were to manifest themselves very dramatically. While the publicised resignation of the Ahali ministers[132] rendered a major blow to the government's increasingly weakening position with uncanny foresight, Zakia George, an Iraqi singer and an ex-mistress of Bakir Sidqi, was chanting:

You who dig up wells
Don't make them very deep
For the days might change
And you yourself might fall in them.

'Like Caesar before the Ides of March', Bakir Sidqi is reported to have received numerous warnings, chiefly from women;[133] but, perhaps overestimating the 'invincibility' of the small army of detectives that usually surrounded him, he paid heed to none of them. On 11 August, the fourth anniversary of the Assyrian revolt, Bakir Sidqi left Baghdad for Mosul *en route* for Turkey. In Mosul he was joined by Muhammad Jawad, the Chief of the IRAF. On the evening of the fatal day, while the two generals were resting at the Air Officers Mess inside Mosul's airport, they were approached by a private who shot them both dead at point-blank range. The assassin was immediately arrested, and Hikmat Sulaiman asked for him and any other suspects to be sent to Baghdad. However, refusing to comply with the Prime Minister's request, General Amin al-'Umari, the military commander of Mosul, who was known for his pan-Arab views, assumed control of the town; and two days later, after succeeding in obtaining the support of the military commanders of Kirkuk and Baghdad, he presented the government with a list of demands, which called for:[134]

(a) the banishment of all officers who supported the coup d'état;
(b) the return of the political exiles;
(c) the removal of Bakir Sidqi's friends from high positions;
(d) the formation of a military court, under the presidency of a close friend of Ja'far Pasha, to investigate the events at Mosul; and
(e) the passing of legislation forbidding participation in politics by army leaders.

With the issuing of this ultimatum, the first circle of Iraqi coups and counter-coups was completed. Realising the impossibility of fulfilling these demands, the Prime Minister tendered his resignation to the King, who on 16 August requested Jamil al-Madfa'i to form a new government.

Thus ended Iraq's first coup government. Given the circumstances of its coming to power and the numerous, though by no means unique, shortcomings of its conduct of affairs, perhaps it was remarkable that it had lasted as long as it had. The coup of October 1936 was clearly no manifestation of a renaissance in Iraq's public administration. Rather, it was yet another attempt, though somewhat different, to gain personal power; and as such the coup government's failure to effect any significant changes in the country's socio-political structure were understandable, if not inevitable.

Chapter 7

Coups and counter-coups

Iraqi governments between August 1937 and May 1941

The assassination of the two main coup leaders and the disintegration
of the cabinet they had brought about marked the end of Iraq's first
coup government. The army, however, was to continue as an effective
instrument of politics. The main reason the King called upon Jamil
al-Madfa'i to form a government was that the latter enjoyed the support
of army officers: namely, Salah al-Din al-Sabbagh, Mahmud Salman,
Fahmi Sai'd, Kamil Shabib, 'Aziz Yamulki, Husain Fauzi and Amin
al-'Umari – all known for their sympathy with pan-Arabism. It is
reported that Jamil al-Madfa'i refused to form a government unless he
received an undertaking from these officers that they would refrain
from intervening in political affairs forthwith.[1] Such an undertaking
was granted, and Jamil al-Madfa'i followed this initial success by taking
over the post of Minister of Defence himself, hoping thereby to shut
off one possible source of rivalry and conflict. At the same time, anxious
to let bygones be bygones, he successfully resisted demands on him to
open an inquiry into the deaths of Ja'far al-'Askari and Bakir Sidqi and
instead showed inclinations to let one murder cancel out the other.[2]
Furthermore, aware of the obvious need for maintaining the maximum
degree of unity within the armed forces, he pledged not to punish those
officers who had collaborated with Bakir Sidqi, and at the same time
appointed the above-mentioned seven officers ('The Seven') to eminent
positions with the hope of silencing them.

But the situation was much too complex to be solved so simply.
First of all, the re-institution of a 'constitutional' government in Baghdad
meant that the considerable, and usually active, number of the country's
political elite who had fled during the Sulaiman government felt able

to return. Apart from former members of the Hashimi cabinet, such as Nuri al-Sa'id and Rashid 'Ali, these included 'Ali Jaudat, Mahmud Mukhlis, Rustum Haidar, Taha al-Hashimi, the former CGS, and a further number of politicians and army officers.[3] With their return, Baghdad once more became the scene of intense political rivalry and intrigue. Taha al-Hashimi, for example, on his return demanded to be reinstated as CGS, the post he had held until the Sidqi coup; but to his disappointment he was offered a seat in Parliament instead, as was Rustum Haidar. A more resourceful rival and intriguer, Nuri al-Sa'id, was thought to be safer out of the country altogether. He was thus offered the legation in London; when that was refused, the British Ambassador was to[4]

> use his influence . . . to persuade Nuri Sa'id to go to London and,
> failing that, to seek your [the Foreign Office] consent to a plan . . .
> to the effect that he should be sent on a mission of mediation
> between the Arabs of Palestine and the Jews . . . if Nuri stayed in
> Baghdad and kept his house open there would inevitably gather
> about him all the disaffected elements in the country who, sooner
> or later, would force him, willy nilly, to make a bid for power.

After much debate between the British Ambassador and Nuri al-Sa'id, Nuri declined to accept the Prime Minister's offer, though he agreed to leave Iraq temporarily for a visit abroad.

Nuri was not the only source of intrigue, however. Hikmat Sulaiman, for example, though believed to be on 'friendly' terms with Jamil al-Madfa'i,[5] was still at odds with some of his former colleagues in the cabinet, namely Ja'far Abu Timman, Kamil Chadirchi, Yusif 'Izz al-Din, and Salih Jabr; and, fearing a come-back of Nuri al-Sa'id (particularly since Nuri was related to the late Ja'far al-'Askari and was bound to seek his revenge), he was now rallying political support against him. In addition, with the return of such forceful characters as Nuri al-Sa'id, King Ghazi's anxieties, which were sedated during the coup government (in a way this seems to have quite literally been the case, since His Majesty was known to have consumed large quantities of whisky with Bakir Sidqi), were now revived.

All of these men, including the Prime Minister himself, are known to have had their supporters among army officers, and that is an important reason why the isolation of the army from political affairs was not an easy task. The officers, for their part, were by no means reluctant to be drawn into political activities. One important reason for this was their reaction against political events in Palestine and their support of pan-Arabism in general. This consciousness must have affected their attitude towards the central government in Baghdad, which was, as they must have been aware, quite incapable of applying significant pressure on the British government and of expressing more than verbal support to the Palestinian cause.

This political involvement of army officers was also reinforced by internal politics within the army itself. In spite of the government's efforts to silence the 'Seven', and the appointment of Husain Fauzi, the most professional and least political among them, as CGS, army officers continued to rally behind political leaders in Baghdad. This attitude was strengthened by the fact that, apart from dismissing 'fifteen-twenty'[6] officers who were closely associated with Bakir Sidqi, the government refused to take measures against other officers who were believed to have collaborated with the coup government. The end result of these actions, or lack of them, was that the army was in fact still very much a platform for and a source of political intrigue; and in that way it remained a political force whose influence was to be sought by those in office as well as those out of it.

Thanks to the inherent weaknesses of the Iraqi political system, there were still more, and naturally more familiar, sources of intrigue. For example, in December 1937 the Madfa'i government decided to hold elections for a new Parliament. Perhaps as was to be expected, these elections departed not an inch from the old familiar pattern. This is how the British Ambassador described the occasion:[7]

> The dumbshow of the Iraqi elections took place some days ago and, as was to be expected, all the Prime Minister's nominees . . . secured their seats in Parliament. It cannot be said that they won them, for, in this country, the unhappy elector has no choice but to vote for the name that is put before him, and outside the Prime Minister's list there were no names. And so Jamil Madfa'i may be said to have assured himself of a robust majority. But I much doubt whether he has thus girt himself with any new strength. Indeed, it is more probable that from now onwards fresh difficulties will begin to gather about him. I mean the kind of difficulty that will sooner or later bring about his fall, for the present calm that always goes before elections is over and the time has come for malcontents to sniff the air for trouble.

Familiar as this type of election was, by following the traditional pattern Jamil al-Madfa'i demonstrated a remarkable lack of political acumen. For, it will be remembered, it was Jamil al-Madfa'i who replaced

'Ali Jaudat as prime minister in 1935, when the latter had to give up
that post largely because of the wave of protest ne had set in motion
through his corrupt handling of the elections. By thus denying his
opponents even a constitutional platform from which they could air their
criticisms, Jamil al-Madfa'i was obviously tempting them to look
elsewhere for support, either to the army or to the opposition circles
that were forming outside, or to both.

This situation was not helped by an unusually dramatic quarrel that
took place in the Senate. On 17 March, speaking in the Senate, Rashid
'Ali attacked the previous Sulaiman government and deplored the
methods that they had adopted to overthrow the Hashimi government.
Angered by Rashid 'Ali's 'double standards', Jamil al-Madfa'i, who had
himself been thrown out of office in 1935 by a tribal uprising engineered
by al-Hashimi and Rashid 'Ali,[8]

> rounded on Rashid Ali, (. . . upbraided him with unparliamentary
> frankness for his own political past. . . .) Some outspoken attacks
> on the work of Yasin's cabinet developed in this manner and the
> surviving members thereof felt obliged to take action to defend their
> reputation. They accordingly submitted a joint petition . . . . when
> this petition came before the Chamber there was a good deal of
> public washing of dirty linen.

Following this debate, the ex-ministers of the Hashimi cabinet blamed
the Prime Minister for breaking a pledge to hold the balance between
them and their enemies; and in turn, they no longer felt obliged to
abstain from openly intriguing against him and his cabinet.[9] Their first
direct target was Mustafa al-'Umari, a former member of the Sulaiman
cabinet and now the Minister for the Interior. They published a leaflet
giving a short account of ten instances in which it was alleged that he
had accepted large bribes.[10]

Such efforts by the opposition to debase the government were made
easier by the existing traditional rivalry between members of the
cabinet themselves and by the fact that the corruption and insolence of
some of these were known to the public. In Mr Edmond's view at that
time,[11]

> any non-official civilian (and many officials), asked about the
> internal situation, would reply: 'There is universal disgust; the
> Prime Minister is flabby, the Minister of Finance insolent and
> overbearing; the Minister of the Interior is corrupt, the Minister for
> Foreign Affairs has a similar reputation. . . . The Minister of Justice
> is a cipher; administrative incompetence is the rule and nobody can

get anything done; corruption is rife; the police have gone to the dogs; and so on'.

It is an unfortunate truth that the feeling of the Iraqi polity was in itself practically inconsequential; and, given the virtual absence of constitutional channels through which the populace could seek to change political realities, perhaps the government could have outlived these adversaries. In the circumstances, the most the public could do was to rally behind disgruntled politicians and thereby add momentum to the political tussle that was raging in the capital.

Unfortunately for the government, their political insensitivity was not confined to their attitude to the sector of population that did not count (i.e. the majority), but was extended to the sector that counted: namely the army. In January 1938 the Prime Minister gave up the post of Minister of Defence in favour of Sabih Najib, a relatively junior officer. This appointment in itself would have sufficed to generate a wave of antagonism within the ranks of senior officers. But to it was also added the 'tactless and over-forceful behaviour'[12] of the new Minister. In order to, as it were, break the backbone of the political blocs within the army, he followed a policy of 'divide and rule'. After depriving the CGS of much of his powers,[13] his target was the 'group of Four',[14] the officers known as the 'Golden Square' who were the most politically active among the 'Seven' – the pan-Arab bloc which the Prime Minister had unsuccessfully tried to 'de-politicise'.[15] While ordering the transfer of the 'Four' to the 'hinterland', the new Minister elevated to comparatively powerful positions a counter-group of officers known for their Iraqi nationalism.[16] Ironically, this move succeeded only in bringing the 'Four' to Baghdad itself, where they made no secret of their divergence with the government: they held regular meetings at the house of Nuri al-Sa'id, which were also attended by a number of important people such as Taha al-Hashimi and Yunis al-Sab'awi.[17]

In February this alliance between the 'Four', who were critical of the government's cool attitude towards pan-Arabism[18] and to the government's opponents was given a further boost when a gathering held in memory of the late Yasin al-Hashimi was turned into a pan-Arab meeting when a number of eminent speakers, including Nuri al-Sa'id, made speeches reasserting their identification with Arab brotherhood and expressing sympathy for the prolonged sufferings of the Palestinian people.

While opposition to the government was growing in strength, the government itself was facing crisis from within. In May Jalal Baban, the Minister of Interior, was implicated in a case of bribery which was serious enough for him to resign, and it was believed that the Prime Minister was considering appointing Muhammad 'Ali Mahmud, a former member of the Sulaiman cabinet, in his place. As soon as the news was heard,[19]

> a deputation of some 30 officers went to al-'Umari and called upon him to visit the Prime Minister at once to explain that the Army objected to the selection of a colleague of Hikmat Sulaiman . . . he was further to say that the Army wanted Nuri back. . . . That night all army units were standing by, not on the order of any supreme commander but by agreement between the unit commanders themselves. The appointment of Muhammad 'Ali was then prevented, but Jamil Madfa'i was elusive regarding Nuri. Since that evening the Prime Minister has been a regular visitor to the Military Club, seeking to cultivate closer relations with the Officers.

In spite of these efforts, it seems that the Prime Minister failed to rally a significant number of army officers behind him; and, having thus failed to join them, he decided to try and beat them. Perhaps he was not so unique in thinking that the worst possible reactions on repression can be forestalled or defused by the introduction of additional repressive measures. Thus, under the pretext of curbing communist activity, of which the British Ambassador says he had not heard,[20] the government added an amendment to the already strict Baghdad Penal Code, which could enable them to impose severe penalties[21] against persons who propagated on behalf of communism, anarchism, nihilism or *similar movements*.[22] Of these 'similar movements', among the first victims were Rashid 'Ali and six others - three of whom were army officers, three lawyers - who were ordered to leave Baghdad and live in a provincial town. There is no evidence that any of those banished was or had been involved in any 'ideological' activity, and it seems that the government's move was based primarily on their desire to generally weaken the opposition. Between them, those exiled represented, in fact, a cross-section of the opposition: Rashid 'Ali[23] was an ambitious politician with a tribal following, three of the others were known former supporters of Bakir Sidqi, while the remaining three were known for their sympathy with pan-Arabism and presumably with the 'Four'.

Clearly, this was a bold challenge to the government's opponents, in the face of which it might have been too optimistic to expect them to remain silent. Not surprisingly, therefore, on 24 December a group of officers, consisting mainly of the 'Seven' and led by Husain Fauzi, the CGS, decided to stage another military take-over. On that evening Husain Fauzi concentrated a strong detachment of armoured cars and cavalry at Hinaidi, on the outskirts of Baghdad. Shortly afterwards, he sought and was later granted an audience with the King, to whom he complained about the general conduct of the Madfa'i government (which he and his colleagues had put in office fifteen months previously) and demanded its replacement by one that should include Nuri al-Sa'id and Taha al-Hashimi. After some hesitation,[24] King Ghazi thereupon called on Nuri al-Sa'id to form a government, which he did the following day.

The fourth coup

Nuri al-Sa'id was not a newcomer to Iraqi politics. He had been in and out of government since the state's foundation in 1920, and by the time of his new appointment he had served in fourteen cabinets, twice as a prime minister. His new government included two Shi'as, and three of its seven members were serving in the cabinet for the first time. These were Taha al-Hashimi (Yasin's brother and ex-CGS), Mahmud Subhi al-Daftari (ex-mayor of Baghdad and Kamil Chadirchi's brother-in-law), and Omar Nadmi (a Baghdad-educated lawyer who had at one time been the Mutasarrif of Mosul).

Like its predecessors, Nuri al-Sa'id's government marked its arrival in power by a plethora of promises of far-reaching reforms; reforms for which a genuine need existed and through which public support would be gained. Less than two weeks after coming to power, the Prime Minister made a broadcast to the Iraqi nation describing the many weaknesses of the state's constitution and, among other things, explaining the urgent need for reforming the country's electoral laws which, in his opinion, had been based on anachronistic legislation. He also spoke at length about how he envisaged true democracy and how, in order to achieve that goal, his government would allow the formation of political parties and give the press the long-awaited freedom it needed so much. [25]

Whether Nuri al-Sa'id was sincere in his promises is a point of little relevance. What is important was that he could not allow the nurturing of a 'liberal monster' which could grow to claim him among its first victims. For the intense intrigue and rivalry that ultimately led to the fall of previous governments were still riddling the Iraqi political system, and it was thus a question of sheer political survival for Nuri al-Sa'id to promote his own supporters and at the same time to endeavour to suppress his oponents.

Now that Nuri al-Sa'id and his supporters were in power, the opposition was taken over by Jamil al-Madfa'i and his followers. There were also, of course, those who supported neither al-Madfa'i nor Nuri, such as the Hikmat Sulaiman group, the Ahali ex-ministers, and the officers who supported Sidqi. Given this set-up, it was not surprising that Nuri al-Sa'id should harbour a feeling of insecurity, which, like many previous leaders, he thought could be diminished by installing his 'men' in Parliament. Therefore the elections for a new Parliament, which were held in February 1939, were little more than a public exercise whose aim was to bring the cabinet's nominees into the Chamber.[26] Discouraged by this attitude of the government, and perhaps fearing for their own safety, the opposition groups seem to have preferred their existing loosely structured alliances, and made no effort to form any political parties.

Later events proved that the opposition's fears of government reprisals were justified. On coming to power in December, the cabinet immediately placed five senior army officers on retirement,[27] while a number of others were transferred from their commands. On 1 March the cabinet ordered the arrest of fifteen officers and civilians, including Hikmat Sulaiman, on charges of plotting to overthrow the regime. Two weeks later the accused appeared before a military court, which found eight of them guilty and sentenced seven, including Hikmat Sulaiman, to death. Unfortunately, the records of this trial have been destroyed, so it is not possible to evaluate the evidence presented before the court. However, the impartiality of the court was quite naturally put to question; and, since the majority of the accused had been participants in the Sidqi coup, opponents of the government viewed the whole affair as an attempt by Nuri to avenge the death of Ja'far al-'Askari as well as his own forced exile in October 1936. Perhaps in gratitude to Hikmat Sulaiman's adherence to the Anglo–Iraqi Treaty while in office, the British Ambassador made persistent and forceful representations on his behalf, with the result that Hikmat Sulaiman's sentence was commuted to five years' imprisonment.[28]

As will be seen later, this harsh treatment of the opposition proved to be one of the reasons for the government's ultimate fall.

In addition to these difficulties, 1939 brought a new set of difficult problems which were of both national and international dimensions, and which shook the foundations of the country's political elite as well as its general public. The first of these was the sudden death of King

Ghazi on 3 April. On that day, His Majesty was supposedly driving from his radio station to Zuhur Palace when his car left the road and hit an electric lamp-post. The King sustained a number of serious injuries, which led to his death an hour later. The details of the accident were so confused and contradictory that opinions then and since have conflicted sharply over the true nature of the King's death. Both Rashid 'Ali and al-Sabbagh,[29] for example, suspected Nuri al-Sa'id of having planned the King's murder, while the general public accused the British intelligence, with or without the co-operation of Nuri. My own impression is that the official version does pose a number of questions.[30]

No matter what the true circumstances of the King's death were, it led to a public outcry which de-stabilised the government and added to the undercurrents of conflict within the ruling elite. The King's personal failings were soon buried, and he was now remembered as the hero of pan-Arabism in general and the Palestinian cause in particular.[31] This was shown very clearly during the procession at his funeral, which the British Ambassador has described vividly:[32]

> From early morning until late at night the main thoroughfares and squares of the town were crowded with mourners, wailing, beating their breasts and tearing their hair in the intensity of their grief. There were as many women and children as men among the crowds and hundreds lay sobbing in the streets . . . tendentious rumours of all kinds were soon in circulation. One that was persistently repeated was the story that the English had killed the King. . . . Another story . . . was that Nuri Sa'id had murdered King Ghazi and several groups of mourners were heard chanting the slogan 'Thou shalt answer for the blood of Ghazi, O Nuri'. . . . The Royal funeral . . . proceeded slowly along the 2 miles route to the mausoleum near Adhamiya. . . . the route was lined by thousands of people. Some stood and watched silently with tears streaming down their faces; others mostly women, abandoned themselves to hysterical griefs, rending their garments and covering their heads and breasts with mud from the gutters. It was strange to see and hear soldiers and even policemen sobbing like children. . . . Reports from Basra and other provincial centres indicated that public excitement was dangerously high and was being worked up to an artificial pitch by official or semi-official encouragement.

Like that of his father, King Ghazi's death dealt a serious blow to Iraq's fragile centre of power. As argued earlier, though of limited effective power, the monarchy provided a balancing, at times crucial, instrument for the country's political structure. A swift containment of the country's 'imbalance' required a vision, a charisma and a determination that King Ghazi's effective successor, 'Abdul-Ilah, seems to have been lacking (in fact, King Ghazi was succeeded by his infant son Faisal, but since Faisal was only four years old, 'Abdul-Ilah, son of the late King 'Ali, was appointed as regent.) A retrospective analysis of 'Abdul-Ilah's personality clearly shows his inability to lead a country through serious crises such as those experienced in Iraq in 1941. The Regent can be summed up, perhaps a little cynically, as the typical 'nice guy'. His intentions, at least from Britain's point of view, were good, but his performance was very weak. It is indeed a damning comment on the political fragility of Britain's position in Iraq that the many comments on the Regent's ineffectiveness and lack of realism, and the absence of any popular support for him, were off-set by the one simple fact that he was pro-British. It was with an irony that was as unconscious as it was strong that Anthony Eden admitted that, while he was 'not . . . a very strong character . . . there can be no question of his loyalty'.[33] It must be rather unusual for the acting head of a state to be commended for his 'loyalty' to another state. In addition, a review of his political career shows that the Regent all too often had to be encouraged in his official duties, or discouraged from rash schemes, by British diplomats. The clearest proofs of this come from a period we will examine later from other angles: for example, when Jamil al-Madfa'i agreed to carry on as prime minister for a month longer than intended (August–September 1941), the Regent failed to use the respite to find a new Prime Minister and, 'though quite willing to air [his] views on what ought to be done, [was] waiting expectantly for me [the British Ambassador] to make all the necessary moves to solve the crisis.'[34] He also had to be encouraged in the assertion of his authority by the British Ambassador, and was told to make himself more popular and even to carry out obvious duties such as distributing decorations, travelling in the country, meeting people and so on.[35] Part of the Regent's reply to these suggestions was the absurdly pathetic announcement that he had decided to make closer contact with the army officers by inviting them to play polo.[36] His judgments seem often to have been unrealistic and even laughably legalistic. For example, his claim in early April 1941 that 'the people in Iraq are getting tired of Palestinian agitators, and that the majority of responsible leaders favour cooperation with Britain',[37] surely shows a somewhat tenuous grasp of reality. However, in all fairness it should be added that, in a crisis, the Regent could show a high degree of courage, as is indicated by his threat to resign and his refusal to dissolve Parliament at the end of January 1941. The fact that, as we shall see, he fled from Iraq does not disprove this. Certainly it appears to be true that after the coup his personal liberty and probably even his life were threatened, and one cannot therefore blame him for decamping. But over all, one must accept the British analysis of him as 'not a strong personality',[38] with a character that was even 'too colour-less to impress itself on the country'.[39]

The second problem that de-stabilised Iraq during 1939 was of international dimensions. While sirens of war were sounding in Europe during the latter half of 1939, the Arab nationalists in Iraq saw an opportunity to achieve the true independence they had dreamt of for so long. The oncoming conflict in Europe would offer them an oppor-tune time to rise against their new masters. The swift German over-running of Poland in September left no doubt in their minds that Germany would emerge victorious in the European conflict that was sure to come. This impression, together with their aspirations for ultimate independence, was further manipulated by the arrival of Palestinian and Syrian political refugees in Baghdad and by an intensi-fication of German activities in Iraq itself. One report claimed that 'The Germans are just pouring money into the land, and we are wondering what 300 of them can be doing in Baghdad alone . . . When one knows that they are only allowed to take 30 Marks out of the country.'[40]

The popularity that Germany and her products were gaining in Iraq is indicated by the fact that both imports and exports between the two countries had doubled between 1935 and 1938. But in addition to the efforts that were made by German officials and residents to strengthen Iraqi–German relations, their attitude to the 'natives', unlike that of the British, seems to have been altogether more respectful. For example, whereas the one German kindergarten that then existed in Baghdad admitted both German and Arab children, there is no evidence that Arab children went to its British counterparts. Similarly, if the tone of a letter that was sent by British residents in Baghdad to the Foreign Office is representative of their attitude towards the local community, it would be very surprising if much love was lost between them and the Iraqi population. Complaining about the increasing influence of Germany in Iraq, the residents ended their letter by saying: 'We Britishers are eating dirt here in a way that is galling to us. You know . . . that no Oriental respects you and fears you (it has to be fear for they can never love) unless you are strong, and if we sit down under this it will be a crying shame.'[41]

The attitude of the Foreign Office itself and of British officials to

Iraqis and to their aspirations seem to have been similarly insensitive. For example, there were quite frequent references to Iraqis, including cabinet ministers, as 'typically Oriental', 'has negro blood', etc. Then, in 1939, the Foreign Office showed remarkable lack of tact by appointing Mr Main, who had been commissioned by the Jewish Agency to write *Palestine at the Cross-Roads*, as the press officer to their Embassy in Baghdad.[42]

These possible animosities between Arab and British residents in Iraq must have been made worse, and were naturally partly caused, by Britain's failure to fulfil her promises to the Arabs made during the First World War; by her support of Zionism and harsh treatment of Palestinian nationalists; by her failure to supply Iraq with the arms it needed; and, more immediately, by the popular belief, no matter how unsubstantiated, about her involvement in King Ghazi's death.

In this anti-British environment, Nuri al-Sa'id's support of Britain surpassed even that of the leaders of her own dominions. Already in April he instructed the Iraqi Legation in Berlin to deliver a strong note to the Wilhelmstrasse protesting against German subversive and propaganda activities in Iraq, with the result that, after being told that his country was an 'appendage of Britain', the unfortunate Iraqi delegate was turned out of his legation premises and offered 'entirely inadequate' alternative accommodation at a rental far beyond his means.[43] At that time, intensive and evidently successful German (and Italian) activities did exist in Iraq, and the Prime Minister's concern was therefore justifiable. But from the point of view of the nationalists, who may or may not have been his 'natural' opponents and who thought it in Iraq's interest not to antagonise the Germans, the Prime Minister's attitude towards the curbing of these activities was an over-enthusiastic one, and the Foreign Office themselves felt that the language used was perhaps rather strong.[44]

Thus, we see Nuri Al-Sa'id, an experienced politician, failing at a crucial time to keep the balance and forestall a reinforcement of the army's intervention in politics that was sure to follow. Perhaps, as the British Ambassador had described him early in 1939, Nuri was 'no longer the man he was'.[45] But if he had felt unable to share the sympathies of the nationalists at that time, he should at least have concealed his own. Instead, when the European war broke out in September 1939, Nuri al-Sa'id, without consulting his colleagues or, more importantly, the 'Seven', preceded Australia, South Africa and Canada in severing diplomatic relations with Germany. On the same day, Dr Grobba was informed that he and his staff must leave Iraq within twenty-four hours, while German nationals of military age were interned and later handed over to the government of India.[46] Further-more, Nuri told the British Ambassador of his intention to declare war on Germany. As the British Ambassador suggested, this over-play of virtuous performance as Britain's friend[47] was met with disapproval from many quarters, including three members of his cabinet (Rustum Haidar, Taha al-Hashimi and Mahmud Subhi al-Daftari), and, more importantly, by the 'Seven', particularly Husain Fauzi, the CGS, and Amin al-'Umari, the commander of the first division. With the arrival of the Mufti of Jerusalem, Hajj Amin al-Husaini (who had left Palestine in the aftermath of the 1936 strike), in Baghdad in October 1939, together with a number of Palestinian and Syrian nationalists,[48] added force was given to the opponents of Nuri al-Sa'id's pro-British policy. Contacts were immediately established between Hajj Amin and the 'Four', as well as with other nationalists, and his political views were now to become all too significant in Iraqi politics.

In addition, there were the cabinet's traditional rivals, consisting mainly of politicians out of office, who would naturally exploit an opportunity to give their opposition a 'patriotic' line. They too now sought the friendship of the 'Four', appealing to them to overthrow 'so and so's cabinet because it is so and so . . . Rustum Haidar because he is a Shi'a . . . the other because he is a traitor . . . and the other because he is a communist, etc.'[49] The cabinet's position was also weakened by the assassination of Rustum Haidar, the Minister of Interior, in January 1940. Both Taha al-Hashimi and al-Sabbagh imply that Nuri had somehow been an accomplice to that murder.[50] But, again, whatever the truth of the matter, Nuri seems to have used the opportunity to clamp down on the opposition, accusing two ex-ministers of having been behind the crime and putting them into prison. Unfortunately for the Prime Minister, these measures, together with the actual incident itself, gave the opposition further cause to work against the government. The Prime Minister was naturally aware of this, and of the unpopularity of his pro-British policy. He was aware too that the most ominous threat to his position came, on the army's side, from the 'Seven', and on the political side from Rashid 'Ali. Thus, in what appears to have been a shrewd move to weaken and/or control both of these forces, quite unexpectedly, Nuri al-Sa'id tendered his resignation to the Regent on 18 February and the recommendation that Rashid 'Ali should be called to form the next cabinet, which should include himself as Foreign Minister and Taha al-Hashimi as Defence Minister. As al-Sabbagh suggests in his memoirs, should this happen, Nuri would thereby associate his most formidable rival, Rashid 'Ali, with his own foreign policy and would therefore stand a better chance of receiving the endorsement of the 'Seven'.[51]

What al-Sabbagh does not add (although he later admits to having fallen into a trap set up by Nuri) is that, should Nuri's scheme fail, it would, as was proved later, lead to disagreement within the 'Seven' themselves, which might result in a split and in ultimate weakening of the group. Nuri knew then that considerable animosity existed between Husain Fauzi, the CGS, and Taha al-Hashimi, the Minister of Defence, mainly owing to the latter's persistent interference in the functions of the CGS and in the daily running of the army.[52] He also knew that Amin al-'Umari was resentful towards him for not having included his cousin, Mustafa al-'Umari, in the cabinet, and for the Prime Minister's suggestion that Amin al-'Umari should be relieved from duties after the latter had a leg amputated in an operation.[53] As was expected, when Nuri resigned, the 'Seven' wanted to have their say in the formation of the cabinet. For that purpose, Husain Fauzi and Amin al-'Umari met the Regent and objected strongly to the inclusion of either Nuri or Taha in the proposed new cabinet. After much debate, the Regent refused the generals' request and instead relieved them of their appointments and placed them on pension. Following this, failing to draw the support of any but one of their other five comrades, Husain Fauzi and Amin al-'Umari reacted by attempting a coup against the government, which was immediately foiled by a successful counter-coup organised by the 'Four'. According to al-Sabbagh, the 'Four' felt compelled to do this in order to maintain the unity of the state and because, to him, Taha was a 'dear friend'; but, quite rightly, he later expresses regret at having done so and at having inadvertently played into Nuri's hands.[54]

As it turned out, the whole affair proved to be a short-sighted blunder, which weakened both the government and the army and was thus detrimental to the welfare of the state as a whole. However, in the short term, with the generals fighting each other rather than him, Nuri's *coup de théâtre* seems to have achieved some of its aims. Though failing to bring Rashid 'Ali (who, perhaps because of his friendship with Husain Fauzi, refused to head or serve in a cabinet that included Nuri) into the cabinet, he succeeded in breaking up the unity of the 'Seven'. With the approval of the 'Four', the Regent called upon Nuri to resume office as prime minister and he agreed, using the opportunity to reshuffle his old cabinet; as a result, three former colleagues were left out, including Mahmud Subhi al-Daftari, who had been one of three ministers opposed to Nuri's foreign policy (the other two being Rustum Haidar, who, as we have seen, had been assassinated a month earlier, and Taha al-Hashimi, who retained his post in the new cabinet and who was a close friend of the 'Four', particularly al-Sabbagh).

As was becoming customary, one of the first acts of the new cabinet was to purge the army of suspected supporters of the fallen generals, while at the same time promoting those who thwarted their move against the government. In this way, though weakening the army *per se* by depriving it of some of its officers, the end result of the staged cabinet crisis was the strengthening of the army's hold, especially of the 'Four', on the cabinet. By this action at such a crucial time in Iraqi history, and by his remarkable lack of vision, Nuri al-Sa'id put the fate of the country in the hands of men who, though driven by unquestionably sincere and patriotic motives to serve the nation and through it the Arab people in general, were of limited political experience and naturally lacking in their understanding of complex international affairs.

The leader, and by far the most powerful, of the 'Four' was General Salah al-Din al-Sabbagh. Salah al-Din was born in Mosul in 1890 where his Lebanese father (who as a merchant had emigrated to Mosul during the middle of the nineteenth century) and Iraqi mother lived. After receiving his school education in Mosul and Beirut, he went to Istanbul where he studied at the Turkish Military College. On graduation in 1915, he was commissioned with the Turkish army and served in the First World War in Palestine and Macedonia. Shortly afterwards he was taken prisoner by the Allies, but was later released to join Amir Faisal's Arab army in Syria. In 1920 he accompanied Faisal to Iraq, and a year later was gazetted in the newly formed Iraqi army. As an officer, he was later reported to be a 'hard worker . . . has good ideas and also quickly picks up and appropriates suggestions put to him'.[55] He was then sent to attend courses in India and England, where he met his English wife. In his memoirs he recalls with evident bitterness how, when he married his wife in 1931, Nuri al-Sa'id, then Minister of Defence, refused to give her a passport and called for Salah's dismissal from the army, not for nationalistic reasons but because Nuri thought that his wife would be superior to Salah and could not be expected to live in Iraqi society.[56] Salah defied Nuri's orders, but his marriage was not successful and in any case his wife died of an illness three years later.[57]

Salah's mixed background, coupled with his experience in Palestine and Syria, seems to have greatly influenced his sensitive nature and given him a broader horizon, extending beyond the geographical frontiers of Iraq. His passionately written and at times moving memoirs reveal a man of rare dedication and idealism. He seems to have been a rock of reliability and friendship, and in his dealings with others reveals a touching sincerity which often verges on naïvety. He glamorised the past achievements of the Arab Empire and, through his euphoric attempts to re-create it, failed to see either the aberrations of his ancestors or the deviousness of some of his contemporaries. Salah's almost child-like sincerity is revealed through the history of his dealing with others, particularly Nuri, whom he appears to have blindly trusted and supported. He makes frank references to Nuri having plotted Rustum Haidar's assassination owing to the latter's knowledge of the true circumstances of King Ghazi's 'accident'.

These references, and al-Sabbagh's implication that he was aware of the inside stories, would suggest that he himself could not have been far removed from the alleged conspiracies. Al-Sabbagh was a main factor in elevating 'Abdul-Ilah to the Regency and in keeping Nuri in office. [58] He implies that this was a sort of *quid pro quo* whose ultimate aim was the serving of the Arab cause. However, in this and other dealings his recollections show how often he was only too easily 'led up the garden path'. A clearly selfless man, al-Sabbagh's most immediate and cherished aim appears to have been the independence and liberation of Palestine and Syria. As he himself expressed it in his last letter from exile to his family, [59]

Had I been an Iraqi nationalist, I would have become more endeared to the English than Nuri al-Sa'id and 'Abdul-Ilah, but it is my sacrifice for beloved Palestine and Syria which led to the condition I am in now.

Driven by such sentiments, al-Sabbagh soon formed a close friendship with Palestinian and Syrian nationalists, particularly with Hajj Amin, whom he respected and admired profoundly. [60] Nuri al-Sa'id was aware of this, and of the decisive influence al-Sabbagh had on other officers and through them on the army. He therefore made consistent efforts to control him. During his attempt to convince the 'Seven' of his plan to delcare war on Germany, for example, he also suggested that Iraq should actually send two battalions (over one-third of the army) either to the Libyan desert or to the Balkans to fight on the side of the Allies *under the command of al-Sabbagh*. [61] Jointly with the rest of his colleagues, al-Sabbagh categorically rejected Nuri's plan, but added that he would support the dispatching of Iraqi troops to Syria and Palestine instead, provided the Allies undertook to grant the two countries their independence at the cessation of hostilities. [62]

Although himself a dreamer of grand Arab schemes and federations, Nuri does not seem to have shared al-Sabbagh's unqualified commitment to the Palestinian and Syrian questions; according to the latter, every time Nuri heard the name of Hajj Amin mentioned he would 'go pale'.[63] Aware of the Hajj Amin's influence on al-Sabbagh, Nuri was naturally anxious to undermine it, and in order to win al-Sabbagh's confidence paid him almost daily visits, reasserting his friendship and inviting his opinion on affairs of state.

Chapter 8

The Rashid 'Ali coup and British intervention

Once the Second World War had broken out, and in particular when the Middle East became involved after the fall of France and the entry of Italy on the side of Germany, British policy in Iraq underwent certain changes. We can distinguish two stages in the development of this policy. During the first, the aim was to attach Iraq to Britain's cause by *political* means, but during the second stage there was a gradual realisation that *military* action would be both necessary and possible.

The events of the first stage can be understood through a study of the attempts of Nuri al-Sa'id to gather sufficient support for his British policy, attempts so blatant as sometimes to be embarrassing to the British themselves, and arousing widespread opposition to him and to Britain among nationalistic Iraqis. As soon as the new cabinet was formed in February 1940, Nuri also revived his attempts to bring Rashid 'Ali into the cabinet, but the latter refused to serve in any government that included Nuri.[1] However, Nuri was not to be discouraged. He appealed to the 'Four' to try and persuade Rashid 'Ali to change his mind, and when that failed Hajj Amin himself was asked to intervene. Subsequently Rashid 'Ali was persuaded to form a cabinet headed by himself; this cabinet was announced on 28 March 1940 with Nuri as Foreign Minister and Taha al-Hashimi as Defence Minister.

Like Nuri al-Sa'id, Rashid 'Ali al-Kilani was not a newcomer to Iraqi politics. Neither were his family unknown to Iraqis. He had first been Prime Minister in 1933, and the family from which he descended had been prominent since the days of 'Abd al-Qadir, the medieval divine. But unlike most of his Iraqi contemporaries, he did not have a military background and actually spent the years of the First World War in the Turkish legal service. He was also an active member of the Committee of Union and Progress (CUP), and there is no record of his having participated in the activities of al-'Ahd or any other Arab nationalist society. After the creation of the Iraqi state he held a number of legal posts, and was a professor at the Baghdad School of Law immediately before his first cabinet appointment as Minister of Justice in 1924.

Compared with the Regent, for example, Rashid 'Ali was an immensely complex character, of whom it is perhaps impossible to form an objective opinion. What from one angle appeared as 'energetic' enthusiasm[2] seemed from another viewpoint to be 'wildness', or at least lack of realism.[3] While it was admitted that he was ready to fight for what he believed in,[4] he was also inclined to be long-winded in speech.[5] Ironically it is possible that the very length of his protestations of friendship for Britain made that country's rather reserved citizens more suspicious of him. There were two conflicting opinions: he was cunning, or very naïve. It was, of course, possible for the British to combine the two, given their unfortunate stereotype of the 'untutored Arab', full of 'native cunning' but ignorant of sophisticated ways. To his people he was seen as an honest and incorruptible leader, yet there are many rumours of peculation on his part (for example, in the misappropriation of charitable bequests when he was Minister of Interior in 1933),[6] which are, inevitably, impossible to assess. Some of the ambiguities in his character are perhaps common to many politicians – for example, whether his motives in urging Arab unity were personal or political. Some of the British comments on him, however, can be fairly firmly attributed to wishful thinking or at times sheer ignorance: for example, the claim that he was unpopular and discredited after his resignation in January 1941; the disingenuous amazement that not one speaker in the Senate supported him when he was out of power;[7] and the apparently unquestioned acceptance of the Regent's statement before Rashid 'Ali's final government that, although Rashid 'Ali combined corruption and cunning by spending £14,000 of secret service or Italian money on bribery and yet proved his unpopularity by failing to stay in power thereby, he (the Regent) had spent money with 'good results'. It would also seem that the actions that led him to be dubbed a 'weathercock lacking both courage and convictions'[8] and 'probably the most unscrupulous intriguer in Iraq'[9] were those of a man who, not unlike the British Prime Minister of the time, believed that any means was justified that served the end most dear to him. Moreover, it appears rather simplistic to claim that he was dominated by the 'Golden Square',[10] and more realistic to say that, as an intelligent Iraqi politician, he realised that he must have a close, almost symbiotic, relationship with the leading figures in the armed forces.

To sum up, Rashid 'Ali is hard to sum up, because he represented a type of politician, perhaps particularly common in the Middle East, who almost consciously tried to make of himself an enigma. A review of his political career shows that, like most of his contemporaries, he was more anti-British when he was out of office than when he was in. It also clearly shows a man with an intense lust after government appointments. When Nuri al-Sa'id did not include him in the cabinet that he formed in January 1939, Rashid 'Ali is reported to have broken down and wept.[11] In addition to being very intelligent and hard-working, he was also a persuasive speaker; but, combined with his intensely ambitious personality, those qualities seem to have won him temporary allies rather than lasting friends. In 1939 he was Nuri's most formidable political rival, and it was therefore natural for him to join the tide of opposition that was moving against Nuri's foreign policy. He soon cultivated a friendship with the Hajj Amin, and through it and his public statements in support of the Arab cause, he came to be highly regarded by and endeared to the 'Four'. This was the main reason why Nuri insisted on associating Rashid 'Ali with the cabinet and, hopefully, with his foreign policy.

Having achieved his immediate aim, Nuri now strove to persuade the new cabinet to adopt his own views on foreign policy. The general attitude of the cabinet, however, was that, while they were willing to comply with the letter and spirit of their treaty with Britain, declaring war was not a treaty obligation. Furthermore, Rashid 'Ali assured the British Ambassador that[12]

> the programme of his Cabinet did not differ in any essentials from that of Nuri Sa'id's. . . . Rashid 'Ali has been at pains to assure me that he aimed at no change of attitude towards Great Britain or the Anglo-Iraqi Alliance, and intended to continue his predecessor's endeavours to maintain and strengthen the closest friendly relations between Iraq and Great Britain. At the same time he had intimated that in order to retain public confidences his Government would have to encourage and lead patriotism of the younger generation.

Nevertheless, at about the same time, Rashid 'Ali told Mr Edmonds that, since Allied fortunes were waning, it would be useless for him to try to rally public opinion to the Allied side, but that he was in any case doing his best to keep a close watch on the activities of the Palestinian and Syrian refugees and other mischief-makers; he added that he had given tribal leaders material with which to combat pro-Nazi talks as well as inspiring pro-Allied articles in the press.[13] However, he emphasised that all his efforts would be useless unless Britain modified her Palestinian policy.[14]

Although Nuri al-Sa'id had failed thus far to obtain the cabinet's support for declaring war on Germany and severing diplomatic relations with Italy, these pronouncements by Rashid 'Ali seem to have satisfied the British, whose view of him was still favourable, if condescending.[15] The British attitude was to change radically, however, after Italy's declaration of war on Britain and France, when the question of cutting off diplomatic relations with Italy was given an added urgency. Nuri knew as well as the British Ambassador that the decisive obstacle in the way to severing diplomatic relations with Italy came from the 'Four'. He therefore persistently sought their support, promising lucrative appointments and generous rewards,[16] but to no avail. He continued his efforts in the cabinet, but apart from the 'half-hearted' support of Taha al-Hashimi, all the ministers continued to reject his plan.[17] By now his campaign to win over his colleagues is reported to have become quite frantic, and in order to demonstrate his disapproval of them, his attendance at their meetings became very rare.[18]

But the tide was firmly moving against him. A continued alliance with Britain seemed to be a bad bet to many Iraqis, given the worsening military position of Britain in 1940-1; moreover, the political and economic pressure she could apply to Iraq was limited, and she could promise little on Palestine or the political development of other Arab lands.[19] On the other hand, the Germans were not short of propaganda material to enhance their image among the Iraqis, and their Arabic radio station in Berlin is believed to have been eagerly received in Baghdad. More significant, through his secretary, Hajj Amin was already establishing contacts with Germany, and by the middle of August he actually succeeded in inducing the Germans to make a political communiqué expressing sympathy with the aspirations of the Arab people.[20]

In the meantime, the 'Four' themselves were in touch with the Axis powers through the Italian and Japanese missions in Baghdad.[21] On the other side of the fence was an increasingly unpopular Nuri, now commonly referred to by 'all classes of people' as the 'untrustworthy Englishman',[22] encouraged by the British Ambassador and supported by the Regent and to a lesser degree by Taha al-Hashimi.

By the first week of October we can observe a change in British thinking. The Chief of the Imperial General Staff was now claiming that 'the situation in Iraq is rapidly deteriorating, and anti-British feeling is growing to such an extent that serious consequences may result if no steps are taken to improve matters'.[23] At about the same time, Mr Edmonds submitted a report in which he advised the British Ambassador that[24]

> it will be wise to cherish no illusions. All the leading Iraqi politicians are Pan-Arab, though the degree of the obsession varies. We cannot have it both ways; the wisdom of His Majesty's Government . . . has decided to make no conciliatory gesture in regard to Palestine; in Iraq we get the disadvantages; we cannot therefore expect from any Iraqi Cabinet, at any rate until we are on the crest of an unmistakable wave of success, much more than a luke-warm implementation of the Alliance.

Short of modifying their Palestinian policy, the Foreign Office were basically left with two alternatives for preventing the situation in Iraq from escalating further: to use direct military intervention,[25] or to use their influence and install a regime that would be able to accede to their demands.[26] The C-in-C, Middle East, however, advised the Foreign Office that the British[27]

> military position in Iraq is weak, and we cannot at present afford troops or air force. Time is past when a comparatively small force might have restored prestige and influence. Unfortunately our diplomacy and propaganda have also been timid and weak. . . . Only remedy for present situation is a much stronger diplomacy and propaganda. . . . It will probably be necessary as first step to replace present Government with one nominated by Regent under our guidance with promise from us of full moral backing and financial support.

With immediate military intervention ruled out, the Foreign Office opted for the second alternative. At this time, it was obvious to all concerned that the Prime Minister as such was of little consequence, and the real political power in Iraq rested with the 'Four'. Therefore only someone who was going to be able to control the 'Four' should be chosen for the next premiership.

For the next two months the British Ambassador's insistence that Iraq should break off diplomatic relations with Italy became even more forceful and direct, but Rashid 'Ali refused to give in. On 15 December Nuri submitted a memorandum to Rashid 'Ali alleging that the cabinet was paralysed by internal conflict and recommending, among other things, the immediate severing of diplomatic relations with Italy and the sending of an Arab delegation headed by Hajj Amin to the United States to campaign on behalf of the Arab cause.[28] Two days later, the Regent called for an urgent meeting of the cabinet and accused the ministers of having lost the unity that was essential for the functioning of government; but Rashid 'Ali rejected the Regent's claim and retorted that the only disagreement was with Nuri al-Sa'id, the Foreign Minister. The same evening, undoubtedly with British approval, the Regent requested the resignation of the Prime Minister, but Rashid 'Ali considered the move unconstitutional and refused to resign.

These exchanges were followed by a session of Parliament when Rashid 'Ali was subjected to a barrage of attacks by pro-Nuri deputies for having defied the Regent's order and for having caused the cabinet crisis. Sensing this antagonism, Rashid 'Ali reacted by refusing to answer questions and then finally stormed out of Parliament, going to the Regent and demanding his approval of the dissolution of Parliament. The Regent refused to sign the dissolution order and instead decided to flee secretly from Baghdad to Diwaniya, the centre of tribal power. Rashid 'Ali was then faced with no choice but to step down, which he did on the following day, after making a statement indicating that his resignation was due to foreign pressure.[29] Consequently, the Regent sent for Taha al-Hashimi, and, after ensuring that he would make a determined effort to control the 'Four',[30] asked him to form the next government, which Taha did on 3 February.

The choice of al-Hashimi for premier was a shrewd move; for, in the circumstances, he was Britain's best hope of controlling the 'Four'. It will be remembered that Taha had been the army's CGS for the last seven years preceding the Sidqi coup. Added to that, through being the Minister of Defence since January 1939, he had maintained close links with the army, and in fact it was his persistent interference with the functions of the CGS that was a main reason for the abortive coup of 1939 and for the subsequent resignation of Husain Fauzi. Nevertheless, this long association with the army had made him, to use al-Sabbagh's words, something of a 'father-of-all' figure to the officers.[31] Both because of this, and his being the brother of Yasin, who was perceived as a great Arab nationalist, the 'Four', particularly al-Sabbagh, had a profound respect for him. Although al-Sabbagh notes that Taha was 'strangely affected'[32] by Nuri, the 'Four' continued to respect him even when relations between them and Nuri had become strained.

However, Taha al-Hashimi does not seem to have been endowed with the strength of character that would have been essential for him to effect as radical a change as the removal of the 'Four' from the political scene. His generally dull memoirs reveal an uninspiring personality and give weight to the British Ambassador's reference to him as being of limited intelligence.[33]

As had been calculated, less than a week after coming to power, the new cabinet informed the British Ambassador that they would endeavour to prepare public opinion for an eventual rupture with Italy, and that it was their intention to transfer some of the 'Four' away from the Baghdad area.[34] By then, the Prime Minister had already sent a mediator to al-Sabbagh to plead with him to accept a transfer to Kirkuk.[35] Declining to accept, however, al-Sabbagh informed the mediator that the army's intervention in politics would cease as soon as the need for it disappeared, and suggested that it was the politician's deviation from what was in the national interest that dictated his (al-Sabbagh's) involvement in politics.[36] However, the Prime Minister continued his efforts to convince the 'Four' of the wisdom of improving relations with Britain and, by implication, of severing relations with Italy. He also repeated his request to al-Sabbagh to accept a transfer from Baghdad, this time to the Persian frontier.[37]

Perhaps inevitably, rather than drawing the desired support, the Prime Minister's insistence precipitated a crisis of confidence between him and the 'Four'. On 28 February, a secret meeting of the 'Arab Committee', headed by Hajj Amin and attended by Rashid 'Ali and the 'Four', decided against breaking off diplomatic relations with Italy. The conference also expressed their doubts of al-Hashimi's allegiance to pan-Arab aspirations.[38] On 17 March Taufiq al-Suwaidi, the then Foreign Minister, returned from Cairo where he had attended a meeting with Anthony Eden, his British counterpart. On his return rumours spread, and were possibly reinforced by Axis agents, that the cabinet intended to remove the 'Four' to provincial posts. On 21 March the Regent informed the British Ambassador of his plan to turn out the government if they were not prepared to deal at once with the 'Four', but the Foreign Office advised the Ambassador to dissuade the Regent from executing his proposal because it might arouse[39]

> violent reactions, not only from the military clique, Mufti and
> Rashid 'Ali, but perhaps also from other elements, and the crisis
> may even involve our own military situation. We have therefore
> some misgivings about bringing matters to a head at this moment
> and in this way, unless indeed Commander-in-Chief Middle East is
> fully aware of the position, and is prepared to accept its possible
> implications.

By this time, however, British military authorities seem to have reached the conclusion that military intervention was necessary. The Chiefs of Staff Committee later recommended that they were 'generally agreed that a forward policy in Iraq was now desirable, with the object of causing a rupture with Italy and of upsetting the extremist clique, which included the Mufti and the "Golden Square" [The Four]'.[40]

The planning of this 'forward policy' was of course an extremely delicate operation. The overriding need was to ensure the establishment of a pro-British Iraqi government that was both legitimate and reasonably acceptable, both internally and externally. But at the same time, Britain wanted to use the occasion to increase rather than reduce the chance of Turkey joining the war on Britain's side (even to the extent of implying that an occupation of Mosul would not be objected to), and, equally, she did not want to tempt Germany to throw so much into supporting Rashid 'Ali that Britain would be forced into a humiliating withdrawal or an 'inconvenient standstill'. There was also a need to avoid actions, or at least the publicity for actions, that might both endanger their safety and offend public opinion in neutral countries (especially America) and in the Arab world.

Against this background, on 30 March, on the instructions of the Regent, the Prime Minister issued an order transferring Kamil Shabib (one of the 'Four') to Diwaniya.[41] Rejecting the order, the Four's suspicion and opposition to the Hashimi cabinet increased until finally, on 1 April, after their units had occupied the telegraph office, telephone exchange and broadcasting stations, they issued an ultimatum to the government to resign. That evening, they extracted a letter of resignation from the Prime Minister and took it to the Regent for endorsement. The Regent managed to elude them, however, and, after hiding in a relative's house that night, he escaped to Basra via Habbaniya and later continued to Transjordan.

The Regent's flight placed the rebels in a dilemma; for without a royal *iradah* neither the Hashimi resignation nor Rashid 'Ali's appointment could be made constitutionally complete. Therefore, after what appears to have been a day of confusion, Rashid 'Ali finally took control in the name of the Government of National Defence at the head of a cabinet of eight other civilians. The first act of the government was to issue two proclamations, the first accusing the Regent of treason, and the second pledging to 'carry on Iraq's national mission, to honour Iraq's international obligations, especially the Anglo-Iraqi Treaty, and to keep Iraq out of the war'.[42]

Although, as a clear manifestation of his government's disapproval of the new regime, the newly arrived British Ambassador, Sir Kinahan

Cornwallis, failed to present his credentials to the Iraqi government, Rashid 'Ali sent him a message in which he[43]

> conveyed profuse assurances of his desire to carry out loyally the treaty of alliance, and indicated that in order to obtain the full recognition of His Majesty's Government he was willing to put through the following plan: the Regent to accept Taha Pasha's resignation and to entrust Rashid 'Ali with the task of forming a new cabinet. The new cabinet then to sanction the Regent's absence from the country for four months and the Sharif Sharaf to act as Regent while the Amir 'Abdul Illah was away. He undertook concurrently personally to broadcast to counter German propaganda, to implement the alliance on a wider basis than before, to stop all agitation about Palestine and Syria and to prepare public opinion for a rupture with Italy.

In spite of these favourable overtures, however, the British Ambassador suspected Rashid 'Ali's motives, and was not sure whether he felt uneasiness about his own position or whether Rashid 'Ali had received German orders to go slowly for the present.[44] The Ambassador therefore advised Rashid 'Ali against summoning Parliament to depose and replace the Regent.[45] Nevertheless, anxious to give the cabinet a constitutional seal, the 'Four' insisted that Rashid 'Ali should go ahead with his plan, and thus an extraordinary meeting of Parliament was held on 10 April, when a joint session of the Senate and the Chamber of Deputies gave a unanimous vote (though out of the total of 135 members only 94 were present) appointing Sharif Sharaf as Regent. Rashid 'Ali used this opportunity to reaffirm again the intention of his government to comply with their international obligations. He pointed out that their[46]

> national movement is entirely an internal movement having no connection whatever with any foreign state. Our relations with foreign states are based on the honouring of our international obligations in accordance with our custom. I declare also that we shall honour the Anglo-Iraqi Treaty. We shall carry out and maintain this alliance and Iraq will continue zealously to fulfil this treaty, both in letter and in spirit.

The British Ambassador thought this to be a shrewd move, because it would appear to have deprived HMG of any right to intervene forcibly in protection of their treaty rights; were they to do so Rashid 'Ali could present it as an attack on the independence of Iraq.[47] He therefore advised the Foreign Office to refuse Rashid 'Ali recognition and see how he reacted. If he denounced the Treaty, Britain could then move in to defend it; and if he accepted it, Britain could move in to use the lines of communications and either find the situation satisfactory after all, or fight from a better position.[48]

Unknown to the Ambassador, however, the Foreign Office had already decided that Rashid was perhaps playing for time; and in any case, on 8 April, in co-ordination with the Chiefs of Staff in London, the Viceroy of India had already set preparations in motion for sending troops to Basra.[49] (The role of the Viceroy of India was that of ruler of a territory that had been much involved with Iraq traditionally, and that provided the only base from which numerous forces could reach Iraq – although one could argue that eventually the role of the light force that reached Baghdad from Transjordan was more important.)

From then on its was clearly only a matter of time before open conflict broke out between the two allies. According to the British Ambassador, on the eve of 11 April he suddenly learned of the un-heralded arrival of HMS *Emerald*, which was due at Basra that evening.[50] The Foreign Office then informed him that, while it was 'appreciated that contemplated action is not entirely covered by our Treaty rights', they clearly regarded Basra as vital. The closing of the lines of communications between Basra and Baghdad were regarded as being of secondary importance,[51] but on 12 April the Committee of the War Cabinet agreed to delay the air and sea-borne troops in order to test the Ambassador's idea of using the lines of communication as a pretext.[52]

The government of India, however, warned that, if the plan was robbed of its characteristics of speed, secrecy and surprise and Rashid 'Ali given time to organise opposition to the landing, it would have to be completely recast, which might take some weeks.[53] Thus it was decided to go ahead with the landing. Because of rumours supposedly going around Basra, the British Ambassador told Rashid 'Ali the news at 6.15 p.m. on 16 April, and reported that the Prime Minister had [54]

> received news well, agreed that passage of troops was treaty right
> and promised all facilities. . . . He agreed also to arrange for suitable
> publicity which would dispel public misgivings. . . . He thought it
> important that the usual compliments should be exchanged by
> His Majesty's ships and shore authorities as a demonstration of
> accord and goodwill.

By 21 April the Ambassador reported with growing confidence an al-most blissful scene of harmony in Basra, with officials returning calls and British sentries and local police controlling military traffic side by side.[55] However, he added that Rashid 'Ali[56]

> kept harping on the question of full recognition. He ascribed any impatient feeling of annoyance which might exist amongst certain officers in the army to our failure to supply their requirements and assured me that all would be satisfied when we did so. . . . He stressed the extreme importance from the Arab point of view of some declaration by His Majesty's Government regarding Palestine and Syria.

It is clear that Rashid 'Ali regarded a conciliation between Britain and his government as possible. But, as pointed out earlier, at that time it was the 'Four' and their supporters in the army whom the British needed to remove from positions of influence; and in the final analysis Rashid 'Ali himself could not push forward a policy that was unacceptable to them. According to the British Ambassador, they were already 'sulky and irritated with Rashid 'Ali, who they feel has let them down'.[57] It was the pressure applied by the 'Four' that led the cabinet to take a decision that evening calling for a limitation of the use of British troops in Iraq. An official note was then sent to the British Ambassador which requested that[58]

(a) All measures must be taken to hasten the immediate onward movement of this force [i.e. the force stationed at Basra which was supposed to be on its way to Palestine] . . . .

(b) Reasonable advance notice to be given of the arrival of further forces, and total strength of forces within the frontier of Iraq at any one time not to exceed one mixed brigade.

(c) The Iraqi Government will not agree to any further troop disembarkation at Basra before recently arrived force has passed across the frontier out of Iraq.

While the Iraqi government was within its rights to take such a stand, the timing of this decision is very curious. It reflects an impulsive approach to the making of political decisions and shows a desperate lack of understanding of the complex process of international relations. It is possible that its authors were encouraged by the recent Axis victories in Greece and Cyrenaica, but it should have been clear to them that, without substantial outside help (as we shall see, Hitler agreed to aid Iraq only on 3 May), the Iraqi army could not withhold its position in an open conflict with British troops which this declaration could provoke. The British Ambassador replied by pointing out that the Treaty did not allow for such limitations and that they were especially unacceptable in wartime. He referred particularly to Article 4, where the Iraqi government promised all facilities and assistance in their power in time of war.[59] The Viceroy of India weighed in with the even firmer line, which he had maintained and was to maintain throughout the crisis: that Britain must 'contemplate effective occupation of Iraq for the rest of the war'.[60] By 28 April Iraqi–British relations were back to the tense situation of four weeks before, with three British ships, carrying a force of 2,000–3,500 men, sailing into Basra, in spite of the Iraqi government's refusal to give them permission to land.[61]

The following day, in a meeting with the Prime Minister and Minister of Foreign Affairs, the British Ambassador was told that, although Article 4 of the Treaty provided for all possible assistance, Article 5 limited the forces that could be *maintained* in Iraq to the two air bases; they also told him that the people had criticised the government for allowing the arrival of the original force and were worried by its non-movement; and that, on the basis of these considerations, they could not allow further forces until the existing ones had been removed.[62] The Ambassador, first, disputed their interpretation of the Treaty; second, he produced the rather hair-splitting argument that the three ships arriving contained not new formations but ancillaries which were part of the force already in Basra; and, third, he stated that the ships would land anyway.[63] The Iraqi government then took the line that the continued presence of British troops was illegal and informed the Ambassador that they could not receive any representation from him until he was accredited to them.[64] That evening, Habbaniya was 'entirely surrounded by Iraqi troops with tanks, armoured cars and anti-tank guns trained on camp'.[65]

Again, this decision by the Iraqi authorities is surprising, since to that date German support for the Iraqi government was confined to verbal statements and promises, which could not have easily been implemented in the absence of any established German supply routes reaching Iraq. Of course, the Axis powers had potentially important roles in Iraqi affairs in this period. First, they acted as an economic and ideological magnet to draw Iraqi politicians – notably Rashid 'Ali and the 'Golden Square' – further away from any sympathy they might have had for Britain. Second, they acted as an irritant provoking, or a convenient excuse inviting, demands and action from Britain. Lastly, they had at least the potential of acting as a counter-force to political or military action by Britain.

In reality, however, none of these potential roles was realised. In the first respect there is very little evidence that the policies of Rashid 'Ali and the 'Golden Square', especially their attitude to Britain, were motivated by anything more than simple Iraqi nationalism or, at most, Arabism. More significantly, it is widely agreed that Italy's military aid to Rashid 'Ali was non-existent, that Germany's aid was both too little and too late, and that too much was asked in return.[66] The Germans had in fact worried about the coup in Iraq occurring before they could effectively aid its instigators; they were also limited in that they could hardly bomb oil fields that they intended to make use of later.

Unlike the Axis powers, the British seem to have been so persuaded of the necessity of intervention in Iraq that they were prepared to use slim excuses, manufacture reasons or, if necessary, simply intervene with no other reason than their perception of military necessity. Thus, by the end of April the Foreign Office thought that, if the Ambassador had to and was able to leave Baghdad, he should go to Basra until the time was ripe for the return of the Regent and his supporters;[67] but the Ambassador replied that he was powerless, and that he had concentrated the British subjects in the Embassy and American Legation, where they could resist a mob but not the Iraqi army.[68] He was then authorised to order any action including aerial attacks to enforce the withdrawal of Iraqi troops.[69]

By 2 May the Iraqi troops encircling Habbaniya had been bombed and the British Embassy were sufficiently concerned to be burning their archives, a scene vividly described by Freya Stark in *The Times* of 27 June; the Iraqi government were now beginning to complain about aerial bombardments of civilians and informed the American Legation that a British plane tried to bomb a mosque at Falluja during prayers.[70] When Turkey offered to mediate, the British inquired whether the Turkish government could be persuaded to arrange a military demonstration near her frontier with Iraq.[71] However, the Turkish reaction to British appeals tended to consist partly of fear, partly of indifference and partly of weary racialism (for example, the Turkish Foreign Minister stated that all Arabs were unreliable – one Arab was much the same as another).[72] By 5 May the British Foreign Secretary confirmed his rejection of Turkish mediation and added the astounding statement that he had left it to the British Ambassador in Ankara to decide whether he should suggest to the Turks that they should occupy Mosul.[73] A link with Turkey from the opposite side occurred when Naji Shaukat, the Minister of Defence, went to Ankara on 7 May, partly to defend his government to the Turks; but it has since been learnt that he also contacted Axis agents and stated that Rashid 'Ali wished to establish relations with them.[74] On 8 May the Reich's representative told the Iraqi government that 'everything depended on Iraq holding out with her own forces for about two weeks'.[75]

Preoccupied with preparations for invading Russia, it is clear that the Reich government had given the conflict in Iraq low priority and had underestimated its strategic importance. Perhaps, had they, as General Smuts was to express it later, 'launched [their] attack on Russia through Syria and Iraq, concurrently with [their] attack from the West, the outcome of the war would have been different'.[76]

In fact, German aid to Iraq was not delayed as much as the German government had feared, and their first planes arrived in Baghdad on 11 May.[77] But the German war-planes were soon crippled by lack of fuel, which the Iraqi government had previously assured the Germans was in great abundance.[78] Nevertheless, their arrival naturally hastened the British desire to bring hostilities to an end by 'every means not – repeated not – involving direct attack on civil population'.[79] Thus, by 14 May it was believed that only Rashid 'Ali and three other ministers (Yunis Sab'awi,[80] 'Ali Mahmud, and Musa Shabandar) tentatively favoured resistance, while the rest were already abroad or applying for Syrian visas. One of the 'Four' (Sa'id Fahmi) had a nervous breakdown, Kamil Shabib no longer participated in the fighting, and al-Sabbagh was 'losing his nerves'.[81] On the other hand, some shipment of arms – though not of men – was now taking place with the acquiescence of Turkey,[82] although Turkey's general attitude was that they would like the conflict solved as quickly as possible, either by negotiations or by immediate vigorous action, with the Turkish Minister of Foreign Affairs claiming that only the latter was of use in dealing with Arabs.[83]

By 18 May Salih Jabr, the ex-Mutasarrif of Basra who had been dismissed by Rashid 'Ali, was appealing for a legitimate government to be set up under the Regent. This suggestion seems to have met with some support in London. The Colonial Secretary agreed with it, and thought that any further delay in setting up a government would be most undesirable, adding further, cynically, that in such an event the Regent could make 'what promises he likes about internal affairs'.[84] This point was further strengthened by Salih Jabr's additional statement that, if the Regent refused or hesitated to form a government, he proposed, in agreement with GOC, Basra, to endeavour to raise revolt among the Muntafiq, Diwaniya and other tribes where he was influential.[85]

So, in theory at least, the spectre of tribal anarchy and a consequent breakdown of law and order, which the British thought an evil second only to an un-cooperative government, was a possibility. The next day the Regent issued his long-awaited message to Iraqi representatives abroad, warning them of messages that might have the effect of putting Iraq under Axis control.[86] On 21 May the Foreign Office appointed Mr de Gaury as *chargé d'affaires* to the Regent.

By this time, the military position of Rashid 'Ali was near collapse. He had had no success in weakening the British hold over Basra and Habbaniya, and was being threatened by a military expedition moving eastwards from Transjordan. It is perhaps a sign of Rashid 'Ali's growing desperation that by the last part of May he was trying to win over the Kurds; but all was now in vain.[87] On 24 May the Prime Minister's family, together with that of Naji Shaukat, left Baghdad, and the government itself was considering moving to another town. The Ministers for Foreign Affairs and Justice fled to Tehran, but Rashid 'Ali was prepared to fight on alone, though the German minister had told him that his government could produce no more aid for two months and had advised him to leave, as he himself was, for Mosul.

Finally, on 30 May the remnants of the short-lived Rashid 'Ali administration, together with the 'Four', the Mufti, German and Italian ministers, and some thirty others, fled to Iran via Mosul, whence some of them later escaped to Germany and played some role in broadcasting from Berlin. Then the administration of Baghdad was taken over by a committee of four under the Lord Mayor, who asked for an immediate armistice, but insisted that its terms should be reasonable as the army would go on fighting rather than lay down its arms.[88]

Ironically, the armistice as finally drawn did not contain that long-held desire – the expulsion of the Italian Legation – perhaps because it was no longer practically necessary. The actual document, signed at 15.30 local time on 31 May, after a meeting which began 'after a long wait, under a white flag at an eerie rendez-vous in water-logged country West of Baghdad',[89] confined itself to purely military matters such as the exchange of prisoners and disposition of troops.

It remained for the Regent to install a new government which would co-operate with the British. In the event, the Regent decided to call upon Jamil al-Madfa'i to form a government, and here the familiar difficulties began again. De Gaury had already realised that, as the Regent's entourage contained three ex-prime ministers (Nuri al-Sa'id, 'Ali Jaudat, and Jamil Madfa'i), whichever one was chosen, the other two would be disgruntled. Apparently, the three men were already ceasing to co-operate and were contacting their followers separately.[90]

Thus ended the first cycle of coups and counter-coups which General Sidqi had set in motion five years earlier. Unlike the Sidqi coup, the rise of the 'Four' was considered a threat to British interests (in fact, it was a conditional threat), and when these, rather than merely the internal stability of a friendly country, were thought to be endangered, Britain had no reservations about invading her ally. As A. H. Hourani expressed it, although in a different context, 'what was important for them was the land and its resources. Those who happened to occupy the land were at best instruments for – or at worst obstacles in the way of – purposes which were no concern of theirs'.[91]

Given the poor state of the Iraqi army, on their own they stood no chance of holding their positions against the invasion of superior British forces. Any gains that could have been drawn during that tense period could only have been secured through the art of diplomacy, of which the 'Four', by the very nature of their profession, seem to have only had a rudimentary understanding. After their inevitable defeat, the new-found 'stability' of Iraq lasted for seventeen years, until General Qasim achieved some of the aims for which the 'Four' had rebelled.

Chapter 9

Conclusions

It is claimed that the Caliph Mu'awiya's dying injunction to his son Yazid was that, in order to keep the people of Iraq quiet, it was essential to give them a new governor every time they wanted one, however frequently. This book should have shown that such advice still would have been of relevance to Iraq during the period under study.

Iraq had for centuries been divided into competing tribes, clans, cities and religious sects. Nevertheless, with the rising tide of Arab nationalism and the final collapse of Ottoman rule in 1918, the idea of the nation-state seems to have appealed to educated Iraqis (particularly those with an awareness of nationalist movements in the Ottoman Empire and Europe generally), who joined in the popular uprising of 1920 that preceded the creation of the state.

The Iraqi state was in fact created in response to the demands of these nationalists, as well as being, of course, in harmony with Britain's own interests in the region. However, from its very foundation, the new state had to be imposed on a diversity of groups that had often risen up in arms against one another. Thus the national unity without which a state could not survive was markedly absent, and the necessary social cohesion had, from the outset, to be based on two external forces: the monarchy, and a rather pervasive British presence. The understandable interdependence that existed between those two forces, and their own bilateral relationship with significant sections of Iraqi society, soon came to be major determinants of the characteristics of Iraq's developing polity. However, though it worked (at least during Faisal's lifetime), this relationship had its own problems and at times could be saved only by the political acrobatics of King Faisal.

Since Britain's own interests often conflicted with those of Iraq, King Faisal often had to attempt to ride both the nationalist and

British horses. The ambiguity of the monarch's position, and his clear dependence on Britain, made it necessary for him to look to the forces within Iraq in order to create a position of strength within the country. As a first step, he gradually accumulated a court party of men who might be called moderate nationalists. A large proportion of these were ex-Turkish and ex-Sharifian officials and officers who had returned to Baghdad after the creation of the Kingdom. Their return to Baghdad had in fact meant that there were more people seeking public appointments than there were jobs to offer, and it was therefore expedient for the King to endow them with power rather than allowing them to drift into an added polarising dimension in a society already riddled with intrigue and rivalry. Nevertheless, once created, this ruling group developed its own problems. They naturally acquired a class interest of their own, but the absence of constitutional methods of achieving political transfer of power and of personal loyalties made it inevitable that members of this group would try to further their own privileges through their relations with the Palace, the British, or, more significantly for our study, the army.

During the first thirteen years of the state's existence, however, with his widely acknowledged political acumen, King Faisal succeeded in averting any serious breakup of this group and managed to maintain a minimum of stability within the country. As if following Mu'awiya's advice, he changed and reshuffled his cabinets very frequently, thereby creating new opportunities for those who were out of office and who were naturally struggling impatiently to return to it, either for the material returns it offered or for the opportunity it would give them to serve the nation. Furthermore, King Faisal is even alleged to have actively encouraged opposition to his government, first to allow an outlet for public dissatisfaction, and second in order to strengthen his negotiating position *via-à-vis* the British.

On the whole, through such tactics Faisal succeeded in enjoying a positive relationship with the British creators and guarantors of his kingdom. But in addition to his reliance on the British commitment and his erratic relationship with the ruling group, the King was naturally aware that, with the existence of such divergent groups and interests within his kingdom, a strong national army was needed to symbolise, as well as to preserve, a minimum degree of cohesion in society and prevent it plunging into utter chaos. Thus, almost immediately after his proclamation as King of Iraq, Faisal turned his attention to strengthening the state's newly established army. In the absence of mass support and a deep-rooted power base, it was natural for the monarchy to attach such an importance to the army. It was for this reason that Faisal insisted on the introduction of conscription in the face of intense opposition from Britain and tribal shaikhs. The debate on conscription focused still further political attention upon the army. Young Iraqi officers, many of whom had in any case come from the same social strata as the ruling elite, were treated with personal favour by the King (such as being congratulated by him personally on their graduation), and altogether the army became the pampered institution of the state.

More significantly, the army soon became the government's main effective instrument in asserting its authority over the diverse sectors of the population. Consequently, the custom of using the army for political ends, which is a basic theme of this work, was well established in the Mandate period, and, as P. Sluglett expressed it, 'one can say that the army featured more prominently in political bargaining than in military action'.[1] In this way, army officers who in any case had their own ambitions for public office, and some of whom were also ardent nationalists (and thus were against the British presence in Iraq – and, perhaps even more strongly, against Britain's policy in Palestine), effectively became an extension of the ruling political group. However, like their 'civilian' counterpart, this officer corps was torn by fragmented loyalties and therefore, in its own way, aggravated the disunity of the nation. Nevertheless, thanks to the skills of King Faisal, all of these undercurrents were somehow suppressed until the early 1930s. Potential sources of discontent among army officers as well as within the ruling group, such as shortage of arms supplies, Britain's policy in Palestine and her presence in Iraq, tribal affinities and conflicting loyalties – all of these were somewhat successfully controlled by Faisal's diplomatic manoeuvres. Perhaps more significantly, while he reigned Faisal came to be regarded as a kind of living embodiment of the Anglo-Iraqi connection, with all its ambiguities and irritations but also with its feelings of mutual regard.

In their own differing degree, all of these circumstances (that is, the issue of conscription, the use of the army as the government's arm in the provinces, the King's special attention to the army, etc.) focused attention on the armed forces. At the end of Faisal's life, the successful crushing by the army of the Assyrian uprising of 1933 made it perhaps the most prestigious institution of the state.

But Faisal was always aware of his own limitations, as well as of the degree of ultimate power that Britain could exercise on Iraq; and had he lived longer he might have been able to restrain the growth of the army's power. After he died, there was no equivalent figure that, while using politicians, could also be used by them to acquire legitimacy and support. He was succeeded by an inexperienced but strong-minded son, which made it possible for Britain and the Iraqi ruling group (including army officers) to grow further away from each other; and this new era of 're-definitions' may well have encouraged Iraqi politicians to seek more basic means to bolster their power and hence to resort to the army.

From then on the army's prestige and confidence increased progressively. The government's reliance on the armed forces was further shown dramatically during the tribal uprising of 1935–6. By then, it must have become obvious to intelligent and ambitious officers like Bakir Sidqi that it was the army officers and not urban politicians who were effectively in charge of Iraq's political 'ship'. The fact that Bakir Sidqi was also keenly ambitious, and came from the same social background as the most successful among the urban politicians (he had in fact been born in 'Askar, the Kurdish village where Ja'far al-'Askari was born), made it perhaps natural for him to resent his relatively less rewarding position and seek to rise against those who reaped the benefits of ruling a state that he and his troops were keeping under control.

Following Sidqi's coup, army officers became firmly recognised as a political force to be reckoned with, and an experienced politician like Nuri al-Sa'id soon found himself using politicised officers as his advisory council. Between 1937 and 1941 a situation developed where an Iraqi government could not come or go without the consent of army leaders, and in particular of those most influential officers known as the 'Golden Square'. Since these four were also commanders of the key divisions of the Iraqi army, no internal force on its own could have budged them from their powerful positions. They stayed at the top of the political pyramid until, for reasons arising from the wartime situation, Britain decided to re-occupy Iraq in May 1941, with the result that the 'Four' and their supporters lost their position of power. Their fall demonstrated the lack of political consciousness in the country as a whole (there was no significant popular uprising for or against them), and the apparent weakness of the Iraqi army, which must have been at least partly caused by the diversion of its leaders to political matters.

To summarise our conclusions, the evolution of the Iraqi political system and state can be attributed to the operation of a number of factors that were specific to Iraq and were not found, or were found only in part, elsewhere in the Middle East: the monarchy and its relations with a foreign power; the competition between British interests and those of the government; and the ethnic and religious differences in

Iraq and the dominance within the army of one religious faction. The combination of these factors provide the basis of an explanation of how Iraq came to be dominated by military leaders acting as personal dictators.

In the light of this, is it possible to say that the case of Iraq confirms or invalidates any of those general ideas about the role of the military that we reviewed in the introduction to this book? Of these models, the only one that seems to have some relevance to the case of Iraq is Hurewitz's idea that inter-communal divisions create a power vacuum into which the most powerful group is usually drawn. The Iraqi army was such a group. The relative weakness of the monarchy in attempting to mediate between conflicting demands, and its increasing dependence upon the army as an instrument of repression of rebellious and conflicting factions, was a major factor in explaining the rise of the army in politics. The presence of the British was a factor that enhanced the weakness of the monarchy and made the army a focus for nationalist sentiment. It acted as a catalyst for nationalism without strengthening the position of the monarch as a nationalist leader. Yet the army was extremely important to the monarchy in that, apart from the RAF (over which, in any case, the Iraqi government had no ultimate power), it was the only instrument at the disposal of the monarchy to consolidate the new state and maintain law and order in it. Thus the army played an essential role, although a negative one. It represented one of the inter-communal divisions, and so was unable to foster or serve a system that created a genuine national polity. It could prevent the evolution of government in the Western tradition, but it could not itself govern other than as a military dictatorship.

Appendices

Appendix I The Programme of the Popular Reform League

Its aims

To endeavour, by means of political, social and economic reforms, to safeguard the public interests and to ensure the progress of the individual members of the community and to put down exploitation.

How these aims will be achieved

1 Foreign policy

The cultivation of closer relations between all Arab countries and the development of intercourse between the peoples' organisations in those countries. The strengthening of friendly relations with the neighbours of Iraq and other foreign countries on the basis of mutual equality.

2 Internal policy

(a) The strengthening of the internal organisation of the state through further development of the army and the air force, through the military training of members of popular organisations and the reform of the police in order that these forces may be fit and ready to defend the country against any external aggression.

(b) The granting of full opportunity for the free expression of thought and the exercise of all progressive democratic liberties.

(c) The spread of culture among all classes of the people in a just manner.

3 Economic policy

To endeavour to raise the standard of living of the people and to ensure to every person the means to obtain the moral and material necessities of life. To ensure to all, in addition, such luxuries as the wealth of the nation may make possible.

(a) The nationalisation of the means of transport, correspondence and communication, of water-supply and electric power, and the organisation by government enterprise of such technical undertakings as the country may require to safeguard the peace and happiness of the people.

(b) The creation of a national bank for the practical control of the finances of the country.

(c) The granting of a monopoly of all land, agricultural and other loans to the national bank in order that the people may be saved from the oppression of the money-lenders. The enactment of laws to punish those who extort exorbitant rates of interest.

(d) The imposition of a sliding scale of taxation on all incomes and inheritances, so that the state may have the means necessary to enable it to carry out essential reforms.

(e) The reclamation of waste-land and its distribution to the peasantry in order that they may directly enjoy its fruits, and the organisation of co-operative enterprise among these people.

(f) The building of model villages, the filling-in of swamps, and the protection of the peasantry from the ill-effects of marshes.

(g) The annulment of oppressive agricultural laws and customs and the enactment of laws to ensure the progress of agriculture, the welfare of the peasants and their protection from exploitation.

(h) The reduction of the salaries of highly paid officials and the just treatment of junior officials and employees.

4 Education

To make elementary education compulsory; to stamp out illiteracy by the creation of institutions for culture and enlightenment - public libraries, cinemas, theatres, concert halls. The development of physical culture through special clubs, and assistance for the poor to continue their education through night schools.

5 Health

(a) To ensure that first consideration is given to preventive medicine and that curative medicine receives second consideration. The general increase of health institutions in all parts of the country, and the increase of public gardens and of children's playgrounds.

(b) To build up healthy dwellings by the following means:

    (i) The planning of towns according to the principles of public health, the building of healthy dwellings and their lease at low rents to officers and soldiers, workmen and minor officials and those in need.

    (ii) To combat intoxication, which harms the health of the public, and the encouragement of marriage.

6 The workers

The enactment of laws to protect the workers, to guarantee their rights, to ensure their progress and to restrict working hours to a maximum of eight hours a day. To encourage trade unions and workmen's organisations and to fix a minimum wage for workers of all kinds.

7 The lives of the people

(a) To enact laws in conformity with modern civilisation to regulate personal status.

(b) To endeavour to bring about the liberation of the women while at the same time preserving the principles of family life.

Appendix II Translation of 'Programme of Policy' issued by the cabinet of Saiyid Hikmat Sulaiman

The new cabinet undertook responsibilities at a time when the people had been reduced to despair. It came to power to do away with the previous state of affairs, and to start a new era of general reform in every sphere of the life of the nation.

This programme, therefore, includes only such undertakings as are to be carried out forthwith or in the near future, in accordance with the principles laid down, as follows:

Foreign policy

The cabinet proposes:

1. To strengthen the co-operation between Iraq and Great Britain, and to continue efforts to ensure that all possible financial, economic and military benefits are derived from the Anglo–Iraqi Treaty of Alliance.

2. To strengthen the ties of friendship and co-operation between Iraq and the Turkish Republic, and to use every endeavour to hasten the conclusion of a non-aggression pact between Iraq, Turkey, Iran and Afghanistan.

3. To continue the friendly relations between Iraq and Iran, and employ every means to strengthen them, and to settle all outstanding questions between the two countries.

4. To strengthen brotherly relations with the Kingdom of Ibn Sa'ud and with the other Arab states; and to maintain and cement the friendly relations between Iraq and all other states.

Internal administration

The amendment of the Civil Servants Law, the Disciplinary Law, and all

191

regulations relating to the engagement and promotion of officials, with a view to ensuring the creation of a civil service on the principles observed by all other civilised nations, taking into consideration the following points:

1 That special care should be taken to select for government appointments only educated youths of good character.

2 To ensure that they carry out their duties efficiently.

3 That the promotion of officials appointed on these lines should be carried out in a regular and impartial manner.

4 The settlement of all disputes among the tribes, whether such disputes arise through land or other questions, with complete impartiality.

5 The settlement of the nomadic tribes who have no lands, by giving each family sufficient land to ensure their livelihood, and to introduce the legislation necessary for this prupose.

Health

To increase the number of hospitals and medical institutions; to engage sufficient doctors to meet the country's needs; to raise the scientific standard of the Medical College, the Midwifery School, the Health Officials Schools, and the Pharmacy School; and to enlarge these institutions in order to increase the number of graduates.

To establish new medical units and special institutions in order to combat diseases which threaten the existence of the nation, such as venereal disease, malaria, and others; to promote child welfare institutions, and to raise their standard by placing them in charge of trained women capable of teaching mothers correct methods of caring for their children.

Prisons

To introduce the latest reforms in the prison system; to educate and train the prisoners so that, when released, they may become useful citizens; and to improve conditions in the reformatory schools.

Municipalities

To improve conditions in the municipalities; to increase the number of public parks, gardens, and sports grounds; to supply municipalities with all the technical assistance required in order to ensure proper town-planning, and an adequate supply of drinking water and electric light in every town and village; to improve labour conditions by encouraging labour unions and by constructing houses for the labouring classes.

Police

To raise the standard and capacity of the police force so that it will be able to perform its duties in the most efficient manner.

Finance

To prepare a permanent cadre for officials in conformity with the country's requirements.

To improve the financial administration so that all the revenues of the state are collected without undue loss of time or giving rise to complaint.

To consolidate the system of financial inspection to ensure effective supervision.

To prepare a general programme of capital works, each of which shall be completed in its allotted time.

To amend all out-of-date financial laws, especially those relating to taxation and, more particularly, income-tax, in order to make it more equitable and logical; to take steps to replace, in time, the present land system by a cadastral system; to take measures to improve the internal and external trade of Iraq in order to balance them as far as possible.

To open spinning and weaving factories to supply the army, the police, and students with their clothing requirements.

To expand the Agricultural and Industrial Bank so that it may be capable of fostering industrial schemes, and improving the quality of Iraqi products.

To supervise the activities of banks, companies, and other economic institutions, and to introduce legislation to ensure the development of Iraq's resources through the employment of insurance money in Iraq.

To settle the land question on principles of equity and public interest, and to divide state lands which are still uncultivated among the people in such a way as to preserve the rights of individuals.

Justice

To ensure equality before the law and to administer justice impartially; to strengthen the spirit of independence and impartiality in administering the law; to reconsider the system of appointing and promoting judges, as well as all questions connected with their transfer and discipline; to raise their standard and broaden their legal knowledge.

To reconsider the laws connected with the constitution of the courts; to reform the present laws of procedure, and the civil, commercial and criminal laws, in a manner consistent with the sound development of the country.

Defence

To lay down fixed rules for the expansion of the army and, more particularly, the air force, and to increase its strength on the most modern lines in order to make it capable of defending the integrity of the country.

To rely as far as possible upon the country's own resources in providing for the needs of the army, and, when important economic schemes are undertaken (such as the construction of roads, bridges and factories, and the establishment of air and other transport companies), to reconcile civil and military needs.

To strengthen the co-operation between the different sections of the community and the army and to popularise military training.

Economic sphere

To pay special attention to productive schemes which increase the country's wealth, such as the undertaking of large irrigation schemes; the improvement of the country's principal roads; the construction of important bridges; the improvement of means of transport and communication; the introduction of reform in the agricultural administration; the improvement of the quality of livestock and measures to combat their diseases; to carry out all schemes which are necessary for the expansion of industry; the construction of an oil refinery; and to develop generally the country's resources.

Education

To popularise education among the younger generation; to raise the standard of educational missions abroad, and limit their training to branches of knowledge which are essential for the rapid development of the country.

To expand education in the villages; to improve industrial education; to abolish secondary school fees; to improve the general knowledge and capacity of teachers of both sexes; to build the required number of government schools on modern lines; to ensure a proper system of examinations; and to lay down a permanent programme for all branches of education.

To hasten the construction of the new Iraqi Museum.

Appendix III Kurdish Petition

1   Improvement of the administration of the northern areas and abolishment of the Regulations for Selection of Administrative Officials as regards the North.

2   Enforcement of the Local Language Law and its amendment as recommended by Amin Zaki Beg.

3   Unification of education in Kurdish areas and the granting of greater authority of the Mudir of Education in the north and a share of the education budget in proportion of the population.

4   Opening of a secondary school, teachers' training college and a technical school in the northern area.

5   Granting a fair share of educational missions to the Kurds.

6   Allotment of a share of night schools, as in the capital, to the Kurds in proportion to their numbers.

7   Reappointment of a Kurdish Assistant Director-General of Interior, who should be a capable Kurd and should be granted wide powers by special regulations.

8   Granting to the Kurds of a share in proportion with their numbers of appointments in headquarters of ministries, central offices and the Palace.

9   Formation of a *liwa* from the Kurdish *qadhas* in the *liwa* of Mosul with its headquarters at Dohuk.

10   Granting of opportunity to the inhabitants of the northern areas for the election of deputies who have true connection with the district and are native of it.

11   Instruction in Kurdish history in Kurdish schools.

12   Improvements in afforestation, fruit culture and tobacco cultivation by the appointment of specialists and the opening of foreign

markets, such arrangements not to be detrimental to merchants or cultivators.

13   Amendment of the capital works programme to include the following projects:

(a) Water project Qarajun and Gobal in the *liwa* of Arbil.

(b) The Zab project in the *liwa* of Kirkuk.

(c) Artesian well projects in the Kirkuk and Arbil *liwas*.

(d) Prolongation of the road from Penjwin to the Persian frontier and arrangements of transit trade thereby.

(e) Opening of a road between headquarters of Sulaimani *liwa* and that of Sharbazher Qadha.

(f) Completion of the road Surdah–Rania.

(g) Improvement of the road Arbil–Koi Sanjak and its extension to Rania.

(h) Opening of a road from Sulaimani to Qara Dagh via Qara Dagh.

(j) Opening of a road from Kirkuk to Koi Sanjak via Shuan.

(k) Opening of a road between Aqra and Barzan and its extension to meet the Arbil–Rownduz road.

14   Preparation for settlement of the Jaf, Herki and other nomad tribes.

15   Appointment of doctors to headquarters of *qadhas* and important *nahiyas* and increase of dispensaries, permanent and mobile.

Appendix IV Anglo-Iraqi Treaty of Alliance, June 30 1930,

and notes exchanged embodying a separate financial agreement, **19 August 1930, with various explanatory notes, both published and unpublished**[1]

Treaty of alliance between His Majesty in respect of the United Kingdom and His Majesty the King of Iraq

Baghdad, 30 June 1930
(Ratifications exchanged at Baghdad, 26 January 1931)

His Majesty The King of Great Britain, Ireland and the British Dominions beyond the Seas, Emperor of India,

And His Majesty the King of Iraq,

Whereas they desire to consolidate the friendship and to maintain and perpetuate the relations of good understanding between their respective countries; and

Whereas His Britannic Majesty undertook in the Treaty of Alliance signed at Baghdad on the thirteenth day of January, one thousand nine hundred and twenty-six of the Christian era, corresponding to the twenty-eighth day of Jamadi-al-Ukhra, one thousand three hundred and forty-four, Hijrah, that he would take into active consideration at successive intervals of four years the question whether it was possible for him to press for the admission of Iraq into the League of Nations; and

Whereas His Majesty's Government in the United Kingdom of Great Britain and Northern Ireland informed the Iraq Government without qualification or proviso on the fourteenth day of September, one thousand nine hundred and twenty-nine that they were prepared to support the candidature of Iraq for admission to the League of Nations in the year one thousand nine hundred and thirty-two and announced to the Council of the League on the fourth day of November, one thousand nine hundred and twenty-nine, that this was their intention; and

Whereas the mandatory responsibilities accepted by His Britannic Majesty in respect of Iraq will automatically terminate upon the admission of Iraq to the League of Nations; and

Whereas His Britannic Majesty and His Majesty the King of Iraq consider that the relations which will subsist between them as independent Sovereigns should be defined by the conclusion of a Treaty of Alliance and Amity:

Have agreed to conclude a new treaty for this purpose on terms of complete freedom, equality and independence which will become operative upon the entry of Iraq into the League of Nations, and have appointed as their plenipotentiaries:

His Majesty the King of Great Britain, Ireland and the British Dominions beyond the Seas, Emperor of India:

For Great Britain and Northern Ireland:

Lieutenant Colonel Sir Francis Henry Humphrys, Knight Grand Cross of the Royal Victorian Order, Knight Commander of the Most Distinguished Order of Saint Michael and Saint George, Knight Commander of the Most Excellent Order of the British Empire, Companion of the Most Eminent Order of the Indian Empire, High Commissioner of His Britannic Majesty in Iraq: and

His Majesty the King of Iraq:

General Nuri Pasha al Sa'id, Order of the Nahda, Second Class, Order of the Istiqlal, Second Class, Companion of the Most Distinguished Service Order, Prime Minister of the Iraq Government and Minister for Foreign Affairs;

who, having communicated their full powers, found in due form, have agreed as follows.

Article 1

There shall be perpetual peace and friendship between His Britannic Majesty and His Majesty the King of Iraq.

There shall be established between the high contracting parties a close alliance in consecration of their friendship, their cordial understanding and their good relations, and there shall be full and frank consultation between them in all matters of foreign policy which may affect their common interests.

Each of the high contracting parties undertakes not to adopt in foreign countries an attitude which is inconsistent with the alliance or might create difficulties for the other party thereto.

Article 2

Each high contracting party will be represented at the Court of the other high contracting party by a diplomatic representative duly accredited.

Article 3

Should any dispute between Iraq and a third State produce a situation which involves the risk of a rupture with that State, the high contracting parties will concert together with a view to the settlement of the said dispute by peaceful means in accordance with the provisions of the Covenant of the League of Nations and of any other international obligations which may be applicable to the case.

Article 4

Should, notwithstanding the provisions of article 3 above, either of the high contracting parties become engaged in war, the other high contracting party will, subject always to the provisions of article 9 below, immediately come to his aid in the capacity of an ally. In the event of an imminent menace of war the high contracting parties will immediately concert together the necessary measures of defence. The aid of His Majesty the King of Iraq in the event of war or the imminent menace of war will consist in furnishing to His Britannic Majesty on Iraq territory all facilities and assistance in his power, including the use of railways, rivers, ports, aerodromes and means of communication.

Article 5

It is understood between the high contracting parties that responsibility for the maintenance of internal order in Iraq and, subject to the provisions of article 4 above, for the defence of Iraq from external aggression rests with His Majesty the King of Iraq. Nevertheless, His Majesty the King of Iraq recognises that the permanent maintenance and protection in all circumstances of the essential communications of His Britannic Majesty is in the common interest of the high contracting parties. For this purpose and in order to facilitate the discharge of the obligations of His Britannic Majesty under article 4 above His Majesty the King of Iraq undertakes to grant to His Britannic Majesty for the duration of the alliance sites for air bases to be selected by His

Britannic Majesty at or in the vicinity of Basra and for an air base to be selected by His Britannic Majesty to the west of the Euphrates. His Majesty the King of Iraq futher authorises His Britannic Majesty to maintain forces upon Iraq territory at the above localities in accordance with the provisions of the Annexure of this Treaty on the understanding that the presence of those forces shall not constitute in any manner an occupation and will in no way prejudice the sovereign rights of Iraq.

Article 6

The annexure hereto shall be regarded as an integral part of the present treaty.

Article 7

This treaty shall replace the Treaties of Alliance signed at Baghdad on the tenth day of October, one thousand nine hundred and twenty-two of the Christian era, corresponding to the nineteenth day of Safar, one thousand three hundred and forty-one, Hijrah, and on the thirteenth day of January, one thousand nine hundred and twenty-six of the Christian era, corresponding to the twenty-eighth day of Jamadi-al-Ukhra, one thousand three hundred and forty-four, Hijrah, and the subsidiary agreements thereto, which shall cease to have effect upon the entry into force of this treaty. It shall be executed in duplicate, in the English and Arabic languages, of which the former shall be regarded as the authoritative version.

Article 8

The high contracting parties recognise that, upon the entry into force of this treaty, all responsibilities devolving under the treaties and agreements referred to in article 7 hereof upon His Britannic Majesty in respect of Iraq will, in so far as His Britannic Majesty is concerned, then automatically and completely come to an end, and that such responsibilities, in so far as they continue at all, will devolve upon His Majesty the King of Iraq alone.

It is also recognised that all responsibilities devolving upon His Britannic Majesty in respect of Iraq under any other international instrument, in so far as they continue at all, should similarly devolve upon His Majesty the King of Iraq alone, and the high contracting parties shall immediately take such steps as may be necessary to secure the transference to His Majesty the King of Iraq of these responsibilities.

Article 9

Nothing in the present treaty is intended to or shall in any way prejudice the rights and obligations which devolve, or may devolve, upon either of the high contracting parties under the Covenant of the League of Nations or the Treaty for the Renunciation of War signed at Paris on the twenty-seventh day of August, one thousand nine hundred and twenty-eight.

Article 10

Should any difference arise relative to the application or the interpretation of this treaty, and should the high contracting parties fail to settle such difference by direct negotiation, then it shall be dealt with in accordance with the provisions of the Covenant of the League of Nations.

Article 11

This treaty shall be ratified and ratifications shall be exchanged as soon as possible. Thereafter it shall come into force as soon as Iraq has been admitted to membership of the League of Nations.

The present treaty shall remain in force for a period of twenty-five years from the date of its coming into force. At any time after twenty years from the date of the coming into force of this treaty, the high contracting parties will, at the request of either of them, conclude a new treaty which shall provide for the continued maintenance and protection in all circumstances of the essential communications of His Britannic Majesty. In case of disagreement in this matter the difference will be submitted to the Council of the League of Nations.

In faith whereof the respective plenipotentiaries have signed the present treaty and have affixed thereto their seals.

Done at Baghdad in duplicate this thirtieth day of June, one thousand nine hundred and thirty, of the Christian era, corresponding to the fourth day of Safar, one thousand three hundred and forty-nine, Hijrah.

(L.S.) F. H. Humphrys

(L.S.) Noury Said

Annexure to Treaty of Alliance

1

The strength of the forces maintained in Iraq by His Britannic Majesty in accordance with the terms of article 5 of this treaty shall be determined by His Britannic Majesty from time to time after consultation with His Majesty the King of Iraq.

His Britannic Majesty shall maintain forces at Hinaidi for a period of five years after the entry into force of this treaty in order to enable His Majesty the King of Iraq to organise the necessary forces to replace them. By the expiration of that period the said forces of His Britannic Majesty to maintain forces at Mosul for a maximum period of five years from the entry into force of this treaty. Thereafter it shall be open to His Britannic Majesty to station his forces in the localities mentioned in article 5 of this treaty, and His Majesty the King of Iraq will grant to His Britannic Majesty for the duration of the alliance leases of the necessary sites for the accommodation of the forces of His Britannic Majesty in those localities.

2

Subject to any modifications which the two high contracting parties may agree to introduce in the future, the immunities and privileges in the jurisdictional and fiscal matters, including freedom from taxation, enjoyed by the British forces in Iraq will continue to extend to the forces of all arms as may be in Iraq in pursuance of the present treaty and its annexure or otherwise by agreement between the high contracting parties and the existing provisions of any local legislation affecting the armed forces of His Britannic Majesty in Iraq shall also continue. The Iraq Government will take the necessary steps to ensure that the altered conditions will not render the position of the British forces as regards immunities and privileges in any way less favourable than that enjoyed by them at the date of the entry into force of this treaty.

3

His Majesty the King of Iraq agrees to provide all possible facilities for the movement, training and maintenance of the forces referred to in clause 1 above and to accord to those forces the same facilities for the use of wireless telegraphy as those enjoyed by them at the date of the entry into force of the present treaty.

4

His Britannic Majesty undertakes to grant whenever they may be required by His Majesty the King of Iraq all possible facilities in the following matters, the cost of which will be met by His Majesty the King of Iraq.

1 Naval, military and aeronautical instruction of Iraqi officers in the United Kingdom.

2 The provisions of arms, ammunition, equipment, ships and aeroplanes of the latest available pattern for the forces of His Majesty the King of Iraq.

3 The provision of British naval, military and air force officers to serve in an advisory capacity with the forces of His Majesty the King of Iraq.

5

In view of the desirability of identity in training and methods between the Iraq and British armies, His Majesty the King of Iraq undertakes that, should he deem it necessary to have recourse to foreign military instructors, these shall be chosen from amongst British subjects.

He further undertakes that any personnel of his forces that may be sent abroad for military training will be sent to military schools, colleges and training centres in the territories of His Britannic Majesty, provided that this shall not prevent him from sending to any other country such personnel as cannot be received in the said institutions and training centres.

He further undertakes that the armament and essential equipment of his forces shall not differ in type from those of the forces of His Britannic Majesty.

6

His Majesty the King of Iraq agrees to afford, when requested to do so by His Britannic Majesty, all possible facilities for the movement of the forces of His Britannic Majesty of all arms in transit across Iraq and for the transport and storage of all supplies and equipment that may be required by these forces during their passage across Iraq. These facilities shall cover the use of the roads, railways, waterways, ports and aerodromes of Iraq, and His Britannic Majesty's ships shall have general permission to visit the Shatt-al-Arab on the understanding that His Majesty the King of Iraq is given prior notification of visits to Iraq ports.

(Initialled) F. H. H.
N. S.

Published notes exchanged

I

His Majesty's High Commissioner in Iraq to the Iraqi Prime Minister and Minister for Foreign Affairs

Baghdad, June 30, 1930

Sir,

I have the honour to inform you, with regard to article 2 of the treaty which we have signed to-day, that it is intended that His Britannic Majesty's diplomatic representative at the Court of His Majesty the King of Iraq shall have the status of ambassador.

I have &c.
F. H. Humphrys

The Iraqi Prime Minister and Minister for Foreign Affairs to His Majesty's High Commissioner in Iraq

Baghdad, June 30, 1930

Sir,

In reply to your note of to-day's date I have the honour to inform you that the Iraq Government, anxious to mark the satisfaction which the appointment of His Britannic Majesty's representative as the first ambassador in Iraq affords them, intend that his precedence in relation to the representatives of other Powers shall extend to his successors. The Iraq Government also intend that the diplomatic representative of His Majesty the King of Iraq at the Court of St James shall have the status of Minister Plenipotentiary during the currency of this treaty.

I have, &c.

Noury Said

II

His Majesty's High Commissioner in Iraq to the Iraqi Prime Minister and Minister for Foreign Affairs.

Baghdad, June 30, 1930

Sir,

In connexion with the treaty signed by us to-day I have the honour to place on record that it has been agreed that all outstanding financial questions, such as those relating to the Iraq Railways and the port of Basra and those which it is necessary to settle for the purpose of the operation of the treaty and of its annexure, shall form the subject of a separate agreement which shall be concluded as soon as possible and which shall be deemed an integral part of the present treaty and shall be ratified simultaneously therewith.

I have, &c.

F. H. Humphrys

III

The Iraqi Prime Minister and Minister for Foreign Affairs to His Majesty's High Commissioner in Iraq

Baghdad, June 30, 1930

Sir,

In connexion with the treaty signed by us to-day I have the honour to inform your Excellency that, in view of the close friendship and alliance between our two countries, the Iraq Government will normally engage British subjects when in need of the services of foreign officials. Such officials will be selected after consultation between our two Governments. It is understood that this shall not prejudice the freedom of the Iraq Government to engage non-British foreign officials for posts for which suitable British subjects are not available.

I have also the honour to inform your Excellency that nothing in the treaty which we have signed to-day shall affect the validity of the contracts concluded and in existence between the Iraq Government and British officials.

I have, &c.

Noury Said

His Majesty's High Commissioner in Iraq to the Iraqi Prime Minister and Minister for Foreign Affairs

Baghdad, June 30, 1930

Sir,

I have the honour to acknowledge the receipt of your Excellency's note of to-day's date regarding the engagement of foreign officials, and to confirm the statement therein recorded of the understanding which we have reached.

I have, &c.

F. H. Humphrys

IV

The Iraqi Prime Minister and Minister for Foreign Affairs to His Majesty's High Commissioner in Iraq

Baghdad, June 30, 1930

Sir,

I have the honour to inform your Excellency that it is the intention of the Iraq Government, in view of their desire to improve the efficiency of their land and air forces, to ask for a British Advisory Military Mission, the numbers of which shall be decided before the treaty comes into force and the conditions of service of which shall be similar to those of the existing military mission.

I have, &c.

Noury Said

His Majesty's High Commissioner in Iraq to the Iraqi Prime Minister and Minister for Foreign Affairs

Baghdad, June 30, 1930

Sir,

I have the honour to acknowledge the receipt of your note of to-day's date on the subject of the British Advisory Military Mission which the Iraq Government intend to invite to Iraq.

I have, &c.

F. H. Humphrys

Notes exchanged with the Iraqi Prime Minister embodying the separate agreement on financial questions referred to in the second exchange of notes appended to the Anglo-Iraqi Treaty of 30 June 1930

I

His Majesty's High Commissioner in Iraq to the Iraqi Prime Minister and Minister for Foreign Affairs

London, August 19, 1930

Sir,

With reference to our conversation in London, I have the honour to propose that the following provisions shall be considered as embodying the separate agreement on all financial questions referred to in the second exchange of notes between your Excellency and myself at the time of the signature of the Treaty of Alliance on the 30th June, 1930.

It is understood that the agreement constituted by this note and by your Excellency's reply thereto shall be included in the instruments of ratification of the Treaty of Alliance and shall become operative on the exchange of ratifications.

1 The Government of the United Kingdom of Great Britain and Northern Ireland shall transfer to the Iraq Government, within the period stipulated in clause 1 of the annexure of the Treaty of Alliance signed on the 30th June, 1930, the aerodromes and encampments at Hinaidi and Mosul at present occupied by the forces of His Britannic Majesty, and the Iraq Government shall accept the transfer thereof (less two 'A' type steel hangers and the ice plants at Hinaidi and Mosul, to be removed by the Government of the United Kingdom) at one-third of the cost price certified as correct by the Air Ministry of the Government of the United Kingdom, of the permanent buildings, plant and structures thereon, no account being taken of the mud buildings which shall be transferred to the Iraq Government free of cost. The Iraq Government shall pay this sum to the Government of the United Kingdom not later than the date upon which the aforesaid transfer is completed.

During the maximum period stipulated in clause 1 of the annexure to the Treaty of Alliance the forces of His Britannic Majesty shall remain in undisturbed occupation of their present stations of Hinaidi and Mosul and at Shaiba and in the use of their existing emergency landing grounds, and the Government of the United Kingdom shall not be called upon to pay higher rental charges in respect thereof than those at present paid.

2 If upon the withdrawal of the forces of His Britannic Majesty from Hinaidi and Mosul in accordance with clause 1 of the annexure to the Treaty of Alliance the Government of the United Kingdom should decide to establish a British air base in the neighbourhood of Habbaniya, then the Iraq Government shall take all possible steps, at no cost to either Government, to arrange for the construction of a railway to connect such air base with the railway system of Iraq.

3 The leases of the sites for air bases to be granted to His Britannic Majesty, in accordance with the provisions of article 5 of the Treaty of Alliance, shall, in so far as such sites are on waste Government land, be free of all rental charges; and, in so far as they are on non-Government land, every facility shall be given for their acquisition on reasonable terms, such acquisition being effected by the Iraq Government at the request and at the cost of the Government of the United Kingdom. The leased lands bases remain in the occupation of the forces of His Britannic Majesty in accordance with the provisions of the aforesaid Treaty of Alliance or of any extension thereof. On the final termination of the leases of the said sites, or of any one of them, the Iraq Government shall either themselves take over the buildings and permanent structures thereon at a fair valuation, having regard to the use to which they have been put, or shall afford such facilities as may reasonably be necessary to enable the Government of the United Kingdom to dispose thereof to the best advantage.

After the expiry of the maximum period stipulated in clause 1 of the annexure to the Treaty of Alliance and so long as the said Treaty of Alliance remains in force the Government of the United Kingdom shall not be called upon to pay any charges in respect of the use of any of the existing emergency landing grounds in Iraq.

4 The following arrangements for the disposal and administration of the Iraq railway system shall be carried into effect as soon as possible and, in any case, within a maximum period of one year from the entry into force of the Treaty of Alliance:

(a) Legal ownership of the railway system shall be transferred by the Government of the United Kingdom to the Iraq Government and registered in the name of the Iraq Government, and simultaneously with such transfer full beneficial ownership shall be vested, by lease or otherwise and a nominal rent and on terms satisfactory to the Government of the United Kingdom, in a special body or corporation having legal personality, to be constituted by a special statute of the Iraq Legislature, the terms of which shall have been agreed by both Governments.

(b) The above-mentioned corporation shall be wholly responsible for the administration and management of the Iraq railway system, and, subject to such limitations as may be imposed in the statute referred to above, shall have sole and exclusive authority to raise new capital by public issue or private loan and to dispose of the revenues of that system.

(c) The capital of the said corporation shall comprise:

(1) Rs 275 lakhs of preferred stock, bearing interest at 6 per cent, such interest being non-cumulative for a period of twenty years from the date of the transfer of the ownership of the system and thereafter cumulative, to be allotted to the Government of the United Kingdom, of which Rs 25 lakhs represents the capitalised value of the debt of the railways to the Government of the United Kingdom on liquidation account;

(2) Rs 45–85 lakhs of similar preferred stock, to be allotted to the Iraq Government, being an amount equal to the loans which the Iraq Government have made to the railways on which interest charges have been waived; and

(3) Rs 250 lakhs of deferred stock also to be allotted to the Iraq Government.

The Iraq Government shall have the option to buy at any time at par the stock allotted to the Government of the United Kingdom.

(d) The board of the corporation shall consist of five directors, of whom two shall be appointed by the Government of the United Kingdom and two by the Iraq Government, and the fifth, who shall be the chairman, shall be appointed by both Governments in agreement. The first chairman shall be the present Director of the Iraq Railways.

(e) The corporation shall be responsible for raising loan capital required for the reconditioning and development of the Iraq railway system, and neither Government shall be under any obligation to guarantee such loan capital either in respect of interest or of capital.

(f) Any loan capital raised by the corporation for the reconditioning or development of the Iraq railway system shall rank before the stock allotted to the two Governments in accordance with clause (c) above.

(g) The Iraq Government, as owners of the equity of the system, shall accept ultimate responsibility for any liabilities relating thereto, not devolving upon the corporation, that may subsequently come to light, and in consideration thereof the Government of the United Kingdom shall transfer to the Iraq Government an amount of preferred stock of a nominal value equal to the amount of any irrecoverable disbursements that the Iraq Government may have to make in the discharge of any of the aforesaid liabilities, the validity of which may have been established to the satisfaction of the Government of the United Kingdom.

(h) In anticipation of the transfer of the railway system and the establishment of the corporation, the Iraq Government shall forthwith grant three-year contracts, on 'treaty' conditions, to such British railway officials as may be recommended therefor by the Director of the Iraq Railways, and shall not terminate any such contracts when granted except with the agreement of the Government of the United Kingdom. The question of granting these officials contracts of longer duration shall be left for the decision of the corporation when constituted.

5 The property in the port of Basra at present held by the Government of the United Kingdom shall be transferred to the Iraqi Government and the port shall be administered by a Port Trust. For this purpose legislation in terms agreed with the Government of the United Kingdom shall be enacted in Iraq for the establishment of a Port Trust having legal personality, and such legislation shall not be amended, except by agreement with the Government of the United Kingdom, so long as any part of the debt owing to the Government of the United Kingdom in respect of the port is still outstanding.

Upon the enactment of the above legislation and the establishment of the Port Trust, the property in the port shall be transferred to the Iraq Government, in whose name it will then be registered, and, simultaneously with such transfer, full beneficial ownership shall be conferred, by lease, concession or other appropriate instrument, the terms of which shall be subject to the approval of the Government of the United

211

Kingdom, upon the Port Trust for the period during which any part of the debt owing to the Government of the United Kingdom in respect of the port remains outstanding.

I have, &c.

F. H. Humphrys

II

The Iraqi Prime Minister and Minister for Foreign Affairs to His Majesty's High Commissioner in Iraq

London, August 19, 1930

Sir,

I have the honour to acknowledge the receipt of your note of to-day's date setting out the provisions to be considered as embodying the separate agreement on all financial questions referred to in the second exchange of notes between your Excellency and myself at the time of signature of the Treaty of Alliance on the 30th June, 1930, and to confirm that your note accurately sets out the agreement at which we have arrived.

I have, &c.

Noury Said

Unpublished notes (arranged in chronological order)

(a)

The Iraqi Prime Minister and Minister for Foreign Affairs to His Majesty's High Commissioner in Iraq

Baghdad, June 30, 1930

Sir,

With regard to the second paragraph of article 8 of the treaty, I have the honour to request that the Iraq Government may be furnished in due course with a complete list of the international instruments therein referred to in order that they may be acquired with the texts of these instruments before the treaty is presented by them to Parliament for ratification.

I have, &c.

Noury Said

(b)

The Iraqi Prime Minister and Minister for Foreign Affairs to His Majesty's High Commissioner in Iraq

Baghdad, June 30, 1930

Sir,

I have the honour to inform you, with reference to clause 4 of the annexure to the treaty which we have signed to-day, that, when the time comes to bring that clause into effect, the Iraq Government will be prepared to agree to the following arrangements for the special guards referred to therein. I do not anticipate that any legislation will be necessary in order to ensure the smooth working of this arrangement, but if there is any point upon which it is found in practice that the existing law is insufficient for this purpose, the necessary legislation will be passed without delay:

(a) The force will consist of not more than 1,250 men, exclusive of British personnel.

(b) Service in the force will be voluntary, and such service will exempt any member of the force from the provisions of any law for compulsory service.

(c) The force will be under the command of a British commanding officer and the requisite number of subordinate British and Iraqi officers, all of whom will hold the commission of His Majesty the King of Iraq. It will also include such British warrant and non-commissioned officers as may be necessary, who shall have the powers normally pertaining to their ranks. The commanding officer will have the power to make rules regarding recruitment, administration, nature of arms, equipment and clothing, method of training, rates of pay and conditions of service.

(d) With regard to discipline, the force, with the exception of the British personnel, will be subject to Iraq military law. The commanding officer and the subordinate British officers will be granted the necessary summary powers, and the commanding officer will have full discretion as to the convening and composition of courts-martial. The sentences of courts-martial of which the commanding officer is not a member will be confirmed by him. In cases in which the commanding officer is himself a member of the court or in which the sentence imposed by the court exceeds one year's imprisonment, confirmation of the sentence will be made by the Minister of Defence.

213

(e) The primary duty of the force will be the protection of such air bases in Iraq as may, with the consent of the Iraq Government, be occupied by the forces of His Britannic Majesty, and this duty will include the task of safeguarding the material and stores of His Britannic Majesty's forces in Iraq wherever they may be. For the purpose of carrying out these duties, the sole executive responsibility for which will rest with the commanding officer, the force will be placed at the entire disposal of the Air Officer Commanding.

(f) It is understood that from time to time it may be necessary, in order that the above duties may be properly performed, that members of the force should receive orders from officers of His Britannic Majesty's forces. Such orders will normally be conveyed to the force through its own officers, but the Iraq Government raise no objection in cases of necessity to such orders being given direct, and will take steps to ensure that in this case all members of the force shall be under an obligation to obey such orders, and that they shall enjoy the same immunities as if the orders had been given by an officer of the forces of His Majesty the King of Iraq. It is understood that any power of command over Iraqi forces which may be given to officers of His Britannic Majesty's forces will only be exercised in relation to the special forces.

(g) The entire cost of the force will be met by His Majesty's Government in Great Britain.

I have, &c.

Noury Said

(c)

His Majesty's High Commissioner in Iraq to the Iraqi Prime Minister and Minister for Foreign Affairs

Colonial Office,
Downing Street, July 15, 1930

Sir,

I am instructed to inform your Excellency that the forces which His Britannic Majesty is authorised to maintain in Iraq in accordance with the terms of article 5 of the treaty shall comprise Royal Air Force units, together with ancillary services.

I am also instructed to inform your Excellency that, whereas it is

provided in clause 4 of the annexure of the treaty that the protection
of the air bases to be occupied by the forces of His Britannic Majesty
in Iraq shall be undertaken by special guards from the forces of His
Majesty the King of Iraq, yet it is understood that His Britannic Majesty
is authorised in time of emergency, in case the special guards should,
after consultation between the two high contracting parties, be considered inadequate for the defence of His Britannic Majesty's air bases
in Iraq, to reinforce such guards temporarily by his own land forces.

I am also instructed to inform your Excellency that the expression
'in transit across Iraq' used in clause 7 of the annexure of the treaty
means transit from any place west of the Euphrates to the Persian
Gulf, or in the opposite direction.

> I have, &c.
> F. H. Humphrys

(d)

His Majesty's High Commissioner in Iraq to the Iraqi Prime Minister and Minister for Foreign Affairs

London, August 19, 1930

Sir,

With reference to paragraph 4 (e) of my letter of to-day's date, I am
authorised to place it on record that, while both Governments anticipate
that the corporation, which will be responsible for the administration
and management of the Iraq railway system, will be able to raise loan
capital for the reconditioning and development of the system without
a Government guarantee, in the unlikely event of the corporation failing
to do so, it is understood that the question of the future administration
and management of the Iraq railway system will call for further discussion between the two Governments.

> I have, &c.
> F. H. Humphrys

(f)

His Majesty's High Commissioner in Iraq to the Iraqi Prime Minister and Minister for Foreign Affairs

London, August 19, 1930

Sir,

In the course of our conversations on the subject of the immunity from taxation enjoyed by the Shaikhs of Mohammerah and Koweit in respect of their date gardens in Iraq, your Excellency and I discussed the method of dealing with this matter in the list of international obligations devolving upon Iraq under article 8 of the Treaty of Alliance signed on the 30th June, 1930, which I have undertaken to communicate to your Excellency before the Iraq Parliament is invited to approve of the ratification of the treaty. As I have informed your Excellency, His Majesty's Government in the United Kingdom approve of your proposal that the Iraq Government should open private negotiations with the shaikhs for the purchase of their properties in Iraq.

It is possible, however, that these negotiations may not have reached finality before the time comes for me to communicate the above list to the Iraq Government. In such event, His Majesty's Government propose to insert mention of the obligation towards the shaikhs in the list, but at the same time to append a footnote to the effect that private negotiations are proceeding with a view to the liquidation of this obligation, and that, if these are unsuccessful, the question will need to be discussed further between the two Governments.

I shall be glad to learn from your Excellency that this procedure will be acceptable to the Iraq Government.

I have, &c.

F. H. Humphrys

(g)

The Iraqi Prime Minister and Minister for Foreign Affairs to His Majesty's High Commissioner in Iraq

London, August 19, 1930

Sir,

I have the honour to acknowledge the receipt of your Excellency's letter of to-day's date, relative to the method of dealing, in the list of international obligations devolving upon Iraq under article 8 of the Treaty of Alliance signed on the 30th June, 1930, with the question of the immunity from taxaton enjoyed by the Sheikhs of Mohammerah and Koweit in respect of their date gardens in Iraq.

I have the honour to inform your Excellency in reply that the procedure indicated in the second paragraph of your letter is acceptable to the Iraq Government.

I have, &c.

Noury Said

216

(h)

His Majesty's High Commissioner in Iraq to the Iraqi Prime Minister and Minister for Foreign Affairs

Baghdad, October 18, 1930

(No. PO 237) (Confidential)

My dear Prime Minister,

Will you please refer to your Excellency's letter dated the 30th June, 1930 addressed to me on the occasion of the signature of the new Anglo-Iraq Treaty, asking to be furnished in due course with a complete list of the international instruments referred to in the second paragraph of article 8 of the treaty.

I have now received from His Britannic Majesty's Government a list of these instruments, of which I enclose a copy for your Excellency's information. His Britannic Majesty's Government desire me to explain that, although an exhaustive examination has been made of the various international instruments to which His Majesty's Government is a party, and which involves them in some degree of responsibility in respect of Iraq, it is possible, although unlikely, that the present list may not prove to be exhaustive, and that instruments which would properly fall within the category envisaged in the second paragraph of article 8 may later be found to have been overlooked.

I should also explain that only those instruments have been included in the accompanying list which might be held to involve a continuing obligation on the part of His Majesty's Government after the entry of Iraq into the League of Nations, and thus to call for the process of substitution contemplated in the second paragraph of article 8, and that no instruments have been included creating obligations of such a character that they must, in so far as the responsibility of His Majesty's Government is concerned, terminate automatically upon the termination of the mandatory regime.

With regard to item 1 on the accompanying list, I would invite your Excellency's attention to the notes exchanged between your Excellency and myself on the 19th August on the subject of the immunity from taxation enjoyed by the Sheikhs of Mohammerah and Koweit in respect of their date gardens in Iraq.

Yours sincerely,

F. H. Humphrys

List of International instruments referred to in the second paragraph of Article 8 of the Anglo–Iraq Treaty of June 30, 1930

1 Undertaking entered into with the Sheikhs of Koweit and Moham-merah in 1914 in respect of their date gardens in Iraq.*
2 The San Remo Oil Agreement, the 25th April, 1920
3 The Anglo-French Boundary Convention, the 23rd December, 1920
4 The Treaty Settlement of Lausanne, the 24th July, 1923
5 The Treaty of Angara, the 5th June, 1926

(i)

His Majesty's High Commissioner in Iraq to the Iraqi Prime Minister and Minister for Foreign Affairs

Baghdad, November 7, 1930

(No. PO 256)

My dear Prime Minister,

Your Excellency recently asked me for an explanation of certain points in the Anglo–Iraq Treaty, which we signed on the 30th June, that seemed to your Excellency liable to misinterpretation.

The first point was the reference to 'common interests' in article 1. Your Excellency enquired whether this term was intended to cover economic and commercial as well as political and military interests. I am to explain that article 1 provides for full and frank consultation between the high contracting parties in regard to all matters which:

(a) Fall within the sphere of foreign policy; and

(b) Affect the common interests of the high contracting parties.

While it is impossible to say that no commercial or economic matter could in any circumstances be of such a character and importance as to fall within the scope of this article (since, to take an extreme example, such matters might conceivably lead to a situation involving a rupture such as is contemplated in article 3), I am authorised to give you an assurance that matters which are purely economic or commercial would fall outside it.

Your Excellency's second enquiry was whether, although it was not specifically stated in article 3, His Britannic Majesty's Government

---

* Private negotiations are proceeding with a view to the liquidation of this com-mitment, If these are unsuccessful, the question will need to be discussed further between the two Governments.

would, in fact, concert with the Iraq Government in the event of a risk of a rupture arising between Great Britain and one of Iraq's neighbours. I am authorised to give you an assurance in the affirmative and to explain that this assurance is implicit in article 1 of the treaty.

Your Excellency further enquired whether the words 'essential communications' occurring in article 5 referred only to air communications. I am authorised to reply that this term is held by my Government to refer to air communications over Iraq and to sea and air communications at the head of the Persian Gulf and in the Shatt-al-Arab.

Finally, your Excellency enquired as to the number of the special guards to be provided by His Majesty the King of Iraq for the protection of air bases under clause 4 of the annexure to the treaty. In reply, I would refer you to your letter dated the 30th June, 1930, on the subject of these special guards in which it was stated that the Iraqi subjects would consist of not more than 1,250 men.

I hope that your Excellency will find these explanations satisfactory.

Yours sincerely,

F. H. Humphrys

(j)

His Majesty's High Commissioner in Iraq to the Iraqi Prime Minister and Minister for Foreign Affairs

Baghdad, January 26, 1931

(No. PO 18) (Confidential)

My dear Prime Minister,

Last November your Excellency asked me verbally for certain explanations of points connected with the Anglo-Iraq Treaty signed on the 30th June last which your Excellency regarded as doubtful. I am now in a position to explain the points in question.

Your Excellency first enquired whether any expenditure that might be incurred by His Majesty the King of Iraq in providing the facilities referred to in the last sentence of article 4 of the treaty would be defrayed by His Britannic Majesty's Government. I am authorised to reply that it appears to His Britannic Majesty's Government that the incidence of cost in each case where the question arises must depend upon the circumstances existing at the time. These circumstances might render it equitable in certain cases that the Iraq Government should bear the whole or part of this expenditure as their contribution to a joint campaign undertaken on behalf of Iraq. In these cases the final decision would be a matter for arrangements between the two Governments at the time. In general, however, His Britannic Majesty's Government consider that if the facilities in question are provided solely in the interests of His Britannic Majesty's Government, any additional expenditure necessarily incurred by the Iraq Government in carrying out the terms of the article should be repaid to them; but His Britannic Majesty's Government would not expect to be asked to pay for the use of existing facilities when the use of such facilities by British forces would not involve the Iraq Government in additional expenditure.

Your Excellency's second enquiry was whether the phrase 'sites for air bases . . . . at or in the vicinity of Basra', occurring in article 5, was correctly translated into Arabic by the dual, i.e. 'sites for two air bases'. I am authorised to reply that the phrase in question contemplates a combined land and sea base at, or in the immediate vicinity of, Basra and a land base near Basra probably at Shaibah.

Finally, your Excellency asked for an assurance that, as it was impossible to guarantee that the list of international instruments covered by article 8 communicated to the Iraq Government was complete, no responsibilities would devolve upon the Iraq Government in respect of any secret agreement concluded between His Britannic Majesty's Government and a third party. I am authorised to reply on this point that His Britannic Majesty's Government have not entered into any secret agreements in respect of Iraq, and that consequently any international instruments that are covered by article 8, but are not included in the list communicated to the Iraq Government, will not include any secret agreements between His Britannic Majesty's Government and a third party.

I hope that your Excellency will find these explanations satisfactory.

Yours sincerely,
F. H. Humphrys

(k)

The Iraqi Prime Minister and Minister for Foreign Affairs to His Majesty's High Commissioner in Iraq

Baghdad, January 29/February 1, 1931

(No. 456) (Confidential)

Dear Sir Francis,

    1 I have received your letter No. PO 18 dated 26th January, 1931,

concerning the elucidation of certain points in the Anglo-Iraq Treaty signed on the 30th June last.

2 The Iraq Government regret that they are unable to concur in the contents of your Excellency's above-mentioned letter in regard to expenditure on the affording of the facilities dealt with in the last sentence of article 4 of the treaty. Right from the commencement of the negotiations for the conclusion of the treaty and until I received your Excellency's letter under reply, I always heard from your Excellency that the expenses of the British Army (? Forces) in the event of a combined expedition would be borne by the British Government. The Iraq Government cannot contemplate a condition arising of a nature leading to concertion of efforts for combined defence in the interest of Iraq alone, but, on the other hand, believe that any combined defence undertaken, whatever the motive, will also be in the interest of the British Government. Had there been no agreement over this fundamental principle, i.e. community of interests between the two parties and 'the existence of' (sic) co-operation for the defence of common interests, the treaty would not have been concluded in its present form, in particular article 4 with which we are now dealing. A point which arrests the attention is that previous treaties did not place on the shoulder of Iraq any such financial obligations; and as the present treaty is (? intended to be) more advantageous to Iraq than the former treaties, it should be less likely to contain provisions which involve Iraq in obligations of this nature. Moreover, it is a common international principle that, when two allied Governments undertake a combined expedition, each Government bears the expenses of her own forces. I shall be very grateful if your Excellency will be so kind as to lay the foregoing considerations before His Britannic Majesty's Government for a reconsideration of the matter, and I also request that you will at the same time point out to them that no Iraq Government can concur in the explanations set forth in your Excellency's letter because they (i.e., the explanations) place on the shoulder of Iraq indefinite financial obligations.

3 The Iraq Government have taken note of the explanation set forth in your Excellency's letter in regard to the location of the two air bases dealt with in article 5 and to the International Agreements dealt with in article 8.

Yours sincerely,

Nuri-al-Said

(l)

His Majesty's High Commissioner in Iraq to the Iraqi Prime Minister and Minister for Foreign Affairs

Baghdad, November 23, 1931

(No. PO 157) (Confidential)

My dear Prime Minister,

With reference to your Excellency's confidential letter No. 456 of the 1st February last, in which your Excellency asked for a further explanation of the views of His Majesty's Government regarding the incidence of cost of the facilities dealt with in the last sentence of article 4 of the treaty of the 30th June, 1930. I have discussed the matter in London, and am now authorised to reply that His Majesty's Government in the United Kingdom would be prepared to indemnify the Iraqi Government against any additional expenditure necessarily incurred by them in the provision of the facilities mentioned in article 4, but would not expect to be asked to pay in respect of the movement or accommodation of the forces of the Iraqi Government, nor would His Majesty's Government expect to be asked to pay for the use of existing facilities when the use of such facilities by the British forces would involve the Iraqi Government in no additional expenditure.

I trust that your Excellency will find this explanation satisfactory.

Yours, &c.

F. H. Humphrys

(m)

The Iraqi Prime Minister and Minister for Foreign Affairs to His Majesty's High Commissioner in Iraq

Baghdad, November 30/December 1, 1931

(No. 4464) (Confidential)

Dear Sir Francis,

The Iraqi Government have noted the contents of your Excellency's letter No. PO 157 dated the 23rd November, 1931, concerning the cost of the facilities dealt with in the last sentence of article 4 of the treaty of the 30th June, 1930, and they find the explanations given therein satisfactory.

Please accept, &c.

Yours, &c.

Nuri-al-Sa'id

Notes

Notes to Acknowledgments

1 'Abd al-Razzaq al-Hasani, *Tarikh al-Wizarat al-Iraqiya* (History of the Iraqi Cabinets), 10 vols, Beirut, 1974.
2 Hanna Batatu, *The Old Social Classes and the Revolutionary Movements of Iraq*, Princeton, NJ, 1978.
3 A. S. Klieman, *Foundations of British Policy in the Arab World, The Cairo Conference of 1921*, Baltimore, 1970.
4 H. Mejcher, *The Imperial Quest for Oil, Iraq 1910–1928*, London, 1976.
5 P. Sluglett, *Britain in Iraq 1914–1932*, London, 1976.

Notes to Introduction

1 May Brodbeck, Models, in *Readings in the Philosophy of Science*, ed. H. Feigl and M. Brodbeck, New York, 1953. See also Abraham Kaplan, *The Conduct of Enquiry*, Michigan, 1963, and Thomas Kuhn, *The Structure of Scientific Revolution*, Chicago, 1970.
2 Morris Janowitz, *The Military in the Political Development of New Nations*, Chicago, 1964, p. 111.
3 Ibid., p. 5, where he refers to five types of civil military relations. See also his Table 1, on p. 10.
4 See for example John J. Johnson (ed.) *The Role of the Military in Underdeveloped Countries*, Princeton, 1962, and also Samuel P. Huntington, *The Soldier and the State*, Cambridge, Mass., 1957.
5 See J. C. Hurewitz, 'Soldiers and social change in plural societies: the contemporary Middle East', in V. J. Parry and M. E. Yapp (eds), *War, Technology and Society in the Middle East*, London, 1975.
6 See also Janowitz, 'Some Observations on the Comparative Analysis of Middle Eastern Institutions', in op. cit.
7 Hurewitz, op. cit., p. 401.

8   This is the notion put forward by S. E. Finer as being negatively
    related to the level of military intervention in the relevant nation.
    See S. E. Finer, *The Man on Horseback, The Role of the Military
    in Politics*, London, 1969.

Notes to Chapter 1

1   According to a report by Major N. N. Bray, then Special Intelli-
    gence Officer attached to Political Department, India, there were
    300 Mesopotamian members of al-'Ahd in Amir Faisal's service.
    'They were nearly all in Turkish military employment. They are
    the leading personalities in the Arab state, and hold all the military
    posts.' FO 371/5230, 14.9.1920.
2   Gertrude Bell, *Review of the Civil Administration of Mesopotamia*,
    London, 1920, p. 132.
3   Already in 1910, a German expert reported 'the oil-bearing district
    of Mosul and Baghdad to be amongst the richest in the world'.
    (As quoted in A. G. Boycott, *The Elements of Imperial Defence*,
    London, 1938, p. 294). British officials were in any case aware of
    the potential wealth of Mesopotamia. This is how a typical
    Memorandum by the General Staff of Mesopotamia referred to
    this issue: 'The future motive power of the world is "oil". The oil
    fields of southern Persia, now under British control, are the most
    inexhaustible "proved" fields in the world. The Mosul province,
    and the banks of the mid-Euphrates, promise to afford oil in great
    quantities, although the extent of the fields is not yet proved.'
    FO 371/5073, 12.11.1919. Apart from oil, even before the First
    World War, Britain occupied a paramount position in the trade of
    what later became Iraq. Of the total import trade of the country,
    Britain's share was between 45 and 50 per cent, and that of India
    about 25 per cent; while Britain was also the principal customer,
    taking some 35 per cent of the exports. FO 371/17858, E 3526/
    190/93, 20.5.1934.
4   For example, in the Memorandum by the General Staff of
    Mesopotamia referred to above, it was noted that, 'with a railway
    and pipe line in the Mediterranean, which is forecasted within the
    next ten years, the position of England as a naval power in the
    Mediterranean could be doubly assured, and our dependence on
    the Suez canal, which is a vulnerable point in our line of com-
    munication with the East would be considerably lessened.' FO
    371/5073, 12.11.1919.
5   For the full text, see P. W. Ireland, *Iraq*, London, 1937, p. 160.
6   Bell, op. cit., p. 128.
7   Ibid., p. 127.
8   Ibid., p. 140.

9 For a study of this rebellion, see W. O. Nadmi, 'The Iraqi Revolt of 1920', PhD thesis, University of Durham, 1974.
10 CO 730/1/15895, C 6247/2740/18, 23.3.1921.
11 Apart from the Arab nationalists and the British striving to further their respective political interests, it was 'reliably reported that letters were received by the 'ulama . . . from 'Ajaimi Pasha acting as agent to Mustafa Kamal Pasha. He talks of a Turk and Arab union against the heretics.' LP & S, 31.12.1920.
12 FO 371/5231, 26.10.1920.
13 LP & S, 48, Intelligence Report no. 4, 31.12.1920.
14 Ibid.
15 *Special Report by H.B.M.G. to the Council of the League of Nations on the Progress of Iraq during the period 1920–31*, Colonial no. 58, p. 14.
16 Air 23/432/BD/39, 21.7.1930.
17 See for example, Air 23/104, SSO, Basra, CD/1/251, 22.5.1926.
18 CO 730/40, Intelligence Report no. 14, 5.7.1923.

Notes to Chapter 2

1 All population figures for 1920 are based on the census conducted by the British military authorities. Details of this census are given in FO 371/5074, and in *Statistical Abstract for the Several British Overseas Dominions and Protectorates, from 1907–21*, no. 56, London, 1924.
2 FO 371/18945, 21.3.1935.
3 G. Bell, *Review of the Civil Administration of Mesopotamia*, London, 1920, p. 129.
4 Ibid., p. 129.
5 All population figures for 1930 are based on the census made by Sir Ernest Dowson, *An Inquiry into Land Tenure and Related Questions*, Iraq Government Report, 1931. These figures are also used as official estimates in *The Iraq Directory, 1936*, Times Press Ltd, Baghdad, 1936, and in the *Statistical Handbook of Middle Eastern Countries*, Economic Research Institute, Jewish Agency for Palestine, 1945.
6 Infant mortality rates for 1929, for example, show that the average rate in the three major cities ran at 334 per 1,000, a rate four to five times higher than that of most Western nations at that time. Also, if we take the annual incidence of malaria, for example, we find that, whereas the total number of reported cases was 36,552 in 1923, it increased to 175,476 in 1926, and although it dropped to 87,476 in 1928 it went up again to 158,902 in 1929 and 151,063 in 1930: Public Health Directorate, *Vital Statistics of Iraq*, 1935, p. 20.

7 Figures on health are based on Colonial Office, *Reports on Iraq Administration*, starting with the year 1922 and continuing until the year 1932.

8 This figure is based on a study of monthly summaries of operations by the RAF in Iraq between August 1921 and November 1932: Air 5/1287/11 J 3/60/A, 1287/3,4.5. 1288/1, 1289/11 J3/60 C, 1290/60 D, 1291/60 E, Air 23, 1618/27, 6496/29.

9 Air 5/1291/60 E, October 1927.

10 FO 406/75, Confidential, E 601/1/93, January 1937.

11 Ferhang Jalal, *The Role of Government in the Industrialisation of Iraq, 1950–65*, London, 1972, p. 1.

12 C. J. Edmonds, *Kurds, Turks, and Arabs*, London, 1957, p. 36.

13 Jalal, op. cit., p. 2.

14 Sir A. Wilson, *Mesopotamia – A Clash of Loyalties*, vol. II, London, 1931, p. 177.

15 FO 371/24556.

16 For more specialised studies of this see S. Haidar, 'Land problems of Iraq', in *The Economic History of the Middle East*, ed. C. Issawi, Chicago, 1966; and H. Batatu, 'The shaikh and the peasant in Iraq', PhD thesis, Harvard University, 1960.

17 Hanna Batatu, *The Old Social Classes and the Revolutionary Movements of Iraq*, Princeton, NJ, 1978, p. 55.

18 D. G. Adams, *Iraq's People and Resources*, Berkeley, Cal., 1958, p. 34. She quotes Locher, a visitor to Mesopotamia in the late nineteenth century, who stated that 'Mesopotamia once yielded food for more than fifty million of people.' *With Star and Crescent*, p. 92.

19 See R. Adams, *The Land behind Baghdad*, Chicago, 1965, particularly Part 2, section 8 ('Islamic Revival and Decline, 637–1900'), p. 84.

20 Walid Khadduri, 'Social background of modern Iraqi politics', PhD thesis, Johns Hopkins University, 1974, p. 7.

21 Albertine Jwaideh, 'Midhat Pasha and the land system in lower Iraq', *St Antony's Papers*, no. 16 (ed. A. H. Hourani), London, 1963, p. 111.

22 See Abd al-Jalil al-Tahir, *al-'Asha'ir al-'Iraqiya* (The Tribes of Iraq), Baghdad, 1972.

23 According to G. Bell, *Review of the Civil Administration of Mesopotamia*, 'the Turks put up leases to auction and encouraged the shaikhs to bid against one another until the amounts bid reached a figure far above the value of the estate. Both the Turkish officials and the farmers knew that they could never be paid, but the officials had the pleasure of exhibiting to the departmental heads at Stanbul [sic] enormous demands from their province which were comfortably interpreted as being synonymous with enormous revenues, while they also enjoyed the satis-

faction of receiving continual bribes from the farmers to induce them not to press for payment. The farmers had to be backed by merchant sureties who took from them large sums. Finally, when immense arrears had mounted up against the farmer, or he had attracted the private enmity of an official . . . the whole erection would topple over. All arrears would be demanded at one blow; the farmer, if a shaikh, would pass from rebellion to imprisonment or exile, the lands and houses of the surety would be confiscated, and the estate would be put up afresh to auction and farmed for a still higher and more impossible rent to the rivals of the supplanted man. Scarcely a year passed without conflict.' p. 22.

24 Bell, op. cit., p. 82.
25 Jwaideh, op. cit., p. 120.
26 Registration of land would not have been in the shaikh's favour for an additional reason to the ones already discussed, namely because, according to the chaotic existing system, there were 'tracts measuring thousands of acres . . . shamelessly recorded as being two or three donums in extent', and the boundaries of holdings were given in 'the vaguest terms quite incapable of practical interpretation on the spot'. Bell, op. cit., p. 84.
27 Jwaideh, op. cit., p. 125.
28 Haidar, op. cit., p. 164.
29 Bell, op. cit., p. 22.
30 Ibid., p. 22.
31 Haidar, op. cit., p. 164. Apart from *miri* and *tapu* (which was in any case ultimately *miri*) land, there were very small areas of land, mainly in and around the cities, that were *waqf* (land held in trust). The rent on *miri* land was one-tenth of the crop of unirrigated land, and where water was supplied by a flow an additional one-tenth was demanded (see Bell, op. cit., p. 86). The state also claimed an owner's share as well as the rent, and altogether its claimed tax usually amounted to one-third of the crop, while the remaining two-thirds were equally divided between the *fallah* (who cultivated the land) and the *sarkal*: Ahmad Fahmi (the Accountant-General), *Report on the Financial Position of Iraq*, Baghdad, 1926, p. 78.
32 Haidar, op. cit., p. 163.
33 C. Issawi (ed.), *The Economic History of the Middle East, 1800–1914*, Chicago, 1966, p. 132.
34 Registration fees for obtaining *tapu sanads* were unreasonably high, in some cases, particularly where holdings were relatively small, estimated to be as much as one-quarter of the estimated value of the holding. Bell, op. cit., p. 85.
35 In addition to paying one-third of the crop to the *sarkal* or shaikh, the *fallah* now had to: (a) pay a deposit to the *sarkal* before each

sowing; (b) own a rifle; (c) distribute 25 kilos out of every 2,000 harvested to each of the following: (i) the *qahwaji* (coffee boy) of the shaikh; (ii) the *subashi* (the shaikh's supervisor); (iii) the *mullah* (the shaikh's clerk); (iv) as *bartil* (bribery) to meet the shaikh's general expenses. Fahmi, op. cit., p. 79. It is also interesting that, when in 1911 the Turkish Government was 'compelled to institute a committee of inquiry to investigate the cause of the rising against Sa'dun Pasha by some of the Muntafiq tribes, . . . this committee attributed the trouble to the fact that 'the arable lands of the tribes were in the hands of a few powerful shaikhs who oppressed the tribesmen'. *Military Report on Iraq*, Superintendent Government Printing, India, 1923, p. 10.

36   H. Batatu, 'The shaikh and the peasant'.
37   Ibid.
38   This can be seen from the following report, for example: 'the process of tribal disintegration was now reverted. The progress of villages towards independence of the surrounding tribe was arrested, comeling [sic] of different tribes was as far as possible forbidden, escape of peasant tribesmen from their shaikh's land was prevented.' *Report on the Administration of Iraq, 1918*, Colonial Office.
39   Ibid.
40   Ibid.
41   Bell, op. cit., p. 54.
42   FO 371/5228, 28.7.1920.
43   FO 371/5228, 13.8.1920.
44   Bell, op. cit., p. 143.
45   For example, the Political Officer of 'Amara wrote in 1918 that 'shaikhs are now rolling in wealth owing to the cheapness of their farm rents under our administration. . . . We have pursued a policy of generosity hitherto which has probably repaid us by inducing the shaikhs to help us to the best of their ability. But where we reduce [rents] the shaikhs do not always reduce for their sarkals and fallahs. . . . One thing seems clear: the policy of backing up the big shaikhs is incompatible with the principle of a wide dispersion of wealth and prosperity. . . . Immediate needs make it necessary and politic to support the big shaikhs. But it will probably be politic in a not very remote future to reverse the procedure.' *Mesopotamian Administration Reports, 1918-1920*, pp. 235-6.
46   Bell, op. cit., p. 76.
47   For example, the following posts were assigned to tribal shaikhs of the Muntafiq region:

Sh. Farhud al-Mughashash, Administrator of the Hammar and 'Aqiqa district;

Sh. Ghayun al-'Ubaid, Qaimmaqam of Police;

Sh. Hamuda al-Bishara, Administrator of ahl-Hasan;

Sh. Sayyid Yusif al-Ba'aj, Administrator of Bani-sa'id;

Sh. Hamad, Administrator of al-Ghamisiya;

Sh. Sulaiman Nasrul-lah, Administrator of Albu-Salih;

Sh. Munshid al-Habib, Administrator of al-Batha;

Sh. Taha al-Ziyara, Administrator of al-Suwaij;

Sh. Ibrahim al-Ba'aj, Administrator of al-Diwaya: 'Abd al-Jalil al Tahir, op. cit., p. 45.

48 For details, see *Report on Iraq, 1925*, Colonial Office no. 21, pp. 144–56.

49 FO 371/5071, Note by Sir A. Hirzel, 3.11.1919.

50 'Abd al-Jalil al-Tahir, op. cit., p. 21. Also, in the financial year 1924–5, for example, the 'Amara shaikhs were given 'substantial tax remissions, specifically because their complaints were reiterated at the somewhat difficult moment of the passage of the [June 1924] Treaty'. CO 696/5, as quoted in P. Sluglett, 'British influence and administration in Iraq, 1914–32', DPhil. thesis, St Antony's College, Oxford, p. 341.

51 See Sluglett, op. cit., p. 331.

52 Proclamation no. 34 of the Civil Administration, 31 October 1914–August 1919, p. 24. For full text see, FO 371/5153.

53 Bell, op. cit., p. 17.

54 To illustrate the degree of the tribes' armed power we list below the composition of a cross section of tribes.

Tribe	Shaikh	No. of men	No. of rifles
(1) *Bani Zaid*	Paramount Shaikh, Umum Sulaiman al-Sharif		
Al-'Udhaimiyin	Sirhan al-Sharrad	325	150
Al-'Umran	Dali al-Kanash	100	50
Al-'Abada	Dajran al-'Aryan	50	30
Bani Humaid	'Auda al-Mandhur	80	40
Al-Jabra	Mansur al-'Uwaiyid	150	100
Al-Judaya	Sulaiman al-Sharif	400	200
Al-Ma'an	Dhabba al-Suwaichil	200	100
Al-Sharahina	Chasib al-Nahi	80	40
Al-Sha'lan	Hatab al-Zunaiyid	300	200
Al-Muhaniya	Abu Zawwa	100	60
(2) *Bani Sa'id*	Paramount Shaikh, Naif al-Masha		
Al-Shams	Naif al-Masha	500	300
Al-Ghashim	Muhammad al-Husain	1,400	300
Al-Kuwami	Naif al-Masha	2,500	1,500
Al-Ma'yuf	Muhammad	1,200	750
Albu Tawil	Humaidi al-'Ali	200	120
Al-'Assaf	Sa'dun al-'Assaf	300	200
Al-Zaibich	'Anad al-Sulaiman	200	100

(3) *Khafajah*	Paramount Shaikh, Umum 'Ali al-Fadhl		
'Abd al Saiyid	'Ali Fadhl	200	150
Al-'Asida	Shi'a al-Dahhan	250	200
Bani Richab	Salih al-Shati	300	200
Al-Chinana	Mizi al-Hasun	200	50
Al-Marawina	Ghafil al-Riyah	300	30
Al-Mashakhil	Ras al-Jirn	200	150
Al-Salim	Muhsin al-Salim	200	120
Albu Shahab	Talib al-Mutlaq	200	40
Al-Talahiba	Shatab al-Manhal	300	200
Al-Tuwainat	'Isa al-Haws	200	80
Al-'Ulaiwi	Farhud al-'Ashian	500	300
Al-'Uwaiyid	'Abbas al-Hutaita	150	100
Al-Sa'id	'Abdullah al-Haiwan	350	300
'Abudat al-Battush	Khala al-Aranis	120	80
Al-Shamki	'Atshan al-Na'ima	300	152

CO 730/150, 68588, 14.12.1919. For a comprehensive distribution of the tribes in southern Iraq, see map in chapter II, p. 42.

55 'Abd al Razzaq al-Hasani, *Tarikh al-Wizarat al-'Iraqiya* (History of the Iraqi Cabinets), vol. III, Beirut, 1974, p. 325.

56 For example, see Air 23/104, SSO, Basra, CD/1/251, 22.5.1926. It should be pointed out, however, that, by the time such attempts were made, agricultural taxation as a source of revenue had become relatively unimportant, particularly after 1931, when agricultural taxation virtually ceased and was replaced by the Istihlak (consumption) law. By that time the larger portion of government revenue from taxation came from customs and excise, which by 1935, for example, constituted 60 per cent of the revenue, whereas that from agriculture made up a mere 17 per cent. See FO 371/20010, 31.1.1936.

57 Air 23/112, Intelligence, SSO, 19.12.1930.

58 The main advantage of this customary land tenure system was the power it gave to the state over the 'distribution' of land, a power that could be (and was) manipulated for political reasons. Thus, *de facto* ownership by certain co-operative shaikhs, for example, could have the backing of the state, while that of hostile shaikhs could be nullified. See Fahmi, 1926, p. 111. Another *Report by the Financial Mission*, appointed by the Secretary of State for the Colonies to inquire into the financial Position and Prospects of the Government of Iraq in 1925, found that 'corrupt practices were extremely widespread in Iraq . . . and that they permeated the whole system of revenue assessment and collection. . . . Collection from the shaikhs and *mallaks* (landlords) is often not made in full, and we find that in the Ministry of Finance there is a

feeling that remission or non-collection has sometimes been due to political consideration. . . . There are also obvious weaknesses in the system by which the government share is assessed. The demand will be made on a powerful tribal shaikh, or landlord, or other local personality. The estimating committee consists of smaller folk who have no disposition to incur the hostility of men of substance. Sometimes it includes intending purchasers of the crop who hope that a pessimistic estimate may find its reward in a discount from the price.' London, 1925, p. 12.

59 FO 624/1/428, November 1933.
60 According to Naji Shaukat, Hikmat Sulaiman, for example, owned an area of land extending over 17,000 *dunums* in the Diyala district, while Rashid 'Ali took control over the *miri* land of the whole area of Shadi where he was aided by small government officials and tribal shaikhs, who themselves became big landlords. One such official is claimed to have acquired 60,000 *dunums* in the Kut *liwa*, while one shaikh, Muhammad al-Shaywd, acquired 200,000 *dunums* and Muhammad al-Kamala, a Muntafiq shaikh, acquired 500,000 *dunums*. Naji Shaukat, *Sira wa-Dhikrayat* (memoirs), Baghdad, 1974, p. 281.
61 FO 371/10334, 5.1.1925.
62 C. L. Harris, *Iraq*, New Haven, Conn., 1958, p. 197.
63 Ibid., p. 197.
64 FO 624/7/623, 9.12.1936.
65 FO 624/1/428.
66 Ibid.
67 Ibid.
68 Air 23/104, HQ/1223, 31.10.1926.
69 Ibid.

Notes to Chapter 3

1 See for example, FO 371/21859, 10.10.1938, and FO 371/20801, 21.4.1937.
2 FO 371/20801.
3 Ibid.
4 Ibid.
5 See chapter VI below.
6 FO 371/20801.
7 FO 371/20802, 14.8.1937. It should be pointed out that, owing to the proximity of Lake Habbaniya to the RAF base at Dhibban, the Hashimi government had been suspicious of Britain's desire to use the lake. Quite naturally, therefore, the Sulaiman government could not have been very willing to reverse the decision of their predecessors on an issue that could have, so easily, brought them severe criticism from the nationalist elements.

8 FO 371/20802, 14.8.1937.
9 FO 371/20801.
10 FO 371/20016, 24.9.1936.
11 Ibid.
12 For a study of this, see H. Mejcher, *The Imperial Quest for Oil, Iraq 1910-1928,* London, 1976.
13 FO 371/17858, 29.5.1934.
14 Ibid.
15 These were the Eastern Bank and the Imperial Bank of Persia, which were entirely British, and the Ottoman Bank, which is an Anglo-French concern. However, the managers of all of these banks were British subjects, as were all their 'higher-grade' employees.
16 FO 371/17858. Other British commercial activities included the following. (1) The business of insurance in 'all its branches is in Iraq almost entirely in the hands of British firms'. (2) The three air-transport companies then serving Iraq (Imperial Airways, KLM, and Air Orient), which were 'all represented in Iraq . . . by British firms'. (3) The London *Times* owned the *Iraq Times*, which was the only foreign newspaper published in the country, and a British company, MacKenzie and MacKenzie, owned the principal book-shop in Baghdad. (4) Even the capital of the Iraq Racing Company was largely British and its salaried officials were British subjects. (ibid.) In addition, it is interesting that, in 1936, 'British officials and officers have a monopoly of the advisory and export posts in the Iraqi Government service . . . and there are today more British subjects in the service of the Iraqi Government than there were in 1932 [i.e. before independence].' FO 371/20801.
17 FO 371/20010, 4.6.1936.
18 FO 371/20010, 13.7.1936.
19 FO 371/20010, 13.7.1936.
20 FO 371/20010, 5.5.1936.
21 Ibid. In fact, during 1936 Iraqi imports from Germany had increased by 19%, but this was due mainly to the appearance of Haavara marks in Iraq. The Haavara was the name of an organisation that was endeavouring to release frozen credits in Germany belonging to Jewish immigrants to Palestine. It is claimed that, during 1936, the equivalent of £165,000 worth of these marks was released through Iraqis buying mainly cement and iron from Germany.
22 FO 371/20010, 5.5.1936. The United Kingdom's exports that suffered most from this competition were cotton textiles, but the Japanese also exported a very wide range of other goods, ranging from electrical equipment to rubber shoes.
23 *The Iraq Directory*, Baghdad, 1936, p. 4; see also C. E. Dawn,

From Ottomanism to Arabism, Urbana, Ill., 1973.

24 Sir Arnold T. Wilson, *Loyalties, Mesopotamia*: Vol. II, *1917–1920*, London, 1931, p. 305.

25 Wilson, op. cit., p. 306.

26 See, for example, A. S. Klieman, *Foundations of British Policy in the Arab World, The Cairo Conference of 1921*, Baltimore, 1970, p. 52.

27 Ibid., p. 102.

28 See Suleiman Mousa, 'King Husain of the Hijaz and the Arabs of Palestine', *International Journal of Middle East Studies*, May 1978, p. 186.

29 Ibid.

30 Klieman, op. cit., p. 134.

31 Klieman, op. cit., p. 150.

32 Ibid., pp. 147–8.

33 Ibid., p. 161.

34 Ibid., p. 161.

35 FO 371/6353, Intelligence Report no. 17, 15.7.1921, *al-Iraq*, no. 338, 8.7.1921.

36 CO 730/17, 16.10.1921.

37 *Report on the Administration of Iraq*, April 1923–December 1924, Colonial, no. 13, p. 9.

38 Ibid., p. 9.

39 Ibid., p. 19.

40 As quoted in P. Sluglett, *Britain in Iraq, 1914–1932*, London, 1976, p. 71.

41 Ibid., p. 155.

42 Ma'ruf al-Rasafi, as quoted in, Yusif 'Izz al-Din, *al-Shi'r al-'Iraqi al-Hadith* (Modern Iraqi Poetry), Cairo, 1965, p. 190.

43 Muhammad Habib al-'Ubaidi, as quoted in Yusif 'Izz al-Din, *al-Shi'r al-'Iraqi al-Hadith* (Modern Iraqi Poetry), Cairo, 1965, p. 191.

44 This is how the expenditure of a typical shaikh, for example, was usually allocated:

10% of total income was spent on guests;

20% on the shaikh's own family;

25% paid to the *'ulama* as *zaka* (alms);

15% on travel to the holy places;

30% paid as interest on loans from city merchants.

A. Fahmi, *Report on the Financial Position of Iraq*, Baghdad, 1926, p. 105.

45 FO 371/5230, 14.9.1920. These ideas were echoed fourteen years later by the British Ambassador, who wrote: 'the tribes have not, however, been the only source of potential disorder, and the most serious, but not the most persistent threat of public disturbance

has always developed from Baghdad.' FO 371/17870, E 1422/1170/93, 5.3.1934.

46 The high degree of governmental dependence on the agricultural sector is indicated by the fact that, even during the first year of the monarchy, 25% of government revenue originated as rents and taxes from agricultural land, produce and animals. By 1925 the proportion of government revenue derived from these sources had increased to 34%, and it did not drop from that level until 1931, when the figure was 19%, the Treasury having started in that year to receive oil royalties. However, even in this post-oil era, an average of around 18% of the government's revenue still comes from the agricultural sector.

47 See, for example, p. 93 below.

48 For example, during the first eight years of his rule, King Faisal made eleven visits to the tribal areas.

49 See, for example, chapter II, pp. 22, 00.

50 See p. 103 below.

51 Muhammad Salman Hasan, 'Foreign trade in the economic development of modern Iraq, 1869–1939', DPhil, thesis, St Antony's College, Oxford, 1958, p. 288.

52 Ibid., pp. 43, 44.

53 Ibid., p. 132.

54 For the purposes of analysis, I classified the inner circle as those members serving in five or more cabinets.

55 FO 371/120017, E 5672/5672/93, 8.9.1936.

56 FO 371/20795, 16.12.1936.

57 FO 371/20015, 30.11.1936.

58 FO 371/20795, 23.12.1936.

59 FO 371/16903, 28.4.1933.

60 FO 371/16908, E 1853/105/93, 25.3.1936.

61 FO 371/16922, Annual Report, 1933.

62 FO 371/17869, E 1604/1038/93, 1.3.1934.

63 FO 371/18949, Review of Events, 1934.

64 FO 371/16903, E 1724/105/93, 22.3.1933.

65 FO 371/16903, E 1724/105/93, 22.3.1933.

66 Ibid.

67 See for example, FO 371/20796, E 7585, 20.12.1937. Even Nuri al-Sa'id was willing to admit that no free elections existed in the country. 'Is it possible,' he once asked, 'for any Member of Parliament, no matter how dignified he might be, and no matter what honourable services he rendered to the country, to be re-elected unless the Government agrees to his being re-elected?' 'Abd al-Razzaq al-Hasani, *Tarikh al-'Iraq al-Siyasi al-Hadith* (Modern Political History of Iraq), vol. III, p. 254.

68 To some extent this classification is somewhat arbitrary, but it

should give some indication of the dominant patterns in the distribution of political privileges in Iraq.

69 FO 371/10833, Intelligence Report no. 12, 11.6.1925.
70 FO 371/17869, E/7699/1038/93, 27.12.1934.
71 It is interesting, for example, that 'Ali Jaudat al-Ayyubi, who considered parliamentary life to be detrimental to Iraq generally, listed this high demand for parliamentary seats as one of the main reasons for his belief. He said 'The truth is that parliamentary life corrupted Iraq for two reasons: the first emanated from the Election Law, and the second from the great demand for seats. Regarding the Election Law, it has given the Government much scope for interference, so much so that deputies are, in fact, appointed rather than elected. Regarding the number of seats . . . their number was limited to 88 until 1935, whereas those seeking seats exceed 2,000. Had a legislative council been established where all provinces were represented, it would have been better and more lasting.' 'Abd al-Razzaq al-Hasani, *Tarikh al-Wizarat al-'Iraqiya* vol. III, Beirut, 1974, p. 34.
72 FO 371/20010, E 851/851/93, 17.2.1935.
73 FO 371/18946, E 5008/278/93, 19.8.1935.
74 Muhammad Bahjat al-Athari, as quoted in 'Abd al-Razzaq al-Hasani, *Tarikh al-'Iraq al-Siyasi al-Hadith* (Modern Political History of Iraq), vol. III, Beirut, 1948, p. 269.
75 Muhammad Rida al-Khatib, *al-Inqilab* Newspaper, Baghdad, 7.2.1937.
76 The only possible exception to this was the Jama'at al-Ahali, but as it was not a political party in the technical sense it has been excluded from this section and will be discussed in a later chapter.
77 For full text, see 'Abd al-Razzaq al-Hasani, *Tarikh al-'Iraq al-Siyasi al-Hadith*, pp. 236–9.
78 Ibid., vol. I, p. 105.
79 Ibid., vol. II, p. 86.
80 'Abd al-Razzaq al-Hasani, *Tarikh al-'Iraq al-Siyasi al-Hadith*, p. 248.
81 Rufa'il Batti, *al-Sahafa fil-'Iraq* (Journalism in Iraq), Cairo, 1955, p. 101.
82 'Abd al-Razzaq al-Hasani, *Tarikh al-Wizarat al-'Iraqiya*, vol. III, p. 101.
83 FO 371/16922, Annual Report, 1932.
84 FO 371/16903, E 1724/105/93, 3.4.1933.
85 FO 371/16922, Annual Report, 1932.
86 LP&S/11&12, Intelligence Report no. 7, 4.4.1932.
87 FO 371/16922, Annual Report, 1933.
88 FO 371/16903, 13.3.1933.
89 FO 371/16903, 10.4.1933.
90 FO 371/17869, 27.12.1934.

91 Batti, op. cit., pp. 17, 18.
92 Ibid., p. 21.
93 Ibid., p. 57.
94 Ibid., p. 58.
95 Ibid., p. 61.
96 Ibid., p. 62.
97 Ibid., p. 81.
98 FO 371/17871, E 2204/2204/93.
99 FO 371/16922, Annual Report.
100 FO 371/17871, E 2204/2204/93.
101 This clause states that 'where, in the opinion of the Political Officer, any person is a dangerous character . . . the Political Officer may, by order in writing, require him to reside beyond the limits of the territories to which this regulation extends, or at such place within the said territories as may be specified in the order . . .'. *Report on the Administration of Iraq*, 1925, p. 153.
102 For full text see *Report on the Administration of Iraq*, 1931, pp. 106–12.
103 FO 371/17858, May 1934.
104 FO 371/17871.
105 Ibid.
106 FO 371/17858.
107 *The Iraq Directory*, 1936, p. 97.
108 FO 371/16889, E5331, 11.9.1935.

Notes to Chapter IV

1 Air 23/439, 12.11.1920.
2 CO 730/18, 15.4.1921.
3 FO 371/20008, E 172/172/93, 13.1.1936.
4 FO 371/2008.
5 CO 730/143, lecture by Sir Percy Cox.
6 Their number was 2,000 during the 1920 revolt, but by the beginning of 1921 'recruits were plentiful for the Levies, some 2,000 men joining in one month'. FO 371/16896, E 5653/7/93, 22.9.1932.
7 In 1920, for example, after an engagement with 600 rebellious Kurds, General Haldane, the British General Officer commanding, maintained that, 'but for this action of the Levies', a large portion of the Mosul Division might have been 'swamped in the wave of anarchy'. FO 371/16896.
8 These were: 1 MBE, 3 OBEs, 5 MCs, 2 MMs; and 4 Assyrians were mentioned in dispatches. E 2048/1/93.
9 CO 730/5, 494, 16.9.1921.
10 *Special Report . . . on the Progress of Iraq . . . 1920–31*, Colonial, no. 58, p. 39.

11 The main conditions were:
1 Any Iraqi of the towns and settled villages of Iraq, between 18 and 40 years of age, may volunteer for army service. The period of service will be two years in the dismounted units and three years in the mounted units.
2 On completion of his period of service a soldier may be permitted to re-enlist for a second period. He will then receive an increase of pay of Rs 5 per month.
3 If a soldier who has completed 12 years' service leaves the army he will be entitled to a post in the civil service (if or when there are vacancies) at a salary of 50% more than his army pay.
4 *Monthly rates of pay from 1 January 1922*:

'Amid	General	RS 2,000
Fariq Awwal	Lt General	1,500
Fariq	Major-General	1,200
Za'im	Colonel	850
'Aqid	Lt Colonel	650
Muqaddam	Major	550
Ra'is Awwal	Senior Captain	450
Ra'is	Captain	400
Mulazim Awwal	Lieutenant	300
Mulazim Thani	2nd Lieutenant	250

	Sergeant	*Corporal*	*Private*
Artillery	Rs 60	50	40
Cavalry	60	50	40
Infantry	55	45	40
Transport	55	45	40

(It is estimated that the rate of exchange then was £1 = Rs 13.5.)
12 According to an intelligence report, the number of ex-Sharifian officers was 190, and that of ex-Turkish officers who did not serve in the Sharifian army was 450. CO 730/1, Intelligence Report no. 11, 15.4.1921.
13 Ibid.
14 *Report on the Administration of Iraq, October 1920–March 1922*, Colonial Office, p. 57.
15 *Report on the Administration of Iraq*, Colonial no. 13, p. 158.
16 CO 730/40, Intelligence Report no. 14, 5.7.1923.
17 CO 730/5, 494, 16.9.1921.
18 *Report on the Administration of Iraq, October 1920–March 1922*, p. 56.
19 King Faisal, for example, gave the title 'Fauj Musa al-Kadhim' (the Musa al-Kadhim Battalion), the Seventh Imam, to the first Iraq Infantry.

20 CO 730/7, Intelligence Report no. 27, 15.12.1921.
21 CO 730/23, Intelligence Report no. 15, 1.8.1922.
22 CO 730/24, Intelligence Report no. 16, 15.8.1922.
23 *al-'Iraq*, no. 764, 21 November 1922.
24 CO 730/40, 33280, 20.6.1923.
25 CO 730/25, Intelligence Report no. 20, 15.10.1922.
26 CO 730/40, Intelligence Report no. 13, 21.6.1923.
27 *Report on the Administration of Iraq*, 1925, Colonial no. 21, p. 104.
28 CO 730/72, Intelligence Report no. 4, 19.2.1925.
29 Air 23/439, 12.11.1920.
30 Air 23/384, IBD/39, 15.9.1922.
31 CO 730/40, 33280.
32 CO 730/96, 19851, 18.11.1926. It is also interesting that Britain had, for example, opposed Faisal's efforts to re-introduce conscription in Syria: 'Conscription was abolished when the Arab Government was established in Syria; nevertheless the Arab Military Council recently drew up a conscription order, including a 6 months exemption fine of 36/-. . . . A delay of 3 weeks on Britain's part in paying the monthly subsidy brought the Military Council to heel and the order did not take effect. There is no punishment for desertion.' FO 371/5071, 15.11.1919.
33 CO 730/94, 13907, 30.6.1926.
34 Given the degree of disunity within Iraq at that time, it is not surprising that conscription was not taken seriously as a potential menace in encouraging national unity, with the multiple difficulties this would have created for British control.
35 It is interesting how the British High Commissioner later combined the attitude of some leading Iraqi politicians with an analysis of their personal ambitions: 'Of the Ministers, Jafar 'Askari hardly counts. Obese and pathetic to British officers, he will complain with tears rolling down his cheeks of his difficulties with his colleagues, their extreme views, their disloyalty. But to Iraqis he appeals for unity to defeat the intrigues of the British who are trying to enslave the country. He dances obediently to the piping of his royal master but the music is not in his soul. Nuri, the imp of mischief, is obsessed with dreams of an absolute monarchy founded on a pretorian army of which he himself is the chief. . . . The first step to the realisation of this simple programme is the introduction of conscription in Iraq. Yasin remains the most sinister figure, dominating the cabinet by his personality and control of the purse, acquiring wealth and pushing Faisal gradually to the precipice.' FO 371/12260, 26.10.1927.
36 CO 730/94, 30.6.1926.
37 CO 730/95, 1.9.1926.

38 'Abd al-Razzaq al-Hasani, *Tarikh al-Wizarat al-'Iraqiya* (History of the Iraqi Cabinets), Beirut, 1974, vol. II, p. 86.

39 Although S. Longrigg provides no evidence to indicate how the army was involved in this controversy, it is probable that high-ranking officers, particularly those with contacts and relatives in the government, were involved. The only clear evidence that I was able to find is an article by Amin al-'Umari (later GSOI in 1936) in the *Iraqi Military Magazine*, no. 1, October 1924, where the author supports the introduction of compulsory service in Iraq.

40 S. H. Longrigg, *Iraq 1900–1950*, Beirut, 1956, p. 179.

41 'Abd al-Razzaq al-Hasani, op. cit., vol. II, p. 105.

42 Ibid., p. 99.

43 Ibid., p. 101.

44 This would have been consistent with the attitude adopted by the tribes to the government right from its formation. See for example chapter III above, p. 39.

45 BHCF, Military, File 4/69 vol. I, Delhi. As quoted in P. Sluglett, 'British influence and administration in Iraq, 1914–32', DPhil. thesis, St Antony's College, Oxford. p. 203.

46 Air 23/384, I/BD/39, 28.8.1928.

47 Ibid., 13.9.1928.

48 Ibid., 8.9.1928.

49 Those present were: Rashid 'Ali, Yasin Pasha, Nuri al-Sa'id, Ja'far Abu al-Timman, Mahmud Ramiz, Sayyid Muhammad Kadhimawi, and Shaikh Mahdi Jawahar. Air 23/384, I/BD/39, 8.9.1928.

50 Air 23/384, 1/BD/39, 8.9.1928.

51 Air 23/384, 1/BD/57, 18.10.1928.

52 Air 23/384, 18.10.1928.

53 Air 23/384, 18.10.1928.

54 CO 730/126, 58003, 1.2.1928.

55 See for example Sluglett, op. cit.

56 FO 371/16903, 1123/14, 16.2.1933.

57 FO 371/16903, 10.11.1933.

58 FO 371/20010, 5.5.1935.

Notes to Chapter V

1 See FO 371/16896, *passim*.

2 FO 371/16896, 22.9.1933.

3 See chapter IV above, pp. 76, 000.

4 FO 371/16894, 18.10.1933.

5 Ibid.

6 FO 371/16894, 18.10.1933.

7 Ibid.

8 Ibid. Also, a former English editor of the *Times* of Mesopotamia wrote of them that they were 'becoming almost more British than the British and that they despised the Arabs in general and the Arab army in particular'. As quoted by K. Husry, 'The Assyrian affair of 1933, part I', *International Journal of Middle East Studies*, vol. 5, 1974, p. 166.

9 FO 371/16894.

10 Apart from the Assyrian community providing most of the personnel for the British-controlled Iraq Levies and thus becoming relatively enriched by the salaries they drew, every Assyrian was presented on discharge with a new rifle and 200 rounds of ammunition. FO 371/16894.

11 Husry, op. cit., p. 100.

12 FO 371/16894.

13 Ibid.

14 Ibid.

15 FO 371/20788, AI (37) 3, 26.1.1937.

16 See particularly Husry, op. cit., part II, pp. 244–60.

17 FO 371/16916, 25.7.1933.

18 FO 371/17871, E 2204/2204/93.

19 R. S. Stafford, *The Tragedy of the Assyrians*, London, 1935, p. 193.

20 The inhabitants of these towns may have remembered the extensive clashes between them and the Assyrians in the Mosul bazaar in August 1923 and the Kirkuk riot of May 1924, 'when an Assyrian levy battalion ran amok in the town, killing and wounding more than 100 Moslem men, women and children by indiscriminate shooting'. FO 371/16894.

21 Stafford, op. cit., p. 201.

22 FO 371/16922, Report by General Rowan-Robinson on the situation in Iraq, E/5555C., 6.9.1933.

23 Stafford, op. cit., p. 204.

24 Husry, op. cit., part II, p. 352.

25 Ibid., p. 352.

26 Lady Paget, for example, described by the British Embassy in Bern as an 'experienced person', who was under the treatment of Dr Kocher, the King's doctor, saw Faisal 'after his return from his motor drive on the day of his death and thought that he was looking particularly well. . . . It appears that he had with him an Indian woman of comely appearance with whom, it is stated, he had intimate relations and with whom he is believed to have quarrelled a day or so before his death. [He had tea at 6] and about 7 he felt suddenly ill and sent for Kocher, his doctor. On his arrival he complained of a burning thirst and on being given something to drink he vomited violently. . . . Later he felt better

. . . but shortly before his death he again complained of a burning thirst and on being given something to drink he again complained of violent pains. [Lady Paget criticised the doctor for not examining the content of his vomit] His death was attributed to arteriosclerosis. . . . No adequate post mortem examination was made . . . his body was embalmed with suspicious celerity and the woman is said to have disappeared the day after his death.' The Foreign Office replied that 'Lady Paget's theory is ingenious and not inherently impossible. . . . I doubt however whether anything would be gained by further pursuing the matter now and it is hoped that Lady Paget will allow the story to die a natural death.' FO 371/16924, 21.9.1933.

The doubts surrounding the cause of the King's death were given particular prominence in the Lebanese and Syrian press, which propounded the view that, far from dying a natural death, Faisal had been killed by the British. See FO 371/16924, 19.9.1933.

27 FO 371/16924, 19.9.1933.

28 King Faisal, for example, had been able to 'keep a check upon the powerful riverain tribes which form so large and important an element in the population of Iraq. By playing the one off against the other, he had curbed their lawlessness, kept them at peace, and held them aloof from the political intrigues of the capital.' FO 371/18945, 17.6.1935.

29 FO 406/46, 4.3.1921.

30 FO 371/16889, 5.9.1933.

31 'Abd al-Razzaq al-Hasani, *Tarikh al-Wizarat al-'Iraqiya* (History of the Iraqi Cabinets), vol. IV, p. 3.

32 Ibid., p. 34.

33 al-Hasani, op. cit., vol. IV, p. 334.

34 This was possible owing to the fact that senators were traditionally appointed to the Senate for a term of eight years, and a change of personalities in the Senate was therefore less frequent than it was in the Lower Chamber. The most outspoken senators for the opposition at this time were Muhsin Abu Tabikh and Maulud Mukhlis. In a speech criticising the government, Senator Mukhlis pointed out that 'the Senate forms that Supreme court . . . and since we [Senators] saw that each Minister . . . does as he pleases and no deputy would hold him to task . . . we feel that enough is enough and now say to the Prime Minister . . . "Stop the Ministers at their limits".' The 'opposition senators' also submitted a written statement to the Prime Minister complaining that 'the country was deprived of its voting rights and so people were brought to Parliament against the legal procedures. Nay, they came due to their personal contacts and blood relations. . . ' . Mahadir Majlis al-A'yan, *Proceedings of the Senate, 1934-5*, pp. 11-12.

35   FO 371/20010, Annual Report, 1935.

36   The government's main supporters in the tribal area of mid-Euphrates were Shaikh 'Alwan Hajj Sa'dun, Shaikh 'Umran Haj Sa'dun, Haj Rih al-'Atiya, Haji Marzouk al-'Awad, and Haji Dakhil al-Sha'lan.

37   In this *fatwa*, Shaikh Kashif al-Ghita preached that 'It is obvious that for the tribes to fight each other and resort to violence is a crime of the first order . . . and is forbidden . . . and that happiness and general wellbeing can be best served by unity, cooperation and solidarity, and that it is the responsibility of the thinkers and leaders of the people to cultivate that spirit amongst them . . . with the hope of uniting this disintegrating nation . . . ' . al-Hasani, op. cit., vol. IV, p. 54.

38   These included a number of influential lawyers such as Taufiq al-Suwaidi, Muhammad Zaki, Jamil al-Wadi, and Nasrat al-Farisi. The government was aware of their activities and tried to control them. For example, in January, when these lawyers attempted to hold a meeting in a private house in Baghdad, on arrival they found the house surrounded by police, and they were not allowed in. They reacted by sending a telegram to King Ghazi complaining that they had been denied 'by the police the right to exercise a most sacred constitutional right, namely the right of citizens to assemble and discuss the affairs of their country . . . ' . al-Hasani, op. cit., vol. IV, pp. 44–5.

   Also, although it seems obvious, it should be pointed out that employment with the government *was* lucrative. For example, in a private letter to Naji Shaukat, Yasin al-Hashimi told Naji of the good news that he had given a job in the Foreign Ministry to his brother, Nasrat, at 90 ID per month. This was at a time when a private in the Iraqi army was earning 1.50 ID per month. *Sira wa Dhikrayat*, (Biography and Memoirs), Naji Shaukat Baghdad, 1974, p. 280.

39   These were distributed mainly in Baghdad and Najaf. FO 371/ 18945, 28.3.1935.

40   al-Hasani, op. cit., vol. VI, p. 30. It is believed that the Iraqi Communist Party started as a clandestine movement in 1932 with its main activities then being the organisation of political meetings and discussions which were mainly held at Basra and Nasiriya. In 1934 this 'movement' moved to Baghdad, where they set up a committee called the 'Anti-Investment and Imperialism Committee' headed by 'Asim al-Fulaij. Owing to the nature of this committee, not much is known about its activities, but it is known that in 1935 it came to the surface first with the issuing of political pamphlets and then later in the year (after the change of cabinet) by publishing a newspaper called *Kifah al-Sha'b*. Safa

'Abd al-Wahhab al-Mubarak, 'Inqilab al-Sittawathalathin' (The 1936 coup), MA thesis, Baghdad University, 1973, p. 90.
41 FO 371/20010.
42 Ibid.
43 FO 371/18945, 21.3.1935. Apart from his resentment of the government for having excluded him from Parliament, Shaikh 'Abd al-Wahid's support for the opposition must have been also motivated by the fact that he had a dispute over land ownership with the Muntafiq shaikhs who were now supporters of and supported by the government.
44 FO 371/18953, 6.3.1935.
45 FO 371/18945.
46 al-Hasani, op. cit., vol. IV, p. 68.
47 According to al-Hasani, the government had in fact ordered an army unit to advance from Baghdad to the tribal areas; but its commander, General Husain 'Alwan, refused to obey. The government then ordered both his arrest and the cancellation of the first orders. al-Hasani, op. cit., vol. II, p. 63.
48 FO 371/20010.
49 See p. 124 below.
50 Those were Nuri al-Sa'id and Muhammad Amin Zaki. It is interesting that later dispatches from the British Embassy make numerous references to the mutual hostility and distrust between Yasin al-Hashimi and Nuri al-Sa'id. In one such typical statement, the Ambassador informed the Foreign Office that 'from time to time, it [relations between Yasin and Nuri] has been somewhat strained. Indeed, on one occasion, I was called in to build a bridge across a gulf which threatened to swallow it up. Political busybodies had persuaded Yasin that Nuri wished to oust him and to take his place, and Nuri that Yasin wanted to be rid of him. Each one had lent an ear to this gossip and had become prickly and suspicious. I was, however, able to convince the one that there was no new evil in the other and so to bring them together again.' FO 371/20010.
51 This was also the view of the British Ambassador, who wrote: 'There is, indeed, little upon which any real hopes of progress may be built. The individual members of the present cabinet have no higher reputation for honesty of purpose or integrity than their predecessors, and in the past they have been just as prone to use public office for private gain.'
52 FO 371/18945, 21.3.1935.
53 This was clearly motivated by the government's wish to reward their supporters without excluding others whose position in tribal or public life made their presence in the Chamber desirable. It is also interesting that, like his predecessor, Yasin included 'most'

of the newspaper editors, thereby securing the government's control of the press.

54 For a complete list of the Kurdish demands see Appendix III.

55 In an interview with *al-Jazira* newspaper, 'Abd al-Wahid declared that the revolt was over longstanding grievances, to which successive governments had paid little attention. He also informed this paper that he had submitted the following demands to the Mutasarrif:

(a) Modification of the constitution to protect the sovereignty of the people;

(b) A freely elected Parliament;

(c) Reform in finance administration and education departments:
    1 reduction of the large salaries paid;
    2 reduction of taxes;
    3 distribution of government lands;
    4 making themselves amenable to ordinary courts;
    5 better supervision of administrative officials;
    6 suppression of administrative officers at Diwaniya;
    7 establishment of hospitals and compulsory primary education;
    8 dissolution of Parliament.

al-Jazira, no. 32, 3 April 1935. As quoted in FO 371/18953.

'Abd al-Wahid also had land disputes with the shaikhs of the Muntafiq tribes for which he later secured a settlement in his favour. See confidential report by C. J. Edmonds, FO 371/20015, 1.6.1936.

56 Also during this time, other shaikhs started to fall out among themselves. For example, 'Sha'lan al-'Atiyah has for the moment broken with 'Abd al-Wahid because the latter will not support his demand for a grant of 25,000 acres of land which he claims was the promised price of his support against 'Ali Jaudat.' Economic considerations were also thought to have caused a fall-out within certain tribes. The same report, for example, continues to refer to 'skirmishes [which] took place at Rumaitha. . . . In the Nasirya liwa tribal unrest is still evident and now shows a tendency to develop into agrarian agitation against the big landlords'. FO 371/18945, 21.3.1935.

57 These were mainly protests against the imbalance of Shi'a representation in government and administration, failures to elect important Shi'a notables, and the fact that there were too few Shi'a judges. They also included protests against negligence of Waqf properties, and poor facilities in health and education in the south. The petition further called for an amnesty for all those who had taken part in recent events (i.e. against the Wahda government of 'Ali Jaudat) and demanded 'that the work of the Land Settlement should be expanded so that by its activities the

stabilization of agriculture will be established. We also demand that the law for the establishment of an Agricultural Bank would be expedited and the alienation of land to their owners without payment of *badals*. We demand that land rents and water rates be cancelled and the substitution of Koda tax on animals by Istihlak and that no tax should be levied on pumps.' FO 371/ 18953, 15.5.1935.

58   The *afrad* of the Muntafiq tribes had, in any case, been restless, and have made several appeals to government officials to review their status on the land. See al-Hasani, op. cit., vol. IV, p. 116.

59   FO 371/18953.

60   FO 371/18953.

61   Ibid.

62   FO 371/20015. Other confiscation or endowment of land (depending on the shaikh's stand *vis-à-vis* the government) that was affected during this period included the reversal in favour of 'Abd al-Wahid of the Raqq al-Haswa decision (and outstanding disputes over land control which 'Abd al-Wahid had with the Muntafiq shaikhs), and the granting to Sayyid Muhsin Abu Tabikh a part of the *miri* land adjoining Ramla, including lands already cultivated by Shaikh Sha'lan al-Salman, chief of Khaza'il. See report by Edmonds in FO 371/20015.

63   FO 371/20010.

64   FO 371/18953, 11.6.1935.

65   FO 371/18953.

66   In a private letter to Naji Shaukat, Yasin al-Hashimi informed Mr Shaukat that 'efforts were being made to bring the size of the army to three divisions' (13.6.1935). In another letter to Mr Shaukat, written on 9 August 1935, al-Hashimi wrote that he 'had at hand a project which would increase the size of the army to four divisions'. [A division then consisted of three infantry brigades, three battalions, one field and one mountain artillery brigade, one engineer company, one signal battalion, one field ambulance, and a divisional motor transport company.] Naji Shaukat, *Sira wa-Dhikrayat* (Memoirs), Baghdad, 1974, pp. 281, 282.

The reliance of, and importance attached to, the army by the government is indicated by the fact that in September 1935, for example, the government paid those serving in the army one month extra pay.

67   FO 371/20020.

68   FO 371/20010.

69   Ibid.

70   Ibid.

71   FO 371/2008, R.A.F. Monthly Intelligence, Summary, 1935.

72   FO 371/20010.

73 Since the aim of this book is not to reconstruct a completely comprehensive history of the period under study, a number of events similar to ones already described have not been included in the body of the text. For example, communist activities, already referred to above, were also evident during the last quarter of 1935. In August and September 'the communist newspaper *Kifah al Sha'b* published violent revolutionary articles. The printing press was raided and confiscated in September and several arrests were made'. In October, 'communist pamphlets were twice scattered about the principal streets of Baghdad in the early morning but were collected and removed by the police before many people were about'. In November, 'pamphlets addressed to soldiers and students were scattered in Nasiriya, communist flags were twice hung on the electric wiring in the main streets of Baghdad, and pamphlets similar to those found in Nasiriya were twice scattered in the main streets'. FO 371/20013, encl. no. 10 in Baghdad dispatch no. 185 dated 15 April 1936.

Apart from communist activities, 1935 saw also sporadic religious riots in the holy cities, particularly in Kadhimain, where in March 1935 a large mob severely damaged the structure of a partially finished new post office and then attacked the government *serai*. One police inspector, one constable and three civilians were killed, and about twenty wounded. FO 371/20010.

74 FO 371/20015, 5.3.1936.
75 Ibid.
76 FO 371/20015, 30.4.1936.
77 Ibid.
78 FO 371/20015, 5.5.1936.
79 FO 371/20015, 5.5.1935 and 7.5.1935.
80 Ibid.
81 Ibid.
82 FO 371/20015, 22.5.1935.
83 Fortunately for the government, the tribes were unable to co-ordinate their revolt against the government and this deprived them of the enormous potential advantage they could have had by uniting their tactics.
84 Ironically, Shaikh Sha'lan al-'Atiya was a prominent leader of the tribal movement against 'Ali Jaudat, which was inspired by the very men who were now in office.
85 FO 371/20015, 10.6.1935.
86 Ibid.
87 Ibid.
88 See Sati' al-Husry, *Mudhakkirati fi' l-'Iraq* (Memoirs), vol. II, Beirut 1966, p. 528.
89 The cabinet, for example, amended the already strict Baghdad Penal Code, adding the following clause: 'Whoever is found in

possession of written or printed matter or other object containing expressions coming within the scope of any of the offences provided for in this section, and there is cause to believe that such matter is intended for publication; or, with intent to give publication thereto, places on goods any mark or inscription referring to any event, person or circumstance of a nature calculated to remind the public of a harmful idea such as might arouse dissension among the various classes of the population or agitation against the Government, or, being a merchant, is found in possession of such goods exposed for sale, shall, unless the court is satisfied that the possession of such matter or object or goods was free from ill intent and was not intended for publication, be punished with the penalty provided for such offence itself.' Draft Law Amending the Baghdad Penal Code, April 1936; as quoted in FO 371/20013, 15.4.1936.

90 This is the agreement which in April 1936 transferred the ownership of the Iraqi railways, hitherto a British concern, to the Iraqi government for an exchange payment of £400,000. Commenting on the terms of this agreement, a senior British diplomat noted that 'first we have got a bit more than we set out to get. I mean that we now have it in writing from Yassin that in the matter of the buying of material, preference will be given to the United Kingdom. I confess that I had expected that Yassin would jib at this, but he did not. . . . Nuri's last minute intervention . . . was a bore and I told him so. . . . Nuri thought it very cunning of us to make Yassin sign one of the notes and laughed incredulously when the real reason for this was explained to him. "You want to tie Yassin down too", he said. When the bill went to the Chamber Nuri came, chortling with delight, to tell me that Yassin was having difficulties with his own friends, who were saying that Yassin had been "led up the garden path". Nevertheless, the bill went through with 60 odd votes against only 3.'

However, although the clauses stipulating preference treatment for Britain were kept secret, it seems that someone, as the British Ambassador put it, had 'let the cat out of the bag', and thus Hikmat Sulaiman and his colleagues in the opposition had received word of it, and quite naturally used the occasion to attack the government. FO 371/19999, 14.4.1936.

91 The offending article in fact criticised the cabinet for:
(a) having deserted the principle for which they stood when out of office and for which their supporters had put them in power;
(b) not having insisted on the amendment of certain 'oppressive' clauses of the Treaty of 1930;
(c) having concluded a secret agreement with Great Britain to buy all railway materials in the United Kingdom. FO 371/19999,

14.8.1936
92   FO 371/20013, 27.8.1936.
93   Ibid.
94   FO 371/20013, 17.9.1936.
95   Ibid.
96   FO 371/16045, 26.12.1931.
97   Through the 'Ahd Party of which he was the head and moving spirit.
98   FO 371/16045, 26.12.1931.
99   Ibid.
100 Ibid.
101 See for example chapter III above, pp. 65, 66.
102 FO 371/20010.
103 FO 371/18945, 30.5.1935.
104 FO 371/20017, 19.6.1936.
105 Ibid.
106 Ibid.
107 FO 371/18945, 30.5.1935.
108 FO 371/20017.
109 As will be seen in the following chapter, the British Foreign Office had in fact seriously considered the possibility of forcing King Ghazi to abdicate in June 1936, but later dropped the idea when no suitable alternative could be found. See, for example, FO 371/20017, 30.6.1936. Britain's irritation with King Ghazi may have stemmed from the public utterances he gave in support of the Palestinian cause and from the fact that he had a radio transmitter in his al-Zuhur Palace from where he broadcast news of Palestinian resistance and also instigated the Arabs of Kuwait to revolt against the British and join Iraq. Sati' al-Husry, op. cit., p. 586.
110 For example, when al-Hashimi 'discovered that Amir 'Abdul-Illah, who had recently taken his sisters to Alexandria for a holiday, had included in his party a well-known Baghdad jockey . . . the Prime Minister telegraphed asking that the jockey should be sent back to Iraq at once'. Also, after the incident of the princess, the Prime Minister ordered the wholesale dismissal of those about the King and was reported to be 'busying himself about replacing them by people who would not be too uncongenial to their master'. FO 371/20017.
111 Air 23/120, 1/Bd/56, 17.7.1930.
112 Ibid.
113 The last available figures give their number as being around 5,300 in 1926. It is however known that by 1929, apart from the RAF, there were no British troops left in Iraq.
114 Their total strength was around 5,000 in 1927. Since that year, however, steps were taken to embody them into the Iraq army, and by 1932 there were only 1,500 Levies left in Iraq – these were

later employed as aerodrome-guards with the RAF.

115 According to Edmonds, 'more than one group of Iraqi politicians had been turning over in their minds the idea of a coup d'état. The first of these had been Ja'far [then Minister of Defence in al-Hashimi Cabinet of 1935–6], who had been thinking last summer [1936] of organising a military coup against Yasin and had discussed it in detail with a high official in Edmonds' confidence.' In the same memorandum, Mr Edmonds continues to give an account of a visit from 'no less a person than shaikh Mahmud [a Kurdish notable]. . . . He told me that on October 27th Yasin Pasha had sent certain Kurdish tribal chiefs out to their districts with instructions to be ready, on a given signal, to mobilize their tribesmen to support himself and Rashid Beg in declaring a republic; the move was to be made immediately on the return of Yasin's brother, Taha, Chief of the Staff. The chiefs had been promised various administrative posts . . . and were actually assembled at the house of one of them in Kifri qadha when the revolution [sic] of October 29th cut the ground from under their feet.' FO 371/20795, 23.12.1936.

116 Ibid.

117 The *Iraq Times*, 30 October 1936.

Notes to Chapter VI

1 Hikmat Sulaiman, as quoted in Yusif Yazbak, *al-Muharrirun* (The Liberators), Beirut, 1936, p. 95.

2 It is interesting that Bakir Sidqi had written to Taha al-Hashimi while in England, advising him to prolong his visit in order to benefit from certain training courses that he could enter; but at the time of the coup Taha al-Hashimi was already in Istanbul, on his way back home from his visit to Europe. It is perhaps ironical that Taha's first recorded reaction to the news of the coup was: 'how tragic that this army which I strove to build into a useful instrument for the State, away from political trends, should effect such a shameful act'. Taha al-Hashimi, *Mudhakkirati*. (Memoirs), Beirut, 1969, pp. 137, 156, 157.

3 It is reported that on this morning Hikmat Sulaiman was waiting at a friend's house (Ra'uf al-Chadirchi's) and was impatiently searching the sky for planes. When they finally arrived at 8.30, he turned to his friend, saying: 'So! Yasin wants to rule the Kingdom for ten years. By God, Sir, he will not rule for ten days.' Then smiling ruefully, he continued: 'Nay, Yasin will not rule . . . even for ten hours'. Yazbak, p. 123. op. cit.

4 FO 371/20014, 16.11.1936.

5 Apart from the generals' letter, the King also received at about the same time a letter which is the only clear evidence we found

of civilian support to the army's move. It was signed by nineteen Baghdadi lawyers and stated that: 'The people, us [the authors] included, have seen the army's declaration which expressed the real wishes of the nation. We, therefore, support the army and pray that Your Majesty will fulfil their demands which are also the demands of the people.' As quoted in 'Abd al-Razzaq al-Hasani, *Tarikh al-Wizarat al-'Iraqiya* (History of the Iraqi Cabinets), Beirut, 1974, vol. IV, p. 219.

6   The following excerpts give the main gist of the generals' letter: 'Your Majesty is no doubt aware of what has befallen your people as a result of the policies of the present Government: policies of destruction, nepotism, exploitation, and unjustified expenditures. They put personal interests before those of the public and showed no regard to the bloodshed of your people, whose lives were lost for no apparent reason except the furthering of personal interest, and in order to satisfy the privileged politicians and leaders. The Government's arrogance even led them to mock our beloved King. . . . The situation in the country continued to worsen, . . . but the Government's policies did not change, and justice was absent amongst your people, while poverty prevailed. All this was in order to promote the well-being of a certain class headed by the members of the present cabinet. So the army which is naturally concerned about the welfare of the country . . . refused to remain silent . . . and we therefore request that . . . the present cabinet be dismissed . . . and a new cabinet, headed by Hikmat Sulaiman, be formed within three hours. Al-Hasani, op. cit., p. 222.

7   FO 371/20014.

8   This is the main part of al-Hashimi's telephone conversation with Sidqi:

> al-Hashimi: Is this what you do Your Lordship: was it not possible that we conciliate?
>
> Sidqi: You know very well the answer: you also know that your cabinet listened to no one.
>
> al-Hashimi: Had you told the King about your move?
>
> Sidqi: His Majesty will be very pleased with the action of his loyal army.

as quoted in Yazbak, op. cit., p. 137.

9   FO 371/20015, 17.11.1936.

10   Ibid.

11   For example, Yasin al-Hashimi had suggested to the King the adoption of an idea of Nuri al-Sa'id, that is, the dispatch of a number of British RAF flights to Qaraghan where they would drop leaflets signed by His Majesty and declare Bakir Sidqi as a traitor. It is claimed that the King replied by saying: 'Do you want to start another Spain here? You must resign!', to which

Yasin replied: 'So! You are a party to the coup.' Denying this, the King answered: 'I am not a party to anything, I am just the father of all.' Yazbak, op. cit., p. 134.

Rashid 'Ali also thought that the King should call on Bakir Sidqi to halt his advance and that, since the ministers all had their adherents among the officers, they should go out and induce them to abandon the movement. Rashid 'Ali's British adviser, Mr Edmonds, however, disagreed and 'impressed on him that he and his colleagues had been taken completely by surprise, that there was no time to do anything, and that in the circumstances it was neither disgraceful nor cowardly to bow to superior force'. FO 371/20015.

12 FO 371/20015.

13 Apart from the severe handling of tribal dissidents, and the reported abuse of power for personal gains, some sectors of the population seem to have been dissatisfied with the government's policies, which interrupted their economic activities. For example, owing to the crop failure in many parts of the world in 1936, there was a considerable rise in prices; but, although Iraq had a record grain harvest in that year, Iraqi farmers could not benefit from these favourable terms of trade to the full, mainly because of the interruption of the existing communications system (as a result of the 'civil war'), which resulted in consignments piling up at various railway stations. See, for example, 'Report on the general trade situation in Iraq at the end of November 1936', FO 371/20013.

14 There were naturally other reasons for these personal jealousies. Kamil Chadirchi, for example, another member of the coup government, is reported to have developed such an antagonism towards Rashid 'Ali, with whom he had served on the Executive Committee of the Ikha' al-Watani Party. It is claimed that after resigning from that party in 1935, Kamil Chadirchi was looking for 'any opportunity to revenge'. Interview with Khayiri al-'Umari, Baghdad, 12 April 1975.

15 FO 371/20803, 1936.

16 FO 371/20803, 1936. Also, it was known that Yasin al-Hashimi held a concession for the exploitation of the 'two best areas yielding the raw materials for the manufacture of cement at Oarachog Dagh and Hit'. FO 371/20010, Annual Report, 1935.

17 FO 371/20014, 21.10.1936.

18 FO 371/20015, November 1936.

19 Ibid.

20 al-Hashimi, op. cit., p. 219.

21 Ibid., p. 158. It is claimed by a veteran Iraqi general who had served with Bakir Sidqi that, after the latter decided to go ahead

with the coup, he weighed the idea of choosing between Hikmat Sulaiman or Rashid 'Ali as the future prime minister, but he was so frightened of Rashid 'Ali's ambitions that he finally decided to choose Hikmat Sulaiman. Interview with Salih al-Juburi, Baghdad, 14 April 1975.

22 al-Hashimi, op. cit., pp. 156–7.
23 Ibid., pp. 156, 157.
24 As quoted in al-Hasani, op. cit., vol. IV, p. 212.
25 These expenses, which came out of the State Treasury, were in fact considerable, and I therefore feel the need to list them in full. Also, the circumstances leading to Sabah's hospitalisation must have made these expenses even less justified. According to British reports, Sabah's injuries were sustained when an Iraqi Air Force plane, which he had borrowed 'against all rules', crashed, killing his servant and causing Sabah multiple injuries. His medical expenses were as follows:

	(*dinars*)
Passage from Iraq to England and back, including passage of Sabah's attendants and conveyance within England	539
Hospital and doctors' fees and cost of medicine	833
Food supplied	141
Transport of food	37
Champagne	60
House and furniture rent	121
Gas, electricity and telephone	101
Wages of servants and nurses and passage of Dr and Mrs Brahm (as companions) from Iraq to England and back	276
Transport incurred by Iraqi Legation in England to arrange lodgings for the patient	11
Crutches, leather shoes, two water bottles and plates	9
	2,128

FO 371/20015, 1936. Not surprisingly, when these expenses were made known to the public they caused a lot of resentment, particularly among 'Sabah's contemporaries in the Iraqi army and air force'. Ibid.

26 See chapter V above. Also, this impression emerged very clearly from the interviews I conducted in Baghdad.
27 For full text of the 1930 Anglo-Iraqi Treaty, see Appendix IV.
28 FO 371/20005, 15.2.1936.
29 Ibid.
30 FO 371/20005, 24.4.1936.
31 FO 371/20005, 9.5.1936.
32 FO 371/20005, 4.5.1936. Similarly, in August 1936 the British

Ambassador told the Foreign Office that 'there was said to be grave disquiet amongst Army officers on this account [delay in arms delivery], and it was broadly hinted that the time was arriving for the Iraqi Government to seek their supplies elsewhere. ... Rashid 'Ali ... had been greatly perturbed while at the scene of operations at Rumaitha ... by the criticism to which the Government was being subjected in the Army on account of their being virtually tied by the Treaty to purchase their war material in the United Kingdom. ... Mr Edmonds had heard similar reports from Sayyid Hikmat Sulaiman and others.' FO 371/20006, 3.8.1936.

33 FO 371/20005, 9.5.1936.
34 FO 371/20005, June 1936. Objectively, as far as the Foreign Office was concerned, these small orders from Czechoslovakia were of little economic or political significance, particularly since there was no security risk involved, as Czechoslovakia was anti-German or at least neutral. But it seems that, for fear of it giving the Iraqi government an idea of their political autonomy greater than they actually had, the Foreign Office acceded to the Iraqi request only after great reluctance.
35 FO 371/20005, 9.5.1936 and 371/20013, 6.11.1936, respectively. It is interesting that, on coming to power, Hikmat Sulaiman, undoubtedly influenced by Bakir Sidqi, himself instructed the Iraqi Military Attaché in London to proceed to Czechoslovakia *immediately* to visit the Skoda factory. Aware of the dissatisfaction of officers in the Iraqi army caused by the delays in arms delivery, and of the objective difficulties that British arms manufacturers were facing in coping with rising demand, the Foreign Office again gave its consent, but only after minuting that Hikmat Sulaiman's more positive attitude towards the Treaty was somewhat negated by this move. See FO 371/20015, 1.12.1936.
36 Interview with Muhammad Hadid, Baghdad, 14 April 1975.
37 Interview with Husain Jamil, Baghdad, 15 April 1975.
38 For example, a British Embassy report makes the point that 'the educated Iraqis follow closely the course of world events', a view that also emerged from the interviews conducted by this writer and from the reading of a considerable number of Iraqi newspapers of that period. The British Embassy referred to it in FO 371/20013, 29.10.1936.
39 FO 371/20014, November 1936.
40 For full text of this programme, see Appendix I below.
41 FO 371/20014, 20.11.1936.
42 S. H. Longrigg, *Iraq, 1900–1950*, Beirut, 1956, p. 250.
43 Out of the seven cabinet posts, they occupied three. These were: Ministry of Economics and Communications (Kamil Chadirchi); Ministry of Finance (Ja'far Abu Timman); Ministry of Education

(Yusif 'Izz al-Din). It will also be remembered that Hikmat Sulaiman himself had in fact joined the Ahali group after his disagreement with Yasin al-Hashimi in 1935, but that was very clearly for immediate political needs rather than a reflection of ideological commitment.

44   In fact, only part of the programme was incorporated into the Programme of Policy, that was later issued by the government. For full text of the government's Programme of Policy, see Appendix II below.

45   In this context, it is worth noting that the Prime Minister was quick to assure the British Ambassador that 'no property of ex-Ministers would be confiscated but it is possible that their titles to some of land which they acquired by irregular means may be cancelled later on'. FO 371/20015, 8.12.1936. As far as I have been able to establish, however, there is no record of any ex-ministers' improper titles to land having been nullified.

46   Yazbak, op. cit., p. 73.

47   Ibid., p. 205.

48   Ibid., p. 210.

49   FO 371/20017, 12.10.1936.

50   Ibid.

51   Ibid. Yasin al-Hashimi himself was also of the opinion that it would be extremely difficult to establish a respectable Council for Regency, and the whole thing would be an extremely risky experiment.

52   For example, the government was interfering in even as mundane an affair as the employment of his chauffeur. FO 371/20017, 13.7.1936.

53   Evidence varies over the King's possible involvement in the coup. In interviews that I conducted with Iraqi veteran politicians, including Husain Jamil, Sadiq Shanshal and Muhammad Hadid, there was a general consensus that the King supported the coup but had no foreknowledge of it. Nuri al-Sa'id, on the other hand, was 'insistent in the expression of the belief that King Ghazi was privy to the Bakir Sidqi movement' (see FO 371/20014). The British Ambassador himself wrote: 'I had watched King Ghazi very closely while he, with his Ministers, was discussing the affair on the morning of the day before, and I am bound to say that I, too, gained the impression that it [the coup] came as no surprise to His Majesty' (Ibid.). Similarly, Sir Francis Humphrys, a former British ambassador, thought that 'the King may indeed have had such fore-knowledge' (Ibid.). Also, Rashid 'Ali suspected the King of 'being privy to the movement' (FO 371/20015). Yasin al-Hashimi thought that 'the King had been *au courant* with the coup in principle, but not necessarily the details' (FO 371/20015,

9.12.1936). Taha al-Hashimi, on the other hand, believed that the King had no foreknowledge of the movement but supported it once it happened (al-Hashimi, op. cit., p. 148). Finally, Hikmat Sulaiman told al-Hasani that 'the King had no fore-knowledge of the coup but was pleased once it happened' (al-Hasani, op. cit., vol. IV, p. 220).

54 According to Bakir Sidqi, however, 'His Majesty advised him [Ja'far] not to go. He, however, insisted on doing so. He even did worse by sending contradictory messages to various senior army commanders. His action in sending out such messages was in itself contrary to military procedure, and, moreover, it was likely to cause mutiny in the army.' FO 371/20015, 29.11.1936.

55 al-Hasani, op. cit., vol. IV, p. 312.

56 Yazbak, op. cit., p. 98.

57 Ibid. Evidence differs concerning the date of this alleged meeting between Bakir Sidqi and Hikmat Sulaiman. It is claimed by Yazbak (op. cit., p. 75) that the meeting was held only three days before the coup, while I was told that the coup was planned a fortnight before it was executed and presumably the Sulaiman-Sidqi meeting took place then (interview with Husain Jamil, Baghdad, 13 April 1975).

   On the other hand, Dr Grobba, then the head of the German Legation in Baghdad, claims that the coup was decided upon in 1933 after the Assyrian revolt when a friendship was forged between Bakir (who was Commander of the troops that suppressed the revolt) and Hikmat (who was the Minister for the Interior), but to me Grobba's claim seems highly unlikely and it is not supported by any other evidence. See Dr Grobba, *Männer und Machte in Orient*, Frankfurt, 1967; translated by Najdat Fathi Safwat, *al-'Iraq*, Beirut, 1969, p. 99.

58 FO 371/20009, 1936.

59 FO 371/20015.

60 In fact, we have found evidence that indicates that the British Embassy was taken by surprise. For example, informing the Foreign Office about the coup, the British Ambassador wrote: 'I am sorry to have to sling that coup d'état at you without a warning. But Hikmat Sulaiman and Bakir Sidqi were unreasonable enough not to warn anyone at all.' FO 371/20014, 1.11.1936.

61 As quoted in FO 371/20015, 14.12.1936. It is possible that the last paragraph of this article was given strength by the fact that General Hay, the head of the British Military Mission, had 'shaken many members of this mission by calling, or rather going out of his way to call, on Bakir Sidqi at the Ministry of Defence on the morning after the overthrow of the Yasin Government and by promising his cooperation'. FO 371/20001, 2.11.1936.

62 FO 371/19994, 26.11.1936.

63 As quoted in FO 371/20015, 29.11.1936.

64 FO 371/20795, 30.1.1937. It is worth mentioning here that it was claimed to me that, perhaps as a sign of his disassociation with Arabism, Hikmat Sulaiman used to wear a *hat* throughout his premiership. Interview with Husain Jamil, Baghdad, 15 April 1975.

65 See, for example, FO 371/20016, 8.6.1936 and 3.6.1936.

66 See, for instance, 371/20016, 21.6.1936, 25.6.1936, 4.6.1936, 12.6.1936, 2.6.1936, 22.6.1936, 28.6.1936, 14.7.1936 and 17.8.1936.

67 As quoted in FO 371/20016, 25.6.1936. In addition to such activities, the Press was unanimous in its support to the Palestinians, and this support was expressed in a variety of ways. For example, on 22 May 1936 most of the daily newspapers carried heavy black borders and contained special leading and other articles about the situation in Palestine. In a representative leader, *al-Bilad* newspaper, for example, concluded its editorial on this occasion by saying: 'O Arabs! old and young, great and humble, high and lowly, rise up as one man and shout with one voice to echo throughout the world "Palestine or death". Act in a praiseworthy manner, and prove to the world that you are a nation of deeds, not of words, and one of sword and lance-bearers, true to the traditions of your worthy ancestors.' As quoted in FO 371/20016, 8.6.1936.

68 For example, on 27 May 1936, Yasin al-Hashimi told the British Ambassador that 'the Iraqi Government were receiving . . . hundreds of requests for help and support from all kinds of organisations concerned in the efforts . . . being made in the interests of the Arab cause in Palestine. He was puzzled to know how to meet these demands. He did not wish to see His Majesty's Government involved in any further embarrassments while they were preoccupied with the situation caused by Italian aggression in Abyssinia; but it was only natural that both the Government and the people of Iraq should feel a deep interest in the position of their brother Arabs. In his recent contacts with his Palestinian friends he had counselled patience and confidence in His Majesty's Government, and had advised strongly against the tactics of violence and disorder which had recently been adopted by some elements of the Arabs in Palestine. . . . He was pleased to see, in a manifesto published a few days ago, that some of the leaders had declared their abhorrence of the killing, arson and other outrages which were being committed in their name. . . . He thought it his duty to give me a friendly and serious warning to the effect that he feared that, in spite of the goodwill which the

Arabs as a whole felt towards the British, His Majesty's Government would see the present happy state of harmony between the two people much damaged if a solution of the problem were not soon found. Was there anything that he could do to help? For the moment the Iraqi Government, both for reasons of internal policy and for the sake of their good relations with His Majesty's Government, upon which they set great store, did not desire to be drawn into taking any action in the matter, but they might not be able indefinitely to resist the pressure that was being brought upon them to champion the Arab cause.' FO 371/20016, 11.6.1936.

69   For example, when on 22 May 1936, most of the daily newspapers carried heavy black borders and contained special articles on Palestine, the Prime Minister told the British Ambassador of the necessity 'for the Government to provide some outlet for public feeling, but that they [the Government] were carefully checking anything likely to lead to violence or disorder'. FO 371/20016, 8.6.1936.

70   For example, when in August 1936 Fawzi al-Qawuqji, an Iraqi ex-officer who was a leader of the revolt in Palestine, attempted to organise in Iraq a band of armed volunteers to join the Arab insurgents in Palestine, he, together with the 100 volunteers he had succeeded in recruiting, were stopped by the police. On this occasion, Yasin al-Hashimi himself told the British Ambassador that 'two lorries, with men and rifles, which had actually set out, had been stopped and turned back by the police. He [Yasin al-Hashimi] undertook to keep a sharp eye open for any further movements of this kind.' Similarly, on another occasion the Prime Minister told the British Ambassador that he 'had decided that the time had come to censor all Sa'id Thabit's [a nationalist known for his support of the Palestinians] communications . . . and to declare the Palestine Defence Committee an unregistered, and therefore illegal, association'. FO 371/20016, 25.8.1936 and 14.7.1936 respectively.

71   *The Times*, for example, reported that 'in Palestine, their [Yasin al-Hashimi and Nuri al-Sa'id's] eclipse has caused dismay, as their joint influence was expected to be of great assistance in furthering the cause of the Palestinian Arabs with the British Government'. *The Times*, 3 November 1936.

72   The position of the Jews in Iraq had in fact been favourable. In the view of Sir Francis Humphrys, a British Ambassador to Iraq, 'Before the war they probably enjoyed a more favourable position than any other minority in the country. Since 1920, however, Zionism has sown dissension between Jews and Arabs, and a bitterness has grown up between the two peoples which did not

previously exist. Events in Palestine are watched closely by the Arabs in Iraq. . . . The wiser and more experienced Jews, while probably sympathising with the general aims of the Zionist movement, openly deplore the unfortunate repercussions which it has had on their position in Iraq. FO 371/17874, 27.12.1934.

During the 1936 revolt in Palestine, the type of the unfortunate repercussions that Sir Francis Humphrys referred to were actually occuring in Iraq, and during the first week of October 1936, for example, there was, as the British Ambassador expressed, such a 'perplexing outburst' of anti-Jewish activities in Baghdad that the Chief Rabbi felt the need to issue a statement to the effect that the Jews of Baghdad had no relation whatever with the Zionist movement. These anti-Jewish incidents consisted of a number of attacks on individuals and, to a lesser degree, of the throwing of hand grenades into Jewish premises or clubs. Altogether, about six people lost their lives as a result of these attacks.

73 FO 371/20804, 8.2.1937. It is interesting that Taha al-Hashimi even suspected the Jews of having had a hand in the engineering of the coup. Taha al-Hashimi, op. cit., p. 185.

74 FO 371/20804, 23.2.1937.

75 Ibid.

76 Ibid.

77 Ibid.

78 Ibid.

79 FO 371/20795, 24.7.1937. Perhaps, as was to be expected, the Iraqi Press reflected the government's indifference to Pan-Arabism. For example, a typical editorial in the *Inqilab* [coup] newspaper told its readers that 'when the position and politics of Iraq are considered, we must not view Iraq as a hostage to Arab unity, but instead, we must view it [Iraq] as an independent country having its daily tasks and international obligations'. *Al-Inqilab*, 2 January 1937.

80 See Appendix II below.

81 See p. 000 below.

82 The treaty of friendship with Turkey was signed in April 1937, and a non-aggression pact between Iraq, Turkey, Iran and Afghanistan was concluded with the signing of the Sa'ad 'Abad Pact on 8 July 1937. See al-Hasani, op. cit., vol. IV, pp. 271, 334.

83 FO 371/20010, 5.5.1936.

84 FO 371/20014, 16.11.1936.

85 FO 371/20795, 18.8.1937. According to al-Sabbagh, by the time of Bakir Sidqi's death, 90% of the high-ranking officers were non-Arab. It is for this reason, and for his general resentment of the government's cool attitude towards Pan-Arabism, that al-Sabbagh, together with other 'Arab' officers, left the country towards the

end of the Sidqi reign. See Salah al-Din al-Sabbagh, *Fursan al-'Uruba fi' l-'Iraq* (Memoirs), Damascus, 1956, p. 76.
86 FO 371/20795, 13.8.1937.
87 al-Hashimi, op. cit., p. 209.
88 Naji Shaukat, *Sira wa-Dhikrayat* (Memoirs), Baghdad, 1974, p. 323.
89 FO 371/20013, 29.10.1936.
90 FO 371/20015, 30.12.1936.
91 FO 371/20015, 8.12.1936.
92 FO 371/20014, 16.11.1936. The British Ambassador described another encounter that he had with Hikmat Sulaiman on the day following the coup. He wrote: 'I called upon the Prime Minister and was with him for about two hours. I went to him . . . full of prejudice, and I found myself, somewhat to my dismay, disarmed by his obvious desire to be friendly and by the apparent sincerity with which he begged for my support. The assurances which he gave me of his desire to have help and guidance from myself left, on the face of them, nothing to be desired.' Ibid.
93 FO 371/20014, 16.11.1936.
94 FO 371/20015, 31.12.1936.
95 FO 371/20015, 19.1.1936.
96 FO 371/20015, 26.11.1936. The refusal of the Foreign Office to grant Bakir Sidqi permission to visit England on these occasions was due to their fears of public reaction at home. For there was a public outcry in Britain following the suppression of the Assyrian revolt, which was conducted with apparent ruthlessness under the command of Bakir Sidqi.
97 Ibid.
98 FO 371/20015, 20.11.1936.
99 Grobba, op. cit., p. 115.
100 Ibid.
101 Ibid. That Bakir Sidqi may have been 'up to' something in Kurdistan can also be extrapolated from British intelligence reports, which reported that he was 'being friendly to the Kurds, who, as there is no Kurdish Minister in the Cabinet, are tending to resort to him when they come to Baghdad'. FO 371/20795, 14.2.1937.
102 See FO 371/20013, 2.11.1936, quoting an article from the *Daily Herald*.
103 In an interview, Salih al-Juburi, a veteran army general, claimed that he himself had seen the letter of invitation that was sent by Hitler to Bakir Sidqi (Interview, Baghdad, 14 April 1975). Mr al-Juburi's claim is given weight by the fact that Dr Grobba was among those who gathered at the railway station in Baghdad to bid farewell to General Sidqi before his departure for Mosul,

en route to Turkey. (In fact, as far as can be seen, Dr Grobba was the only member of the diplomatic community in Baghdad who had come to the station that morning.) See photograph in Najdat Fathi Safwat, *al-'Iraq fi Mudhakkirat al-Diblumasiyin al-Ajanib* (Iraq in the Memoirs of Foreign Diplomats), Beirut, 1969, p. 129.

As far as the possible involvement of the British in the assassination of Bakir Sidqi is concerned, their implication was claimed by Husain Jamil, a veteran Iraqi politician, and Yusif Yazbak, a veteran Lebanese journalist. According to Yazbak, in addition to Sidqi's flirtation with the Germans, the British had become aware of a plan he had apparently drawn up to attack Kuwait. According to this alleged plan, Kuwait was to be attacked two or three days after his departure, so that the blame would be laid on the generals leading the attack and not on him. Interviews with Husain Jamil in Baghdad on 15 April 1975, and with Yusif Yazbak in Beirut on 27 April 1975.

104 As an indication of the degree to which Iraq's general importance was publicised, one might mention an article by the well-known American journalist Eliot Janeway entitled 'The oil fields of Near East: life-line of the British Empire', which states that 'the strategic oil field that feeds fuel to the British and French navies not only is one of the pillars of the post-war alliance between England and France, but it also occupies another and no less vital position. It lies half-way along the route to India. Thus it shares with the new Singapore naval base first rank in the British Empire's system of defence.' Janeway even suggests that Britain's abandoning of the sanctions imposed upon Italy for her war upon Abyssinia was *quid pro quo* for Italy's giving up an oil concession acquired in north-western Iraq to IPC. FO 371/20008, 1936.

105 FO 371/20895, 24.7.1937.

106 There is a consensus of opinion that Hikmat Sulaiman had intended to invite Nuri al-Sa'id to join his cabinet, but felt unable to do so after the murder of Ja'far al-'Askari. See for example, al-Hasani, op. cit., vol. IV, p. 232, and FO 371/20015, 29.10.1936.

107 FO 371/20014, 16.11.1936.

108 FO 371/20015, 30.11.1936.

109 FO 371/20013, November 1936.

110 FO 371/20013, 29.10.1936.

111 FO 371/20014, 16.11.1936.

112 FO 371/20015, November 1936.

113 After his death, even the Iraqi press, with the exception of his own newspaper, *al-Difa'*, did not express any admiration for him or any regret at his death. See FO 371/20895, 18.8.1937.

114 FO 371/20015, November 1936.

115   FO 371/20895, 3.7.1937.
116   FO 371/20801, 1936.
117   FO 371/20798, 6.1.1937.
118   'Abd al-Qadir Isma'il, for example, who according to British reports was a man 'who, in the past, has shown leanings towards Communism', and who had been one of the founders of the Popular Reform League. FO 371/20014, 20.11.1936. See also Longrigg, op. cit., p. 252.
119   Longrigg, op. cit., p. 251.
120   Ibid., p. 252.
121   Although no specific names are given, a number of documents make a general reference to these violent methods of handling political opposition. This view was also confirmed throughout the interviews that I conducted in Baghdad. It is also known that two determined attempts were made in February 1937 to kill Maulud Mukhlis, a senator known for his sympathy with pan-Arabism. FO 371/20795, 14.1.1936.
122   FO 371/20795, 3.7.1937.
123   Ibid.
124   Ibid.
125   During the army's suppression of the tribal revolt of 1935–6, for example, it is claimed that Bakir Sidqi had 'a portable gallows rigged on a Ford car which he took with him everywhere in order to expedite executions'. *The Times*, 3 November 1936.
126   See, for example, FO 371/20795, 14.1.1937.
127   FO 371/20015, November 1936.
128   It was claimed by a deputy who raised a question of this subject that Baghdad had a total of 200 foreign female dancers who, in view of the deputy (Nasrat al-Farisi), were taking away around 2,000 ID per month and, more seriously, had posed the capital with a possible source of physical and moral disease. In reply to this question, the Prime Minister told Parliament that it was natural for such things to exist in the country and that it was not the state's business to control people's morality. See Mahadir Majlis al-Nuwwab, *Proceedings of Parliament, 1937*, p. 108.
129   The 'Arab' group within the army was led by what became since known as the Golden Square: that is, a group of four Iraqi officers who were to play a decisive role in the shaping of Iraqi politics during later years. These were Salah al-Din al-Sabbagh, Fahmi Sa'id, Kamil Shabib, and Mahmud Salman.
131   FO 371/20795, 12.6.1937.
132   In fact, the ministers concerned distributed copies of their letter of resignation 'widely in the Holy Cities and on the Euphrates'. In their letter they criticised the government for its harsh treatment of the tribes, for the interference of Bakir Sidqi in the

running of the state, and for its failure to implement the 'reform' programme. FO 371/20795, 3.7.1937.

133 FO 371/20895, 18.8.1937.

134 FO 371/20795, 18.8.1937.

Notes to Chapter VII

1 Mahmud al-Durra, *al-Harb al-'Iraqiya al-Biritaniya* (The Anglo–Iraqi War, 1941), Beirut, 1969, p. 89.

2 FO 371/21846, 25.12.1937.

3 Jamil al-Madfa'i himself was exiled after the Sidqi coup and returned to Baghdad only after being requested to do so by the officers who revolted against the Sulaimani government in August 1937. Also, Salah al-Din al-Sabbagh was among the 'Arab' officers who left Iraq during the last months of the Sulaimani government.

4 FO 371/21846, 25.12.1937.

5 Ibid.

6 FO 371/21846, 1.7.1938.

7 FO 371/21846, 25.12.1937.

8 FO 371/21846, 30.3.1937.

9 Ibid.

10 Ibid.

11 FO 371/21846, 1.7.1938.

12 FO 371/23214, 21.1.1939.

13 al-Durra, op. cit., p. 93.

14 See p. 164.

15 See p. 150.

16 al-Durra, op. cit., p. 93.

17 It was at such a meeting attended by Nuri al-Sa'id, Taha al-Hashimi, Rustum Haidar and a number of officers including the 'Four', that it was decided to 'entitle the army to express its opinion in *every* decision concerning the formation or fall of cabinets. In this way, the army would become dominant and would fill the vacuum created by King Faisal's death,' (my emphasis). Salah al-Din al-Sabbagh, *Fursan al-'Uruba fi' l-'Iraq* (Memoirs), Damascus, 1956. pp. 70, 133; and Taha al-Hashimi, *Mudhakkirati* (Memoirs), Beirut, 1969, p. 254.

18 Al-Sabbagh, for example, gives the government's cool attitude towards pan-Arabism as a main reason for his decision, jointly with his colleagues, to organise the December 1938 coup. An indication of the government's cool attitude towards pan-Arabism was seen in August 1938, after the *fatwas* were issued by leading Shi'a and Sunni divines, declaring that all Arabs were in honour bound to join their brothers in Palestine in their struggle, but the government refused a public procession in support of these *fatwas*

and the press was told to give them no support. The Minister of Foreign Affairs also gave an undertaking to the British Ambassador that his government would do their best to ensure that money was not sent from Iraq to the Palestinian insurgents. FO 371/23214, 21.1.1939.

19 FO 371/21846, 1.7.1938.
20 FO 371/21846, 4.5.1938.
21 The accused was liable to a maximum penalty of seven years' imprisonment; if the offenders were soldiers or policemen, the maximum penalty was death. Ibid.
22 Ibid.
23 FO 371/23200, 27.12.1938.
24 For example, the British Ambassador claimed that he had heard from 'many quarters that . . . King Ghazi at first summoned Hikmat Sulaiman, and it was only after Hikmat had declared his inability to form a Government that the premiership was offered to Nuri'. FO 371/23200, 27.12.1938.
25 'Abd al-Razzaq al-Hasani, *al-Asrar al-Khafiya li-Harakat al-Tahrir Sanat 1941*, (The Secrets of the 1941 Liberation Movement), Sidon, 1971, p. 25.
26 Ibid.
27 al-Durra, op. cit., p. 97.
28 FO 371/23200, 17.3.1939.
29 See al-Sabbagh, op. cit., p. 76, and Rashid 'Ali's memoirs in *Majallat Ahkir Sa'a*, Cairo, 1957, as quoted in Isma'il Yaghi, *Harakat Rashid 'Ali* (The Rashid 'Ali Movement), Beirut, 1974, p. 35.
30 This is well beyond the scope of the present inquiry, and the only possible additions that might be made to the many hypotheses that have been presented since consist mainly of two points. First, although the British Foreign Office showed an impressive stamina for producing painstakingly detailed accounts of sometimes seemingly trivial matters, and although public scepticism over this affair led to the murder of the British Consul in Mosul by angry demonstrators, there is a conspicuous absence of any recorded lengthy analysis of the circumstances surrounding the King's death in the British archives. Second, the following reference to a conversation about King Ghazi, which was made by the Foreign Office some days *before* the accident, is, to say the least, very curious: 'In any case, Sir Maurice Peterson [then Ambassador to Iraq] with whom Mr Baxter discussed the other day the relative merits of the various members of the Royal Family in case *any emergency might arise*, was very definitely in favour of the Amir Zaid' (my emphasis). FO 371/23200, 4.4.1939.
31 See chapter V above, p. 118.
32 FO 371/23201, 11.4.1939.

33 FO 371/27072, 27.5.1941.
34 FO 371/27082, 11.11.1941.
35 FO 371/27080, 13.9.1941.
36 Ibid.
37 FO 371/27062, 1.4.1941.
38 FO 371/24558, Note on Iraqi Personalities, undated.
39 FO 371/27064, 11.4.1941.
40 FO 371/23216, 4.4.1939.
41 FO 371/23216, 16.4.1939.
42 FO 371/23202, 17.10.1939.
43 FO 371/23203, 24.5.1939.
44 See for example FO 371/23202, 14.4.1939.
45 FO 371/23200, 3.1.1939.
46 FO 371/23203, 6.9.1939 and 7.9.1939.
47 See for example FO 371/27061, 6.2.1941.
48 Their combined number is estimated to have been 400–500.
    Yaghi, op. cit., p. 55.
49 al-Sabbagh, op. cit., p. 71.
50 Ibid., p. 134, and al-Hashimi, op. cit., p. 341.
51 Ibid., p. 134, and al-Hashimi, op. cit., p. 341.
51 See al-Sabbagh, op. cit., pp. 121–33.
52 It will be remembered that one of the reasons for the army's coup
    against the Madfa'i government was the persistent interference of
    Sabih Najib, then Minister of Defence, in the functions of Husain
    Fauzi, who was also then the CGS. See chapter V above, p. 154.
53 al-Durra, op. cit., p. 109.
54 See al-Sabbagh, op. cit., pp. 207–13.
55 FO 371/23217, June 1939.
56 al-Sabbagh, op. cit., p. 113.
57 FO 371/23217, June 1939.
58 al-Sabbagh does not give details of how he helped in promoting
    'Abdul-Ilah to the regency, but he makes this claim in various
    parts of his Memoirs.
59 al-Sabbagh, op. cit., p. 301.
60 Ibid., pp. 109–20.
61 al-Sabbagh refers to the meeting at which Nuri tried to persuade
    him and his colleagues to agree to declare war on Germany and to
    send Iraqi troops to the Balkans or the Libyan desert. The 'Seven'
    then told him that even Ireland was maintaining a neutral policy
    and advised him to do likewise. He continues to relate a rather
    amusing part of the conversation when Husain Fauzi, then CGS,
    apparently inquired of Nuri: 'So . . . you want me to send two
    Iraqi army battalions to the Balkans. Let's say that while these
    troops were marching through Aleppo they would be stopped by
    a local man who might ask them: "Well brother! where are you

going?"; then the Iraqi soldier would reply: "To the Balkans to fight the Germans". What do you expect the Aleppine to say? "Well done! and this is Syria and Palestine!!' al-Sabbagh goes on to argue that this exchange was the reason why Nuri relieved Husain Fauzi from his duties later (al-Sabbagh, op. cit., pp. 114–15.

62 al-Sabbagh, op. cit., p. 114.
63 Ibid., p. 112.

Notes to Chapter VIII

1 Salah al-Din al-Sabbagh, *Fursan al-'Uruba fi' l-'Iraq* (Memoirs), Damascus, 1956, pp. 131, 136.
2 See, for example, the British Ambassador's telegram to the Foreign Office in FO 371/24557, 17.2.1940.
3 See the Ambassador's dispatch to the Foreign Office in FO 371/27067, 30.4.1941.
4 FO 371/27072, 26.5.1941.
5 FO 371/27067, 3.4.1941.
6 See FO 371/27072, 21.5.1941.
7 FO 371/27063, 8.3.1941.
8 FO 371/24561, 7.7.1940.
9 FO 371/24558, undated.
10 FO 371/27064, 7.4.1941.
11 Taha al-Hashimi, *Mudhakkirati* (Memoirs), Beirut, 1969, p. 229.
12 FO 371/24558, 29.5.1940.
13 FO 371/24561, 10.6.1940 and 16.5.1940.
14 Ibid.
15 FO 371/25558, 29.5.1940.
16 Mahmud al-Durra, *al-Harb al-'Iraqiya al-Biritaniya* (The Anglo-Iraqi War, 1941), Beirut, 1969, p. 164.
17 al-Sabbagh, op. cit., p. 142.
18 Ibid., p. 279.
19 The following means for economic pressure were considered but were not expected to be effective:
(a) insistence on payment of £300,000 owed to Britain by the Iraqi government for Hinaidi buildings;
(b) refusal to supply dollars;
(c) refusal to permit further shipments under Credit Agreement;
(d) withdrawal by Indian government of rupee credit facilities for Japanese imports into Iraq;
(e) refusal of credit facilities by local British banks;
(f) blocking of the Iraqi balance with the Eastern Bank, London;
(g) tightening-up of contraband control;
(h) restriction of shipping calling at Iraqi ports.

20 For full text see 'Uthman Kamal Haddad, *Harakat Rashid 'Ali al-Kilani* (The Rashid 'Ali Movement), Sidon, undated, p. 30.
21 al-Sabbagh, op. cit., p. 143.
22 Ibid., p. 112.
23 FO 371/24558, 9.10.1940.
24 FO 371/24561, 10.10.1940.
25 FO 371/24561, 10.10.1940.
26 Economic pressures such as the blocking of the oil royalty payments and the removal of currency reserves, block credit, etc., were considered; but, apart from removing currency reserves (in fact, out of I.D. 900,000 in Baghdad, 220,000 had been transferred to Habbaniya and 100,000 to Mosul by 9 April), these considerations were thought to be generally ineffective and were therefore soon dropped. See FO 371/27062, 5.4.1941 and 3.3.1941.
27 FO 371/24558, 1.10.1941.
28 Isma'il Yaghi, *Harakat Rashid 'Ali* (The Rashid 'Ali Movement), Beirut, 1974, p. 64.
29 FO 371/27061, 31.1.1941.
30 See al-Hashimi, op. cit., pp. 385, 423.
31 al-Sabbagh, op. cit., p. 214.
32 Ibid., p. 136.
33 See for example FO 371/27063, 1.3.1941.
34 FO 371/27061, 7.2.1941.
35 al-Sabbagh, op. cit., p. 208.
36 Ibid., p. 210.
37 Ibid., p. 216.
38 Ibid., p. 218.
39 FO 371/27062, 24.3.1941.
40 FO 371/270162, undated.
41 FO 371/27062, 31.3.1941.
42 FO 371/77076, 24.6.1941.
43 Ibid.
44 FO 370/27063, 7.4.1941.
45 FO 371/77076, 24.6.1941.
46 FO 371/27064, 11.4.1941.
47 Ibid.
48 Ibid.
49 FO 371/27064, 8.4.1941.
50 FO 371/27064, 11.4.1941.
51 Ibid.
52 Ibid.
53 FO 371/27064, 12.4.1941.
54 FO 371/27065, 16.4.1941.
55 FO 371/27065, 21.4.1941.

56 Ibid.
57 Ibid.
58 Ibid.
59 Ibid.
60 Ibid.
61 FO 371/27067, 28.4.1941.
62 FO 371/27067, 29.4.1941.
63 Ibid.
64 FO 371/27067, 30.3.1941.
65 Ibid.
66 For example, it is reported that, during the hostilities, Grobba presented Rashid 'Ali with a three-point treaty which demanded the immediate transfer to Germany of: (a) all oil concessions, (b) Baghdad railway concession of 20 km each side, and (c) all aerodromes. FO 371/27075.
67 FO 371/27067, 30.4.1941.
68 Ibid.
69 FO 371/27067, 1.5.1941.
70 FO 371/27068, 7.5.1941.
71 Ibid.
72 FO 371/27068, 4.5.1941.
73 FO 371/27069, 5.5.1941.
74 FO 371/27068, 7.5.1941.
75 L. Hirszowicz, *The Third Reich and the Arab East*, London and University of Toronto Press, 1966, p. 156.
76 As quoted in M. Khadduri, *Independent Iraq*, Oxford, 1960, p. 234.
77 According to British intelligence, a total of 80 German planes had arrived in aid of Iraq and at least 10 of these were destroyed in action. FO 371/27073, 29.5.1941.
78 See for example Haddad, op. cit., p. 97.
79 FO 371/27069, 11.5.1941.
80 For further details on Sab'awi's ideas, see Khaldun S. al-Husry, in *Intellectual Life in the Arab East, 1800–1939*, ed. M. R. Buheiry, Beirut, 1981.
81 Haddad, op. cit., p. 115.
82 FO 371/27070, 18.5.1941, and Hirszowicz, op. cit., pp. 170, 217.
83 FO 371/27069, 14.5.1941.
84 FO 371/27070, 19.5.1941.
85 Ibid.
86 FO 371/27071, 20.5.1941.
87 FO 371/27071, 23.5.1941.
88 FO 371/27072, 30.5.1941.
89 FO 371/27073, 31.5.1941.
90 FO 371/27071, 22.5.1941.

91 A. H. Hourani, 'The decline of the West in the Middle East', in *The Modern Middle East* (ed. R. H. Nolte), New York, 1963, p. 40.

Notes to Chapter IX

1 P. Sluglett, *Britain in Iraq 1914–1932*, London, 1976, p. 261.

Notes to Appendix III

1 FO 371/18945, 28.3.1935.

Notes to Appendix IV

1 FO 371/21092.

Bibliography

British Government documents used or consulted

Public Records Office

FO 371 files on Iraq from 1920 to 1941; FO 624 boxes, nos 4, 7, 8, 21, 23, 24 and 26; FO 406/46, March 1921; FO 406/75, January 1937; CO 730 and 732 files on Iraq, nos 1–126; WO 208 files nos 1563 and 1560; Air Ministry files on Iraq, series Air 5, 20 and 23.

India Office Library

LP&S files, series 11 and 12 for the year 1932–1941.

It was also possible to see transcripts of the Baghdad High Commission files through the kindness of Dr Peter Sluglett who had consulted the originals in New Delhi.

Official publications

Bell, Gertrude, *Review of the Civil Administration of Mesopotamia*, HMSO, London, 1920.
Colonial Office, *Report on Iraq Administration, 1922–32.*
Dowson, E., *An Inquiry into Land Tenure and Related Questions*, Iraq Government Report, 1931.
Fahmi, A., *Report on the Financial Position of Iraq*, Baghdad, 1926.
A History of Mesopotamian Railways during the War, Government Central Press, Bombay, 1921.
The Iraq Directory, Times Press, Baghdad, 1936.
Military Report on Iraq, Superintendent Government Printing, India, 1923.
Le Mondain Egyptien et du Moyen-Orient, l'Annuaire de l'Elite, Cairo, 1949.
Public Health Directorate, *Vital Statistics of Iraq*, 1935. *Report by the Financial Mission*, HMSO, London, 1925.
Reports on the Administration of Iraq for the years 1918–25, Colonial Office.
Special Report by H.B.M.G. to the Council of the League of Nations on the Progress of Iraq during the period 1920–31, Colonial no. 58.

Bibliography

Statistical Abstract for the Several British Overseas Dominions and Protectorates, from 1907–21, no. 56, HMSO, London, 1924.
Statistical Handbook of Middle Eastern Countries, Economic Research Institute, Jewish Agency for Palestine, 1945.

Primary Arabic documents

The Royal Palace files for the years 1938 and 1939, the National Records Office, Baghdad.
The Cabinet files for the years 1935–41, the National Records Office, Baghdad.
Proceedings of Parliament for the years 1935–41, the National Records Office, Baghdad.
Proceedings of the Senate 1934–5

Personal interviews

The following Iraqi veteran politicians and officers were interviewed by the author in Baghdad during the spring of 1975:
Husain Jamil
Muhammad Hadid
Sadiq Shanshal
Salih al-Juburi
Other people interviewed were:
'Abd al-Razzaq al-Hasani
Khayri al-'Umari
Yusif Yazbak

Works in Arabic

'Abd al-Aziz al-Kassab, *Min Dhikrayati* (Memoirs), Beirut, 1962.
'Abd al-Jalil al-Tahir, *al-'Asha 'ir al-'Iraqiya* (The Tribes of Iraq), Baghdad, 1972.
'Abd al-Rahman al-Bazzaz, *al-'Iraq Min al-Ihtilal Hatta al-Istiqlal* (Iraq from Occupation until Independence), Baghdad, 1967.
'Abd al-Razzaq al-Hasani, *Tarikh al-Wizarat al-'Iraqiya* (History of the Iraqi Cabinets), 5 vols, Beirut, 1974.
'Abd al-Razzaq al-Hasani, *al-Asrar al-Khafiya li-Harakat al-Tahrir Sanat 1941* (The Secrets of the 1941 Liberation Movement), Sidon, 1971.
'Abd al-Razzaq al-Hasani, *Tarikh al-'Iraq al-Siyasi al-Hadith*, (Modern Political History of Iraq), 3 vols, Beirut, 1948.
'Abd al-Razzaq al-Hasani, *al-'Iraq Qadiman wa-Hadithan* (Iraq: Ancient and Modern), Beirut, 1973.
'Abdullah Fayyad, *al-Thawra al-Iraqiya al-Kubra* (The Great Iraqi Revolution), Baghdad, 1974.
'Ali al-Wardi, *Dirasa fi Tabi'at al-Mujtama' al-'Iraqi* (A Study in the

Society of Iraq), Baghdad, 1965.

'Ali Jaudat al-Ayyubi, *Dhikrayat 'Ali Jaudat* (Memoirs), Beirut, 1967.

'Ali Mahmud al-Shaikh 'Ali, *Muhakamatna al-Wajahiya* (Memoirs), Beirut, 1967.

Al-Maja'la al-'Askariya ('The Army Journal'), Baghdad, 1924–37.

S. A. W. al-Mubarak, 'Inqilab al-Sittawathalathin' ('The 1936 Coup'), MA Thesis, Baghdad University, 1973.

Anwar 'Abd al-Malik, *al-Jaysh wal-Haraka al-Wataniya* (The Army and National Movements), Beirut, 1971.

Fadhil Husain, *Tarikh al-Hizb al-Watani al-Dimocrati* (History of the National Democratic Party), Baghdad, 1974.

Fa'iq Batti, *Sahafat al-'Iraq* (Iraqi Journalism), Baghdad, 1968.

Ghassan Tuwaini, *Mantiq al-Quwwa* (The Logic of Force), Beirut 1954.

Husain Muhammad al-Shabibi, *Min Watha'iq al-Hizb al-Shuyu'i al-'Iraqi* (From the Documents of the Iraqi Communist Party), Baghdad, 1974.

Isma'il, Yaghi, *Harakat Rashid 'Ali* (The Rashid 'Ali Movement), Beirut, 1974.

Khalil Kanna, *al-Iraq Amsuhu Waghaduhu* (Iraq: Past and Future), Beirut, 1966.

Khayri al-'Umari, *Hikayat Siyasiya* (Political Anecdotes), Cairo, 1969.

Khayri al-'Umari, *Shakhsiyat 'Iraqiya* (Iraqi Personalities), Baghdad, 1955.

Kamil Chadirchi, *Min Awraq Kamil Chadirchi* (Memoirs), Beirut, 1971.

Kamil Chadirchi, *Mudhakkirat Kamil Chadirchi wa-Tarikh al-Hizb al-Watani al-Dimocrati* (Memoirs and the History of the Democratic National Party), Beirut, 1970.

Khurshid Shaukat Rawanduzi, *Mashkilat Shatt al-'Arab* (The Problem of Shatt al-Arab), Baghdad, 1970.

Mahmud al-Durra, *al-Harb al-'Iraqiya al-Biritaniya* (The Anglo-Iraqi War, 1941), Beirut, 1969.

Mufid Nuri, *Dirasat fi' l-Watan al-'Arabi* (Studies of the Arab World), Mosul, 1972.

Muhammad Mahdi Kubba, *Mudhakkirati fi Samim al-Ahdath* (Memoirs), Baghdad, 1966.

Muhammad Salman Hasan, *al-Tatawwur al-Iqtisadi fi' l-'Iraq* (The Economic Development of Iraq), Beirut, 1965.

Muhammad Salman Hasan, *Dirasat fi' l-Iqtisad al-'Iraqi* (Studies of the Iraqi Economy), Beirut, 1966.

Naji Shaukat, *Sira wa-Dhikrayat* (Memoirs), Baghdad, 1974.

Najdat Fathi Safwat, *al-'Iraq fi mudhakkirat al-Diblumasiyin al-Ajanib* (Iraq in the Memoirs of Foreign Diplomats), Beirut, 1969.

Najm al-Din al-Suhrawardi, *al-Kitab al-Abyad* (The White Book),

Baghdad, 1966.

Nuri al-Barazi, *al-Badawa wal-Istiqrar fi' l-'Iraq* (Nomadism and Settlement in Iraq), Baghdad, 1969.

Rashid 'Ali al-Kilani, *Mudhakkirati* (Memoirs) in *Majallat Ahkir Sa'a*, Cairo, 1957.

Salah al-Din al-Sabbagh, *Fursan al-'Uruba fi' l-'Iraq* (Memoirs), Damascus, 1956.

Sati' al-Husri', *Mudhakkirati fi' l-'Iraq* (Memoirs), 2 vols, Beirut, 1966.

Sa'id Hamada, *al-Nidham al-Iqtisadi fi' l-'Iraq* (The Economic System of Iraq), Beirut, 1938.

Su'ad Khairi, *Min Tarikh al-Harakat al-Thawriya al-Mu'asirah fi' l-'Iraq* (from the History of the Contemporary Revolutionary Movements in Iraq), vol. I, Baghdad, 1·974.

Taha al-Hashimi, *Mudhakkirati* (Memoirs), Beirut, 1969.

Talib Mushtaq, *Awraq Ayyami* (Memoirs), Beirut, 1963.

Tawfiq al-Suwaidi, *Mudhakkirati* (Memoirs), Beirut, 1969.

'Uthman Kamal Haddad, *Harakat Rashid 'Ali al-Kilani* (The Rashid 'Ali Movement), Sidon, undated.

Yusif 'Izz al-Din, *al-Shi'r al-'Iraqi al-Hadith* (Modern Iraqi Poetry), Cairo, 1965.

Yusif Yazbak, *al-Muharrirun* (The Liberators), Beirut, 1936.

Iraqi newspapers

A wide range of newspapers was consulted, but the only ones to need a full reference are:

al-Ikha al Watani, Baghdad, 1934 and 1935.

al-Inqilab, Baghdad, 1936 and 1937.

Works in other languages

'Abd al-Malek, A., *Egypt: Military Society*, New York, 1968.

al-Marayati, A., *A Diplomatic History of Modern Iraq*, New York, 1961.

Adams, D. G., *Iraq's People and Resources*, Berkeley, Cal., 1958.

Adams, R., *Land Behind Baghdad*, Chicago, 1965.

American Political Science Review, June 1953.

Batatu, Hanna, *The Old Social Classes and the Revolutionary Movements of Iraq*, Princeton, NJ, 1978.

Batatu, H. 'The shaikh and the peasant in Iraq, 1919–1958', PhD thesis, Harvard University, 1960.

Bedler, A., *Military Rule in Africa*, New York, 1973.

Be'eri, *Army Officers in Arab Politics and Society*, Jerusalem, 1969.

Bell, G., *The Letters of Gertrude Bell*, 2 vols, New York, 1927.

Berger, M., *Military Elite and Social Change: Egypt Since Napoleon*, Princeton, NJ, 1960.

Bienen, H., *The Military Intervenes – Case Studies in Political Development*, New York, 1968.

Birdwood, Lord, *Nuri as-Said*, London, 1959.

Boycott, A. G., *The Elements of Imperial Defence*, London, 1938.

Brodbeck, May, Models in *Readings in the Philosophy of Science*, ed. M. Fiegl and M. Brodbeck, New York, 1953.

Collingwood, R. G., *The Idea of History*, Oxford, 1961.

Craig, G. A. *The Politics of the Prussian Army*, Oxford, 1964.

Daalder, H., *The Role of the Military in Emerging Countries*, the Hague, 1962.

Dann, U., *Iraq Under Qassem*, Jerusalem, 1969.

Dawn, C. E., *From Ottomanism to Arabism*, Urbana, Ill., 1973.

Edmonds, C. J., *Kurds, Turks and Arabs*, London, 1957.

Eisenstadt, S. N., *Modernization: Protest and Change*, Englewood Cliffs, NJ, 1966.

Erskine, S., *King Faisal of Iraq*, London, 1935.

Feigl, H., and Brodbeck, M., *Readings in the Philosophy of Science*, New York, 1953.

Finer, S. E., *The Man on Horseback: The Role of the Military in Politics*, London, 1969.

Fisher, S. N., (ed.), *The Military in the Middle East: Problems in Society and Government*, Columbus, Ohio, 1963.

First, R., *The Barrel of a Gun*, Harmondsworth, Middx, 1970.

Gibb, H. A. R., and Bowen, H., *Islamic Society and the West*, vol. I, Oxford, 1950.

Gurr, T. R., *Why Men Rebel*, Princeton, NJ, 1970.

Haddad, G. M., *Revolution and Military Rule in the Middle East*, vol. II, New York, 1971.

Haidar, S., 'Land problems of Iraq', in *The Economic History of the Middle East 1800-1914* (ed. C. Issawi), Chicago, 1966.

Halpern, M., *The Politics of Social Change in the Middle East and North Africa*, Princeton, NJ, 1970.

Harris, G. L., *Iraq*, New Haven, Conn., 1958.

Hirszowicz, L., *The Third Reich and the Arab East*, London and University of Toronto Press, 1966.

Hourani, A. H. 'The decline of the West in the Middle East', in *The Modern Middle East* (ed. R. H. Nolte), New York, 1963.

Hourani, A. H., (ed.), *St Antony's Papers*, London, 1963.

Huntington, S. P., *The Soldier and the State: the Theory and Politics of Civil Military Relations*, Cambridge, Mass., 1957.

Huntington, S. P., (ed.), *Changing Patterns of Military Politics*, New York, 1967.

Hurewitz, J. C., 'Soldiers and social change in plural societies: the contemporary Middle East', in V. J. Parry and M. E. Yapp (eds),

Bibliography

War, Technology and Society in the Middle East, London, 1975.

Husry, K., 'The Assyrian affair of 1933, part 1', *International Journal of Middle East Studies*, vol. 5, 1974.

Husry, K. in M. R. Buleiry (ed.), *Intellectual Life in the Arab East, 1800-1939*, Beirut, 1981.

International Journal of Middle East Studies (ed. S. J. Shaw), Cambridge University Press.

Ireland, P. W., *Iraq*, London, 1937.

Issawi, C., (ed.), *The Economic History of the Middle East 1800-1914*, Chicago, 1966.

Jalal, F., *The Role of Government in the Industrialisation of Iraq, 1950-65*, London, 1972.

Janowitz, M., *The Professional Soldier*, New York, 1960.

Janowitz, M., *The Military in the Political Development of New Nations*, Chicago, 1964.

Janowitz, M., and van Doorn, Jacques, (ed.), *On Military Intervention*, Rotterdam, 1971.

Johnson, J. J., *The Military and Society in Latin America*, Stanford, Cal., 1964.

Johnson, J. J., *The Role of the Military in Underdeveloped Countries*, Princeton, NJ, 1962.

Jwaideh, A., Midhat Pasha and the land system of lower Iraq, *St Antony's Papers*, no. 16, (ed. A. H. Hourani), London, 1963.

Journal of the Iraqi Medical Profession, vol. IV, no. 2, June 1956.

Kaplan, A., *The Conduct of Enquiry*, Michigan, 1963.

Kennedy, G., *The Military and the Third World*, London 1974.

Khadduri, M., *Political Trends in the Arab World*, Baltimore, 1972.

Khadduri, M., *Independent Iraq*, Oxford, 1960.

Khadduri, W., 'Social background of modern Iraqi politics', PhD thesis, Johns Hopkins University, 1974.

Kirk, G., *The Middle East in the War, Survey of International Affairs*, Oxford, 1954.

Klieman, A. S., *Foundations of British Policy in the Arab World, The Cairo Conference of 1921*, Baltimore, 1970.

Kuhn, Thomas, *The Structure of Scientific Revolution*, Chicago, 1970.

Luttwak, E., *Coup d'Etat*, London, 1968.

Lenin, V. I., *The State and Revolution*, Peking, 1973.

Liebknecht, K., *Militarism and anti-Militarism*, Cambridge, 1973.

Lindsay, A. D., *The Modern Democratic State*, Oxford, 1962.

Lipset, S. M., and Solari, A., *Elites in Latin America*, Oxford, 1967.

Longrigg, S. H., *Iraq 1900-1950*, Beirut, 1956.

Luckham, *The Nigerian Military*, Cambridge, 1975.

Main, E., *Iraq: From Mandate to Independence*, London, 1935.

von der Mehden, F. R., *Politics of the Developing Nations*, Englewood Cliffs, NJ, 1969.

Mejcher, H., *The Imperial Quest for Oil, Iraq 1910-1928*, London, 1976.

Mousa, Suleiman, 'King Husain of the Hijaz and the Arabs of Palestine', *International Journal of Middle East Studies*, vol. 9, 1978.

Nadmi, W. O. 'The Iraqi revolt of 1920', PhD thesis, Durham University, 1974.

Nolte, R. H. (ed.), *The Modern Middle East*, New York, 1963.

Parry, G., *Political Elites*, London, 1969.

Parry, V. J., and Yapp, M. E. (eds), *War, Technology and Society in the Middle East*, London, 1975.

Popper, K. R., *The Poverty of Historicism*, London, 1961.

Potash, R. A., *The Army and Politics in Argentina 1928-45*, Stanford, Cal., 1969.

Pye, L. W., and Verba, S. (eds.), *Political Culture and Political Development*, Princeton, NJ, 1965.

Reynolds, C., *Theory and Explanation in International Politics*, London, 1973.

Roosevelt, K., *Arabs, Oil and History*, New York, 1969.

Sassoon, D. S., *A History of the Jews in Baghdad*, Lechworth, 1949.

Schumpeter, J. A., *Capitalism, Socialism and Democracy*, London, 1966.

Shwadran, B., *The Middle East, Oil and the Great Powers*, New York, 1959.

Sluglett, P., 'British influence and administration in Iraq 1914-1932', DPhil. thesis, Oxford University, 1972.

Sluglett, P., *Britain in Iraq 1914-1932*, London, 1976.

Spencer, W., *Political Evolution in the Middle East*, Philadelphia, 1962.

Stafford, R. S., *The Tragedy of the Assyrians*, London, 1935.

Vagts, A., *A History of Militarism*, New York, 1959.

Vatikiotis, P. J., *The Egyptian Army in Politics*, Bloomington, Ind., 1961.

Vatikiotis, P. J., *Politics and the Military in Jordan*, London, 1967.

Wheeler-Bennett, J. W., *The Nemesis of Power: The German Army in Politics 1918-45*, London, 1964.

Wilson, A. T., *Loyalties, Mesopotamia*, 2 vols, London, 1930-1.

Wright, M. C., *The Power Elite*, New York, 1956.

Index